THE LONGEST YEAR

THE LONGEST YEAR

YEAR

America at War and at Home in 1944

VICTOR BROOKS

Carrel Books

Carrel Books may be purchased in bulk at special discounts for sales promotion, corporate gifts, fund-raising, or educational purposes. Special editions can also be created to specifications. For details, contact the Special Sales Department, Carrel Books, 307 West 36th Street, 11th Floor, New York, NY 10018 or carrelbooks@skyhorsepublishing.com.

Carrel Books® is a registered trademark of Skyhorse Publishing, Inc.®, a Delaware corporation.

Visit our website at www.carrelbooks.com.

10 9 8 7 6 5 4 3 2 1

Library of Congress Cataloging-in-Publication Data is available on file
Cover design by Anthony Morais
Cover photo credit: Library of Congress

ISBN: 978-1-63144-023-6
Ebook ISBN: 978-1-63144-032-8

Printed in the United States of America

CONTENTS

Preface

During the more than two centuries of American existence as a nation, politicians, historians, and average citizens have chosen a few specific years as particularly crucial to who we are and what we have become as a people and a nation. The year 1776 is an obvious choice, as it represents the birth of the United States; 1865 represents the rebirth of a divided nation; 1945 witnessed the end of the most massive war in modern history; and 1968 witnessed political discord, major assassinations, and significant generational conflict. However, it is also true that the period immediately before or after these seminal years might have been as important, or even more so, than the original iconic twelve-month span. The year 1777 may very well have been the most important period in the War of Independence, as it produced the victory at Saratoga, which brought France into alliance with the still-struggling infant republic. The Union victories at Atlanta, Mobile Bay, Franklin, and Nashville in 1864 did far more to end the military capacity of the Confederacy than any battle in 1865. Much of the discord that made 1968 such a tense year was incubated in a 1967 generational confrontation in such locales as San Francisco (the "Summer of Love") and the antiwar rallies on numerous college campuses.

Much of the concept for this book is based on a similar premise: the climax and eventual Allied victory in 1945 was based heavily on the enormously important events of 1944, which pushed the two main Axis powers, Germany and Japan, from still relatively confident belligerents in late 1943 to nations reeling toward defeat by January of 1945.

This book does *not* have the word *decisive* in its title because the list of truly decisive decisions made by the Axis and Allies stretches over the length of the six-year conflict in which the German failure to conquer Great Britain in 1940 and the Japanese inability to sink the American carrier fleet at Pearl Harbor in 1941 are in many respects as decisive as almost any event in 1944. Therefore, I have chosen the title *The Longest Year* as a narrative of the American experience in a multimonth period, of which the iconic "Longest Day" of Operation Overlord is roughly at the midpoint of this chronicle. Regarding sheer drama, a book on 1944 is an author's dream, with the main challenge being the necessity to keep multiple critical simultaneous events in some readable context.

For sheer drama in any war, it is difficult to match the spectacle of two of the largest invasions in history: Operation Overlord in Normandy and Operation Forager in the Marianas were evolving almost simultaneously at opposite sides of the world, while, just for good measure, another American army was liberating Rome. On another dramatic plane, the heroic stand of an outnumbered, outgunned garrison against the fury of a massive German offensive set in a Christmas card-like setting of the small Belgian town of Bastogne had elements of Valley Forge, the Alamo, and Gettysburg all rolled into one.

I first began to see the possible need for a chronicle of the American experience in 1944 when I was writing my two previous World War II books, *The Normandy Campaign* and *Hell Is Upon Us: D-Day in the Pacific*. I was able to include minor references to what was occurring in the other theater in each of these two narratives, but I was already developing an interest in presenting the American war of that year on a wider platform. Then, one of my favorite military history authors, Winston Groom, published *1942: The Year That Tried Men's Souls*. Groom created a seamless, multifront narrative of that critical period of World War II, and I began to see an opportunity to utilize my background on 1944 to produce a similar chronicle of another decisive year of the war.

There is a phenomenal delight and satisfaction in having the opportunity to describe, and sometimes link, the multiple battles and critical decisions that permeated 1944. I had the freedom to change the scene of action from Pacific sea battles to the hedgerows of Normandy to the explosion of juvenile delinquency on the American home front without skipping too many beats. World War II was experienced by just over one hundred thirty million Americans ranging from frontline troops who faced imminent death, to frazzled war workers asked to work yet another overtime shift in a bomber factory, to a new mother who discovered that the rubber pants to help keep her newborn baby diapers dry were out of stock with no date when, or if, a new shipment would arrive. Each of these Americans felt the emotion, depression, and triumph of some aspect of the war, and each dreamed of the day when their country would become "normal" again. This book is largely the story of these one hundred thirty million people, for whom 1944 would be a year that was never to be forgotten.

Two of these people would have more than a minor impact on my life, especially in view of their activities in 1944. At the beginning of this year, my father, an Army Air Force captain, was busy unpacking after a transfer from his former base to a new posting at a field near Rome and Utica, New York. He had started the war working on his doctorate in his hometown of Philadelphia and was now about to experience winters undreamed of in southeastern Pennsylvania, a fact about which he complained frequently to his family. In turn, a young, recent high school graduate of a Utica high school had accepted a secretarial position at the same base, looking for the adventure that seemed very likely in her new environment. Sometime during this snowy winter of 1944, these two people became a couple after a number of officers' club events, and they announced their engagement at Christmas and married the following June, after V-E Day and before V-J Day. Nineteen months later, I became an early member of the Baby Boom generation and was soon regaled with tales of World War II from an army of relatives in Philadelphia, Utica, and many points between. All of these people experienced 1944 in different ways, and some of their relatives did not survive the year that was the bloodiest in American history since 1864.

This book, then, is the story of many of these one hundred thirty million people and also, to some extent, the people of Allied nations such as Britain, who befriended and often married them, and the young men of Germany and Japan who fought against them, sometimes with chivalry and other times with cruelty thought unthinkable in a "modern" twentieth-century world.

Although I am an author, I am also a very avid reader of everything from history to horror, science fiction books to baseball and football preseason magazines. I sincerely hope that you enjoy reading this book as much as I enjoyed writing it. There is a magic in books, from older adults enjoying again a special work from an earlier time to a certain seven-year-old in my home who has just discovered a new book series for kids. I hope that this work gives you, the reader, that sort of satisfaction.

Acknowledgments

One of the challenges yet rewards of pursuing dual careers as a teacher and a writer is that it enables me to acknowledge two groups of people who greatly influence what I do. On the academic side, a career of forty-three years at Villanova University has created a multitude of relationships where former students have become university officials and former officials have become colleagues.

The Reverend Peter Donohue, O.S.A., Villanova University President, is not only an excellent administrator but also a formidable presence in the world of Theater. The Reverend Kail Ellis, O.S.A., Vice President for Academic Affairs, has constantly encouraged my work while revealing his own enormous knowledge of history and politics. Dr. Adele Lindenmeyr, Dean of Arts and Sciences, and Dr. Edward Garcia Fierros, Chair of the Department of Education and Counseling, my academic home, have been unfailingly supportive of my research projects, while Anne Feldman has been a major contributor to this project by her almost magical ability to turn my written drafts into a readable manuscript ready for publication. The extensive level of academic support I receive at Villanova has been matched by my editor at Carrel Books, Niels Aaboe. I hope that

The Longest Year will be merely the first of several projects with this cutting-edge publishing house, where writing history really seems to matter.

Finally, I would like to dedicate this book to my children, Matthew, Gregory, and Stephen, and to my eight-year-old grandson, Liam D'Arcy Brooks, who is munching a candy cane and putting the final decorations on our Christmas tree as I write these lines. Liam and his fellow twenty-first-century children are facing a world of excitement and wonder largely due to the sacrifices of the Americans who populated the world of 1944 and preserved a free society beyond their own lifetimes.

Prologue
December 1943

On a Tuesday morning in December 1943, one hundred thirty million Americans across the four time zones of the forty-eight states wakened to a late autumn day that reflected the size and diversity of the republic. Cold weather and snow-covered sheets in parts of the north contrasted with the balmy warmth of the rapidly growing population centers of Florida and California. As families sat down to a breakfast that would seem enormous to many of their twenty-first-century counterparts, children and parents vied for control of the two major communications outlets of their era as they reached for their favorite section of the morning newspaper or scrambled to turn the radio dial to a favorite program. They were quickly reminded of the importance of this particular date, December 7, the second anniversary of Pearl Harbor.

A nation that continued to be both traumatized and energized by the abrupt transition from peace to global war twenty-four months later was now coping with the challenge of defeating two rapacious empires whose leaders had seemed to have jettisoned any vestige of humanity or civilized behavior and were still loudly proclaiming that their form of state gangsterism was the logical wave of the future for the entire planet.

Two years earlier, each newspaper article or evening radio newscast seemed to announce a new setback against the Axis powers that increasingly dimmed the impending holiday festivities. Japanese forces captured Wake Island in what initially seemed a Pacific replay of the siege of the Alamo as the garrison of Marines, little larger than the Texan contingent in the old San Antonio mission, initially thwarted enemy landing attempts and then broke radio contact as the final Nipponese landing surged into the last machine-gun pits and headquarter dugouts. Initially, the Japanese assault commander had planned the same fate for the survivors as Santa Anna's edict on the eve of the final assault on the Alamo: "in this battle there will be no prisoners." However, as the leathernecks were tied up in groups on the island airfield in preparation for their execution, a last-minute "Christmas edict" from the Emperor spared the garrison, an act generally unknown in America until many months later.

In that last month of 1941, newspaper and radio accounts had focused on the courage of Captain Colin Kelly, who had allegedly sunk a Japanese battleship as a final act of defiance as his dying *Flying Fortress* plunged toward ground in the newly invaded Philippine Islands. In actuality, no Japanese battleship had been within several hundred miles of Kelly's plane, but his courage in remaining at the controls of his fatally damaged plane, allowing other crew members to bail out, would survive the intrusion of factual material of a relatively unsuccessful mission. The bravery of Kelly and other American and Filipino defenders of the islands was ultimately not enough to parry the better tactics and weapons of the Japanese, and now survivors among the twenty-five thousand original defenders of Bataan and Corregidor were enduring attacks against their own section of hell, a reality that would begin to become public knowledge only in the early months of 1944.

During the two years since Pearl Harbor, Adolf Hitler made the stunning decision to declare war on America, although it had no treaty obligation with Germany's Nipponese ally to do so. This decision was now gradually beginning to haunt the leaders of the Third Reich. Soon after Pearl Harbor, Americans strolling beaches or boardwalks along the Atlantic coast were horrified to see distant tankers burst into flame on the darkened sea as they became new victims of what gleeful U-boat crew-men called the "happy times." Now, in late 1943, those celebrations were far fewer as the U-boats themselves were becoming the prey of a vastly expanded American destroyer fleet.

Even the earlier outrage at watching American soldiers captured by the third major Axis member as they were marched as prisoners past the Coliseum was long since avenged by the surrender of Italy in September, as fascism had been overthrown, and an American Army was gradually pushing northward toward the Eternal City.

By December of 1943, the United States was a wartime nation on a march toward perceived ultimate victory, although most citizens recog-nized that bloodshed and disappointment lay ahead. As the second year of war edged toward a close, the American government began releasing fairly accurate figures on the cost of the war thus far, and, while that cost was hardly trivial, it was still far short of the halfway mark of the costs of the Civil War or even those of the entire span of the much more recent Great War that was now universally called World War I. Just over twenty-nine thousand Americans had paid the supreme price for defending the repub-lic, a figure almost evenly divided by the army ground and air forces on the one hand and naval and Marine personnel on the other side. The total of men wounded in action was far higher on the Army/Air Force side of the ledger, as thirty-five thousand personnel had been injured compared to six thousand sailors and Marines, most of whom were wounded at Pearl Harbor or during the Guadalcanal Campaign. At least twenty-nine thousand Americans were known or suspected to have been captured at Bataan, Corregidor, or the Kasserine Pass or during the air battles that were now swirling over the skies of Europe. While loved ones at least had the consolation of knowing that these men (and some women) were alive, the level of their relief depended almost entirely on which of the Axis enemies had captured them. The personnel captured by the Germans were hardly well-fed, but at least they were regularly visited by neutral Red Cross officials, were able to supplement their diet with American food parcels, and had relatively regular contact with their families. On the other hand, while the nurses captured on Bataan and Corregidor were treated relatively decently by their Imperial captors, the servicemen who had come under Japanese control were often suffering privations, torture, and humiliation that would not be fully chronicled until the closing months of the war.

As Americans prepared to enter the third year of a conflict that was now almost universally referred to as World War II, millions of citizens engaged in a guessing game centered on the end dates of the conflicts with Germany and Japan. Two years earlier, news media analysts discussed the probability of German superbombers raiding New York City or Japanese carrier planes strafing the streets of Los Angeles. Now, in December of 1943, those threats seemed increasingly remote, and slogans such as "End the War in '44," "Home Alive in '45," and "The Golden Gate in '48" merely differed on when the war would end, not which side would win.

The most optimistic prediction—that the war would end in the upcoming year—was based on a combination of realism and wishful thinking. Virtually all Americans believed that 1943 had been a disastrous year for the Axis. Italy had dropped out of the Axis and, in effect, switched sides. Germany had lost one entire army at Stalingrad and much of a second army in Tunisia, while a high-risk roll of the dice at Kursk had produced a third disaster and initiated a long Wehrmacht retreat westward toward the borders of the Reich. By December, a Red tide was lapping at German defense lines only one hundred miles east of the outer borders of Germany, while rumors circulated that Axis allies Finland and Romania were quietly attempting to make a deal with the Allies before the Red Army engulfed them.

Meanwhile, one hundred miles south of German-occupied Rome, the American Fifth Army and the British Eighth Army loomed as a potential major threat if the Allies could break out of rain-soaked mountains and lunge northward toward the Eternal City. Even as severe winter weather seemed to stalemate Allied operations in Italy, their very presence forced the German high command to station substantial forces on that front that were desperately needed in the east to hold the Soviet juggernaut at bay.

One significant element of the news media and American public opinion in late 1943 was that they hoped and expected that the great European land battles foreseen in the coming year might actually prove to be unnecessary. Their eyes increasingly looked to the skies and to the massive Allied bomber fleets that, according to some reports, were turning Germany into a vast wasteland that was gradually reverting to Stone Age conditions.

One of the wonders of Allied strategy in late 1943 was that the American and British air chiefs had turned a roiling feud over bombing strategy into a public relations bonanza. As British bomber crews were decimated by losses in daylight raids, the Royal Air Force had switched to nighttime bombing of the European continent, and, as large-scale American forces reached Britain, they advised their Yank counterparts to do the same. However, senior American commanders were convinced that the much more heavily armed Fortresses and Liberators could challenge Luftwaffe interceptors in daylight, and they felt confident that their "precision" bombing was the key to aerial victory.

Then, almost magically, a seemingly major row between Allies was turned into a propaganda bonanza with a new slogan—"Round the Clock" bombing. The Allied air forces were now committed to Round the Clock bombing of the enemy as British area bombing and American precision bombing would combine to devastate the Germans on such a titanic scale that the expected 1944 ground invasion of mainland Europe would not even be necessary. Thus, in the closing weeks of 1943, similar to factory workers toiling in alternate shifts in the same plant, bombers displaying RAF roundels and AAF stars droned over the Reich and returned to Britain with mildly inflated estimates of the damage they had inflicted. American newspapers and magazines published "exclusive" testimonials from citizens of neutral countries residing in the Reich that Berlin and other large cities were only one step from becoming unlivable shells. Photos of German mobile soup kitchens feeding homeless citizens against a backdrop of piles of rubble attested to a German reversion to Dark Ages culture. During the new year of 1944, surely this rain of fire would decisively affect the ability of the Wehrmacht to continue the war unabated.

While substantial numbers of Americans in late 1943 saw a real possibility of a German collapse before the end of the coming year, the general mood regarding the Pacific War tended to be less sanguine although guardedly optimistic. While a wide range of people from journalists to factory workers belived that Hitler might be pulled from power by generals, courtiers, or even an open insurrection, there was little expectation that Emperor Hirohito would share that fate in the foreseeable future.

In December of 1943, the vast majority of Americans were convinced that the Pacific War would most likely end only after a time-consuming march back across the ocean, culminating with a ground invasion of the Nipponese homeland from a springboard of the eastern coast of China. Most Americans believed that, compared to the dark days following Pearl Harbor, the United States was in an incalculably better strategic position in December 1943. There was an almost unanimous feeling that the war against Japan had turned a corner and that there was virtually no chance of either an American defeat or even a heavily compromised negotiated settlement. Pearl Harbor, Wake Island, Bataan, and Corregidor were too fresh in memory to conceive of anything short of massive payback in kind to a nation and populace that seemed incapable of functioning as a modern, civilized entity. Yet thousands of miles still separated the most forward American positions and the halls of the Imperial palace.

In December 1943, Japanese thrusts at Alaska, Hawaii, and Australia were now counted as absolute failures: the archvillain of Pearl Harbor, Admiral Yamamoto, was dead, and there was no chance that the Nipponese would dictate terms of peace in the White House. However, a figurative bamboo curtain still seemed to surround the land of the rising sun, and the Pacific War was currently being fought in a no man's land between America and Japan.

During the Civil War, the back-and-forth maneuvering of the two primary eastern armies created a form of no man's land at some point between Washington and Richmond. Areas around the Rapidan and Rappahannock rivers, much of the Shenandoah Valley, parts of rural Virginia that would be nicknamed "Mosby's Confederacy" after the famed "Gray Ghost"—all became part of a malleable, moving universe of war under permanent control of neither Union nor Confederacy. Now, in late 1943, a contested borderland between Japan and America had emerged in places such as the Solomon Islands, New Guinea, and parts of the Central Pacific. However, while the fact that Washington and Richmond were only one hundred miles apart somewhat limited that war's no man's land, Virginia, Pacific distances were often measured in thousands of miles, and picturesque nineteenth-century towns and countryside were replaced by the "Green Hell of New Guinea" and the coral specks of land in a seemingly endless sea in which reality and myth seemed to intersect.

Until the final few weeks of the year, much of the Pacific War in 1943 seemed to revolve around the hazy no man's land in a back-and-forth struggle that lacked the drama and large-scale impact of their 1942 predecessors such as Bataan, Midway, Guadalcanal, and Savo Island. Then, just as Americans prepared for Thanksgiving celebrations, newspapers, radio newscasts, and movie news clips announced that a massive American Central Pacific offensive had begun in the obscure location of the Tarawa Atoll.

While the battle for Guadalcanal had seesawed for six months, the army assault on Makin Island and the Marine battle for Betio were lightning strikes that turned white coral into a red landscape in a few dozen hours.

The invasion of Makin by the 27th Army Division initially seemed to progress according to schedule, but, as the Japanese perimeter shrank, the intensity of the battle escalated and stretched from mere hours into days. While expertly concealed Nipponese defenders whittled away at the GIs a Japanese submarine slipped through the screen of American destroyers to torpedo the escort carrier *Liscombe Bay,* which quickly sank to the bottom of the sea with eight hundred crew members. Their deaths pushed the Makin operation death toll to nearly one thousand.

Meanwhile, one hundred miles to the south of Makin, the 2nd Marine Division was bleeding to death in the aching brilliance of Betio Island's coral sands. As American families began sorting out their holiday decorations, four battalions of leathernecks clambered down the sides of their transport ships and boarded landing craft that would carry them through a stunningly beautiful tropical lagoon that fronted the northern beaches of Betio. Initially, wary invasion troops relaxed slightly at the sight of the island's seeming implosion under the firepower of naval and Marine aerial attacks and the big guns of the supporting fleet. Then grim reality began to displace optimism as the new amphibian tractors that were carrying the invaders toward shore struck coral reefs that were supposed to be sitting in much deeper water. Soon hundreds of Marines who expected to disembark on dry land found themselves wading, and in some instances drowning, in a nautical killing ground between the outer reefs and Betio's palm-lined beaches. Now the Japanese garrison, who were themselves Imperial sea soldiers, blasted away at their American counterparts.

Elite fighting men of two nations were now embarking on a seventy-six-hour carnival of death that featured an intensity far beyond that of earlier island battles. Unlike the large, jungle-dominated islands of the Solomons, Betio was essentially a coral rock roughly the size of an American university campus. While Japanese defenders on previous island targets obliged the American invaders by launching human-wave assaults that rapidly depleted the garrison, the Imperial troops on Betio hunkered down to inflict maximum Marine casualties. As one American correspondent noted, "On Tarawa, the Japs dug in as only that burrowing people can dig in; their officers told them that a million Americans could not take that place." Japanese defenders watched their adversaries wade slowly and painfully through the water in what seemed like almost a film in slow motion, as blood mixed in larger quantities with the azure sea.

By dusk on their first day in this tropical hell, the Marine presence in Betio was limited to a twenty-foot-wide strand of beach fronted by a ring of strong points filled with Imperial troops determined to push the Marines back into the sea. Then, as the sun rose on the second day of battle, much of the Japanese garrison made a grievous error that would plague them all throughout the coming year of 1944. The Imperial troops on Betio were experts at creating fortifications with minimal tools and resources, but at heart they were still driven by a Samurai spirit that rebelled at a defensive mentality. Now young men in mustard-colored uniforms, some of them wielding swords, charged out of their expertly crafted defenses and stormed toward the beaches. They were met by equally intense young men in green dungarees who may not have carried swords but parried with bayoneted rifles, pistols, and even fists. Dozens of leathernecks dropped in injury or death, but far more of their tormentors dropped around them, especially when Japanese swords were countered by expertly handled flamethrowers that, according to one officer, "curled Japs like celluloid."

Over a period of three days, the Japanese perimeter gradually contracted, but impending victory was coming at a steep price. A generation earlier, 956 Marines had died in a month-long duel with the kaiser's troops at Château-Thierry, and two men fewer than those had paid the supreme sacrifice in the jungles of Guadalcanal. Now, in only a few dozen hours, 1,027 leathernecks were dead and 2,557 seriously wounded in the capture of one small stretch of coral. When the grisly toll of soldiers on Makin Island and sailors on Liscombe Bay were added to the soaring casualty list, the statistics showed that the capture of Tarawa Atoll had resulted in over two thousand American deaths, a total that had occurred in a time not much longer than the Day of Infamy itself two years earlier. As the shockingly high casualty lists began reaching American media outlets in the early part of December, some newspaper and magazine analysts wondered whether the war in the upcoming year of 1944 would present a long series of costly battles and campaigns resulting in similar bloodshed in the Civil War during 1864. An editorial in *Life* magazine asked, "Was not such a fight [Tarawa] this costly for a patch of sand two miles long and eight hundred yards wide? The famous tenacity of the Jap is not equal to the tenacity of an American aroused [but] there is no cheap short cut to victory."

While the news of the Tarawa campaign alternately thrilled and shocked Americans on the home front, Franklin Delano Roosevelt was mixing wartime cocktails for the leaders of the other two most powerful nations arrayed against the Axis. At the end of November, the president's plane left an airfield in Cairo; dipped low over Jerusalem, Bethlehem, Jericho; and the Jordan River; and flew into the heart of the old Persian Empire to meet with the master of the much newer Soviet Empire. Roosevelt and British Prime Minister Winston Spencer Churchill had received an invitation to meet with Josef Stalin in the rambling, spacious Soviet embassy in Tehran, a venue that the field marshal insisted was as far as he could travel while handling the day-to-day planning of the massive Russian-German confrontation on the Eastern Front.

The venue Stalin chose also had the additional bonus of placing his two Allied counterparts in quarters that bristled with every form of 1940s listening device that technology could provide, a simple fact of doing business for the often paranoid Soviet leader. Stalin mixed massive eavesdropping with a surprising level of geniality that alternated between lavish banquets and extended drinking sessions in which the themes for mutual toasts never seemed to run short.

The marshal praised America's industrial production and massive aid for his nation and admitted that this largesse had been one of the key factors in the Russian ability to turn back Nazi attempts to conquer the Soviet Union. A highlight of the conference occurred when Churchill presented the marshal with a fifty-inch, two-handed sword made by the Wilkinson Blade Company; the weapon had taken two days to forge, had a pommel with a gold rose of England, and had been commissioned personally by King George VI and designated as the Sword of Stalingrad. In a rare moment in which genuine emotion seemed to replace his usual cynicism, Stalin kissed the weapon as Roosevelt held the scabbard and lauded the marshal's "heart of steel." The concluding joint statement about the decisions made at the Tehran conference was a message designed to stir fear in the hearts of Hitler and his minions: "No power on earth can prevent our destruction of the German armies by land, their U-boats at sea and their war planes from the air. Our attacks will be relentless and increasing day by day."

One of the first beneficiaries of this joint statement of purpose was an engaging, articulate American Army officer who on the morning of Pearl Harbor had been a relatively obscure, middle-aged colonel working from a tiny desk in a nondescript location in the War Office in Washington. Now, two years later, the three major Allied leaders celebrated Winston Churchill's sixty-ninth birthday, while Roosevelt cheerfully mixed martinis and old-fashioneds for his counterparts. Somewhere in this alcohol-infused festivity, Josef Stalin rather coldly cornered the American president, asking for a specific date and the name of the commander of the long-promised second front in Europe. On a North African stopover on his way back to Washington, the commander-in-chief sat in an automobile at the Tunis airport, invited General Dwight Eisenhower into the car to join him, and blurted out a single sentence: "Well, Ike, you are going to command Overlord." If no other event had occurred in the upcoming year of 1944, the single event of the invasion of German-occupied Northern Europe would have ensured that year as one of the most remarkable in American history. The last full year, and the bloodiest twelve months of the American war experience, were about to begin, and life in the United States would never be completely the same afterward.

CHAPTER I

A Gathering
of Eagles

During the cold, short days of January 1944, lights shone brightly
far into the night at the two major centers of decision making
in the American capital. In the warm, homey atmosphere of the private rooms of the White House, Franklin Roosevelt alternated between
showing off his world-class stamp collection, mixing his favorite cocktails, and discussing military strategy with senior civilians and officers
in the now-burgeoning American military establishment. With the only
exception being George C. Marshall, the president engaged in a first-
name give-and-take with the secretaries of War and Navy and the top
tier of generals and admirals who were tasked with implementing the
Allies' "unconditional surrender" directive against Nazi Germany and
the Japanese Empire. In a time of numerous new studies on Abraham
Lincoln and the Union prosecution of the Civil War, Roosevelt may
have compared his role as commander-in-chief in a global conflict with
his predecessor's attempts to restore a fractured nation in an equally
bloody and massive conflict eight decades earlier.

In January of 1864, the Union Army of roughly one million men
was largely resting and refitting after an 1863 campaign season that,
while beginning disastrously, had finished with the capture of the entire

Confederate Army at the vital port city of Vicksburg; it had defeated Robert E. Lee's most ambitious foray into the North at Gettysburg and seriously crippled a second rebel army in the hills around Chattanooga. Lincoln was just about to name the hero of Vicksburg and Chattanooga, Ulysses S. Grant, as his Commanding General, and, whereas the rebels still held substantial portions of their seceded confederation, there was something between hope and expectation among citizens of the North that the coming year, 1864, would turn the course of the Civil War irrevocably against the rebellion.

Now, in early 1944, Franklin Roosevelt was sitting in the same office as Lincoln had sat, planning strategy of a war that was global instead of national, with both mighty allies and fanatic enemies, capable of flinging into battle forces that were many times the size of those that fought the War Between the States. Like Lincoln, who had entered the Civil War with an essentially constabulary force army of only sixteen thousand men, the current commander-in-chief had received news of the outbreak of World War II in charge of an army smaller than that of Portugal with equipment shortages that forced war-game participants to use broomsticks in place of rifles, stove pipes to substitute for mortars, and bags of flour standing in for bombs in mock air attacks. However, now the nation that had entered the war with only a few dozen modern bombers and essentially no first-line tanks had become the "Arsenal of Democracy," which meant that American aircraft factories could replace in a few hours the equivalent of all the planes lost at Pearl Harbor; they were also forced to find increasingly creative names of ships, as most traditional designations had already been used. Ironically, the president who sat in the Oval Office in January 1944 had approximately sixteen months left in his life, the same destiny that faced Lincoln at the same point in 1864.

While Abraham Lincoln had to develop a strategy with his most trusted generals to recapture all or part of eleven seceded states, Franklin Roosevelt had to supervise construction of a plan to first eject the Axis powers from the huge segment of the planet that they had annexed and looted during the past four years, and then, most likely, smash into their homelands, which were defended possibly to the last person, in an orgy of almost theatrical self-destruction. Thus, Roosevelt would have to call upon his generals and admirals, and in this modern war, his scientists and engineers as well, to force an unconditional surrender and occupation on two nations that had enjoyed ample opportunity to turn large segments of their population, from children to grandparents, into excellent candidates for suicide warriors.

If the war could somehow be limited to a relatively conventional clash of arms, Roosevelt and his commanders enjoyed a growing cornucopia of military assets. The Armed Forces were still expanding toward an approximate ceiling of twelve million active-duty personnel, divided roughly between 8.5 million Army and Army Air Forces personnel and 3.5 million sailors and Marines. Two years earlier, success or failure in defense of the American protectorate in the Philippines hinged on the ability of a single regular Army regiment, two regiments of native Filipino constabulary, thirty-five bombers, one hundred fighter planes, and a few platoons of light tanks. Now the Army and its Air Force were moving toward a grand force that had essentially peaked at eighty-eight divisions and an Air Force that would soon be capable of dispatching one thousand bombers escorted by hundreds of modern fighters on a single mission.

Just over eighteen months earlier, the navy had been forced to face a potential Japanese threat at Hawaii centered on approximately ten aircraft carriers with only three flattops of their own and had later spent harrowing periods when only one carrier was combat-effective in the entire Pacific battleground. Now, in 1944, fleet operations in the march across the Pacific were centered on four carrier groups deploying fifteen or sixteen fleet and light carriers by summer, with several scores of smaller escort carriers forming a formidable second tier of aerial power. Battleships listed as "sunk" at Pearl Harbor were now being extracted from the mud of the harbor bottom and paired off with a bevy of new "fast" battleships to theoretically outgun anything the Japanese Navy could throw into their path.

Ungainly Vindicator ("Wind Indicator") torpedo bombers that had been nearly annihilated at Midway were now serving as training planes, replaced by Avengers capable of 50 percent more speed and twice the bomb load, while the stately Wildcat fighters, forced to deal with deadly

Japanese Zeros in uneven duels, had given way to superb Hellcats that were already shooting down enemy planes at a ratio of twenty to one.

In a similar vein, the Army Air Force in early 1944 was undergoing enormous changes in fighter and escort missions as the feisty but outperformed Airacobras and Warhawks were now giving way to the deadly trio of the twin-engine P-38 Lightning, the bottle-shaped workhorse P-47 Thunderbolt, and the streamlined, elegant P-51 Mustang. The Army Air Force now largely matched or exceeded Luftwaffe speed, performance, and pilot quality over the frigid upper atmosphere of occupied Europe.

While the technical breakthroughs since Pearl Harbor had virtually guaranteed that American soldiers and Marines would fight the 1944 Pacific battles with a substantial technological edge over their Nipponese opponents in almost every aspect of the battlefield, the plans for the coming year's campaign in Europe were complicated by both anticipated and unanticipated disadvantages against the German ground forces. The American divisions that would be fighting the European ground battles of 1944 were the most mobile in the history of warfare. Massive infusions of jeeps and trucks into almost any infantry unit meant that with relatively minor transfers of vehicles, entire army divisions would become completely motorized and change the speed of warfare from walking speed to motor-propelled speed. This change was already emerging in 1943 and in the coming year would set up some astounding breakthroughs at speeds hardly envisioned even in the great German Blitzkrieg of 1940.

Almost every American soldier would go into battle in 1944 equipped with the superb eight-shot M1 Garand rifle that spewed firepower far beyond the ability of the World War I-era bolt-action rifles that were standard for every other major army in 1944. The infantry GIs would be supported by an artillery array that was well-organized, dependable, and, in certain cases, capable of annihilating an enemy formation in a short time span.

However, while American ground forces would routinely outgun the enemy in the coming Pacific battles, the campaigns in Europe would be considerably less one-sided because of a number of American shortcomings and newly emerging German tactics.

While the GIs fighting in Europe in the coming year would employ excellent rifles and be supported by superior artillery and imaginative tactical air support, these advantages would be partially challenged by several realities. First, while the American M1 Garand could outgun the German Mauser, the Wehrmacht (the unified armed forces of Germany from 1935 to 1946) changed the rules by pouring vast numbers of short-range automatic weapons into its infantry companies. While the M1 could outgun the Mauser, it, in turn, fired less rapidly than the new "storm rifles," machine pistols, and "burp" guns that many Germans now carried. Also, while American machine guns were relatively rapid and effective, the potent German Mg-1942 could double or triple the firepower of the GIs' support weapons and spread terror across the front lines. One of the most controversial segments of 1944 ground battles in Europe was the huge philosophical difference between American and German armored practices. The GIs would enter the ground battles of 1944 supported by thousands of standard M4 Sherman tanks. The Shermans were reliable, in huge supply, and supported by relatively high speed and automatic rotating turrets. When the Americans came up against the standard German battle tanks of 1944, the Panzer IV, the enemy enjoyed the advantage of superior armor, while the Shermans could fire more quickly. However, in one of the most underreported American military gaffes of 1944, armor planning officers chose to concentrate on massive production of the Sherman while freezing introduction of the far faster, better armored, more powerful Pershing, which only entered the theater in small numbers in the final weeks of the war. On the other hand, the Germans were introducing *two* upgraded models beyond the Mark IV, the Mark V Panther, and the Mark VI Tiger.

The Panthers were introduced in relatively large numbers in the 1944 battles and were clearly superior to the Shermans, but the perceived scourge of the battlefield was the Tiger and its even more imposing cousin, the King Tiger, which dwarfed the Shermans and seemed like prehistoric creatures rolling around the roads and fields of Northern Europe. Luckily for the American forces, the Germans fielded only small numbers of Tigers in the battles for Northern Europe in 1944; there were only eighty available to challenge the D-Day invasion, but the failure to match those behemoths with new Pershings would become a major issue in the coming campaign.

At the beginning of 1944, the American Army had a realistic ceiling of ninety divisions and would need to deploy at least twenty of these units in the Pacific against the Japanese, while the Wehrmacht fielded three hundred divisions. However, the initially shocking disparity in formation numbers was softened by a variety of mitigating factors. First, German casualties in four years of multifront fighting had been astronomical, and the High Command was in the process of cutting most divisions down to two regiment units, which, in turn, were often consistently below authorized strength owing to a shortage of replacements. Therefore, at best for the Germans, their combat divisions would field perhaps 60 percent of the personnel of an American equivalent, and, as the year went on, even this number was usually maintained only for the most elite German units. Second, a huge portion of the German Army was now tied down by garrisoning occupied countries that the Allies had no intention of immediately liberating or deploying in keeping Axis nations from switching sides if the Allies appeared to be winning. Thus, Denmark, Norway, Romania, and Hungary were filled with German troops that were of little immediate benefit in repelling an Anglo-American invasion of the Continent. Third, and probably most important, the bulk of the German Army opened 1944 deployed on the Eastern Front awaiting another in a series of Soviet offensives that had already positioned the Red Army dangerously close to the eastern frontier of the Reich. Hitler could, and did, pull some of his most elite Eastern Front divisions into France in an attempt to smash the efforts of the Anglo-American invasion but was essentially robbing Peter to pay Paul. As elite SS Panzer divisions rumbled westward to challenge the invasion of France, those units were leaving gaping holes on the Eastern Front that would be difficult to fill.

Even on the projected battlefield of France in 1944, the American divisions that were expected to be deployed in Operation Overlord were not planning to be entering battle alone. Britain and Canada would combine forces to deploy an entire army group, which, in turn, would be supplemented with free French and Polish units that would add several more divisions to the final tally. However, unlike in World War I, when the Americans solidified an already enormous British- and French-allied Army, the most prominent contingent of the 1944 battle for Western Europe would be the combat units from the United States, who, unlike in 1917 and 1918, would have to fight their way into France, rather than transition from welcoming parades at Allied-held ports to a trench line already held by a huge army. Without an enormous American military contingent, French people had little hope of liberation, and British soldiers had faint prospects of returning to the Dunkirk beaches from which they were evacuated in 1940. The Americans and Germans were already dueling for possession of the forbidding mountainsides of southern Italy; now the major clash of armies loomed in the fields and hedges of France. While the long-awaited invasion of Northern Europe presented enormous challenges for American war planners, there was expectation of combat in a relatively finite area of land that had topography and climate similar to much of those of the United States, with the somewhat comforting prospect that an even larger Soviet Army would be slamming into the enemy from the rear. The planning for the 1944 campaign against the Japanese provided almost none of those comfort zones.

After the successful battles for the Solomon and Gilbert island chains during the year just ending, American strategic planners could begin to focus on bigger, more rewarding operations during 1944. However, while there was at least a slim hope that a combined Anglo-American and Soviet offensive just might "end the war in '44," more than a few American military strategists, average citizens, and combat personnel were hearing a less optimistic "The Golden Gate in '48," concerning the time prospects for V-J Day. The year 1944 just might be the climactic year in the war against Germany; the coming twelve months was seen at best as a major, but not final, step in the demise of the Japanese war machine. Ironically, while the Americans had suffered a nasty bloody nose in their first confrontation with the German Army at Kasserine Pass the preceding February and were now engaged in a near stalemate in southern Italy at the beginning of 1944, United States forces had not tasted any form of defeat against the Japanese since the disastrous moments of Savo Island in August of 1942.

The year 1943 had seen the Americans victorious at Guadalcanal: they pushed the Imperial Army backwards across most of New Guinea, successfully ambushed and killed Admiral Yamamoto, the architect of Pearl Harbor, and most recently had annihilated the Japanese garrison in the Gilberts. However, optimism for future success in 1944 was mitigated by the realization that the Nipponese had gained such massive new territories in both the war against China and in the first six months after Pearl Harbor that it seemed enormously optimistic to see Americans at the gates of the Emperor's Palace in the reasonably near future. However, within the limitations of this sobering reality, there was hope in early 1944 that this year would at least push Japan a giant step nearer defeat.

The leaders who would plan operations for the Pacific War in 1944 were by now confident that American forces could beat Japanese forces in the vast majority of stand-up battles in the coming year. The Americans had better fighters, better bombers, better rifles, better tanks, better submarines, and better aircraft carriers than their adversaries. American strategists had carefully noted that in initially seesaw battles on the ground, in the air, and at sea, enemy impatience encouraged them to turn nearly or actually suicidal and deplete their strength from some form of banzai attack that usually resulted in ten or twenty Nipponese casualties for every American equivalent.

However, the senior officers planning Pacific operations for 1944 still saw victory primarily through the prism of a physical invasion of the Japanese home islands, and, with seemingly no chance of a negotiated surrender, they envisioned the battle of Japan as occurring well beyond the next twelve months. Their best hope for a decisive battle during the coming year revolved around an attempt to capture a Nipponese possession that was so important they could not afford to give it up and, thus, entice the launch of the Imperial Fleet, which had been largely on the sidelines since Guadalcanal or even Midway, to sortie from its bases and engage in a decisive battle that would hopefully end in total American victory. These planners would get their wish on not one but two occasions in 1944, but there was much more in store for the year in the Pacific War than they initially expected.

This Gathering of Eagles—composed of the generals and admirals who would plan and command the battles that would make 1944 the decisive year of World War II—was, of course, more figurative than literal. At no other point in the year would virtually every senior commander sit in the same room and discuss operations, concerns, and opportunities. However, World War II was a period of emerging revolution in communications, and telephones, teletype, radio, motion pictures, and other relatively recent breakthroughs allowed a speed of communication that even modern-thinking Civil War commanders could only dream about.

One of the most important constitutional duties performed by the president of the United States is to serve as commander-in-chief of all American armed forces, and the sixty-two-year-old New Yorker sitting in the Oval Office in 1944 now commanded the largest military force ever fielded by the United States. Franklin Roosevelt, in this year of decision, was late in his unprecedented third term in office and had held office in a seemingly never-ending crisis atmosphere caused by the greatest economic meltdown in the nation's history, followed immediately by the largest military effort ever attempted. The incumbent president presented one of the most complicated personalities of any other leader in the history of the Republic. He was affable, kindly, truly concerned about less fortunate people, and bipartisan enough to have appointed Republicans to some of the highest offices in the government. On the other hand, he was often devious and untruthful and could be mean and petty. He had been in office so long that many of the young servicemen and servicewomen he commanded could barely remember any other occupant of the White House.

During 1944, Roosevelt's health was probably deteriorating far more rapidly than either he or his personal physician would admit. Official pronouncements of sinus infections, bronchitis, and other minor maladies led to screening for worse issues, such as high blood pressure, erratic heartbeat, and ever-lengthening recovery periods from illnesses. Yet, while photographs and films of the president depict a person who sometimes looked ten or even twenty years older than his true age, it appears that his ability to make critical military decisions was not yet significantly compromised.

Unlike his distant cousin and earlier counterpart, Theodore Roosevelt, FDR had never been involved in an actual battle but had been a voracious reader of military and naval history and had served as Assistant Secretary of the Navy during World War I. Franklin Roosevelt had realized the potential threat of Nazi Germany and an increasingly fascist Japan much earlier than most other political leaders and had begun a serious rearmament program only a year before Pearl Harbor. His choices for appointments to senior command positions both before and after Pearl Harbor had been generally apolitical and intuitive and, more often than not, produced competent leaders in key positions. The commander-in-chief occasionally micromanaged to the extent of suggesting some military operations and some personnel promotions, but, compared to his closest ally, Winston Churchill, Roosevelt allowed far more autonomy to his senior decision makers. By 1944, numerous Republican leaders may have loathed his domestic politics but generally gave tacit support to his role as commander-in-chief as basically being above party issues.

The most important personnel decision that Roosevelt had made in relation to the war was his selection of George Catlett Marshall as the senior commander of the United States Army. On the surface, the civilian commander-in-chief and the senior officers in an American Army that fielded 8.5 million men and women seemed a partnership of opposites. While Roosevelt was often jocular, exuberant, and informal and loved conversation, his senior military commander exuded at least an external aura of control and dignity that would have been applauded by the chronicles of ancient Rome.

George C. Marshall turned sixty-three years old on December 31, 1943, and, thus, was very much a contemporary of the commander-in-chief. He was born in Uniontown, Pennsylvania, as a distant cousin to the famous Supreme Court Justice John Marshall. Growing up in the home of a Civil War veteran, he began developing plans to attend West Point, but with mediocre high school grades and a Democrat father engaged in feuds with the local Republican congressman, he shifted his priorities to Virginia Military Institute instead. At VMI, Marshall emerged as a very good student and an all-league football player who utilized those two skills to demonstrate excellent ability for planning and tactics, from fighting Filipino guerillas to planning the great American St. Michael offensive in 1918.

He began attracting Franklin Roosevelt's notice as an organizer and administrator of New Deal Civilian Conservation Corps camps before transitioning into chief of the War Plans division of the War Department. In September 1939, as reports filtered into the White House describing the massive German invasion of Poland, the president promoted Marshall to full general as Chief of Staff of the then less-than-robust American Army of two hundred thousand men.

While Roosevelt and Marshall developed an excellent working relationship, with the president supplying the funding and the general supplying the expertise to increase the army ground and air forces to forty times their prewar levels, their relationship seemed closer to the Jefferson Davis-Robert E. Lee partnership than the Lincoln-Grant alliance of 1864–65. Marshall, like Lee, was noted for his intuition, courtesy, and consideration, even toward low-ranking enlisted personnel, but in the 1944 era, journalists noted a certain detachment from too much frivolity or exuberance, a barrier of reserve which few people really crossed, and a lack of really intimate friends that made him, like Lee, "revered fondly but from afar."

Marshall took every opportunity to go out in the field to meet troops, asking which school they attended or what they planned to do after the war. He almost always ordered that any extra seats on any plane on which he flew be used for ambulatory wounded and cordially greeted military police personnel who guarded him on his trips with "I'm General Marshall. Glad to have you with us." When Marshall traveled to Army stations or encampments, commonly orders were forwarded to muster no guard of honor and to prepare a room in a regular visiting-officer quarters, and he even refused to have a regular aide-de-camp as an exclusive position.

George Marshall had been preparing for the current war years before Pearl Harbor as he crisscrossed the nation, visiting military bases and quietly making notations in a small notebook about midlevel officers who either clearly possessed or clearly lacked the attributes of a commander of large bodies of men. Now, some of these earlier captains, majors, and lieutenant colonels held generals' ranks and were commanding the forces beginning to defeat the Axis powers. The commander-in-chief and his senior military commander had achieved an excellent, if very formal, relationship, but one based on mutual respect and admiration, rather than affectionate feelings. In some respects, both men were responsible for this formality. The limitation on their relationship that could primarily be tied to Marshall's side was that the general's reserved personality and personal dignity and gravity simply could not melt in the presence of the chief executive. Roosevelt's natural affability and joviality simply did not mesh well with Marshall's serious persona, and, in one memorable instance, in which the president felt comfortable enough to address the general as "George," Marshall's response of an icy stare raised the level of tension in the room. On the other hand, the president had some role in the lack of personal engagement when he made it clear to all comers that because of his World War I position, he was a "navy man" through and through. When he referred to the army, it was always "them"; when discussing naval matters, the terms always centered on "us" and "we." The president's office was replete with paintings of ships, models of ships, artifacts of ships, and nothing indicating that the United States even had an army. Perhaps the bright side of this reality from Marshall's perspective was that, in turn, Roosevelt never either micromanaged nor second-guessed any decision the general made concerning army activities in the war.

The navy that the commander-in-chief referred to in the personal "us" or "we" was now under the command of an admiral who seemed to have almost nothing in common with George Marshall except four stars on his shoulder. Admiral Ernest D. King was, in 1944, a sixty-five-year-old, hard-drinking, hard-swearing, chain-smoking, and, according to rumors, frequently womanizing "old salt," who in a real-life irony of Greek theater or Shakespearean proportions, headed a household composed of a probably long-suffering wife and a large bevy of daughters who seemed impervious to his vaunted wrath. While King was brusque, opinionated, and profane, when the press or other outsiders were not looking, he was loyal and gracious to junior officers on his staff, enjoyed a gruff camaraderie with enlisted men, and got along splendidly with his commander-in-chief.

Roosevelt promoted King to the position of commander-in-chief of the United States Fleet a week after Pearl Harbor, and the man who would eventually have nearly four million naval personnel serving under him set up shop in a bare third-floor office in the Navy Department building, equipped with only two chairs and a broken table. The new commander of the United States Navy displayed a versatile background in submarine duty, battleship service, and, near his fiftieth birthday, as a navy pilot. Now, in the president's office, amidst naval decoration and a pall of haze created by the two chain smokers, Roosevelt and King were plotting the annihilation of both German Kriegsmarine and the Imperial Japanese Navy.

A third major service had emerged during the past four decades and now determined to break from its parent organization. The relatively recently retitled Army Air Force was a new organization with personnel who looked longingly and jealously at the totally independent Royal Air Force of their ally, Britain, and the Luftwaffe of their major European enemy, Germany. While personnel of those services visually demonstrated their independence in the stylish "aviation blue" uniforms, USAAF personnel could only add distinction patches and insignia on traditional army khaki and olive drab. However, their commanding general now had a seat on the Joint Chiefs of Staff, and Henry "Hap" Arnold was not about to play second fiddle to either of the "senior" services.

Hap Arnold was slightly younger than either the president or the commanders of the army and navy, but the fifty-seven-year-old Pennsylvania native, who apparently outdid even Ernest King in alcohol and smoking excess, was forced to trade his "younger than his age" appearance for the heart of a man twenty years older. Arnold had actually learned to fly from the Wright brothers and was a pilot in World War I, followed by a long list of "firsts," such as the institution of airmail service, air-to air-refueling, and air forest fire patrols. In 1941, as chief of the Army Air Corps, Arnold was able to negotiate a partial separation of air and ground forces with tacit approval from the president that a complete "divorce" would follow the end of the war. Meanwhile, if Arnold could not yet issue blue uniforms, he could hire fashion designers to produce the "smartest" uniform of any

American service, lure top band leaders like Glenn Miller into forming an Air Force swing orchestra, and wine and dine Hollywood executives into having Air Force films display the most handsome actors and most glamorous starlets.

At the beginning of 1944, Hap Arnold most likely knew that the American Air Force had not accomplished the precision, pinpoint destruction of enemy assets that had been promised or often erroneously reported. However, in early 1944, the air force finally seemed to be receiving the hugely increased numbers of bombers and the long-range escort fighters that could possibly knock Germany out of the war before D-Day, or at least ensure that the invasion of Europe was a success. Then, with the promise of the delivery of the futuristic B-29 Superfortress, his airmen could begin to destroy the Nipponese war machine and render a ground invasion of Japan superfluous.

Each of these three senior American military leaders had been given considerable autonomy by their commander-in-chief to implement plans designed to make 1944 the climactic year of World War II. Unlike Adolph Hitler and even Winston Churchill, Franklin Roosevelt allowed his senior "Eagles" enormous leeway to develop a winning formula to defeat the enemy. Even at meetings of the Joint Chiefs of Staff, Roosevelt's place was taken by his surrogate, Admiral William Leahy, a convivial, experienced diplomat who played cards frequently with the president and had served as his ambassador to Vichy, France, and offered the dual bonus of providing a second Mariner to offset the technical advantage of Marshall and Arnold versus King, while also serving as a conduit between the president and his commanders. As Chairman of the Joint Chiefs of Staff, William Leahy was technically the most powerful uniformed officer in the United States, but the admiral's presence, in reality, created a pragmatic environment, whereby senior American military commanders could fight the campaigns of 1944 with little direct civilian intrusion. Yet, the president, as their civilian superior, could be a "virtual" presence in their relatively collegial decision making. The pragmatic president of a pragmatic nation had, in essence, set in motion a command structure that could turn 1944 into the decisive year of World War II.

CHAPTER II

The Ghosts of Hills and Rivers

In the winter of 1944, as Franklin Roosevelt's senior military commanders met to plan and plot the multifront 1944 assault on the Axis, a small, wizened, almost elf-like figure swaddled in layers of olive drab and civilian clothing sat staring at looming hills and listening to the sounds of battle as he composed a chronicle of a battle. Ernie Pyle was the most famous and popular war correspondent in American journalism, and the reality that he was twice the age of the warriors around him had forced the writer to admit that he must leave this particular corner of hell for a rest in his home in the warm, dry air of Albuquerque, New Mexico.

Ernie Pyle's primary weapons were a pen and a typewriter, and he had come to Italy to narrate an expected, dramatic Anglo-American drive up the Italian boot, a drive to be climaxed by a festive capture of the first Axis capital to fall, the Eternal City of Rome. Instead, Pyle and the dirty, unshaven GIs around him were stuck in mountainous terrain eighty miles south of the Coliseum and the Vatican, engaged in an endless shootout with talented, highly motivated German defenders under a leaden sky that alternately spat rain and snow at the huddled men of the Fifth Army. Pyle frankly told his readers to ignore the official blithe communiqués that the American forces were "steadily gaining ground" or "pushing up the peninsula." In actuality, they were accomplishing the drive only in the context of the "movement of a worm," and Pyle insisted that what he saw was "from a worm's eye view." He said that the world around him contained no shred of glamour, "only tired, dirty soldiers who were alive and didn't want to die; shocked, silent men wandering down the hill from battle, chow lines and atabrine tablets and foxholes and burning tanks, tents and shirts gray-black from months of wearing, and a sound of constant cussing."

Pyle admitted that when he first arrived on this front a few months earlier, "I sat in my tent alone and gloomed with the desperate belief that it was actually possible to lose this war." Now, he admitted that he veered back-and-forth in an emotional tug-of-war. On the one hand, the patent sense of frustration and helplessness at fighting in a virtually impossible battle environment led him to believe, "Our soldiers might have voted to go home immediately, even if peace was less than enemy surrender, but now the attitude was gradually shifting to a demand for total victory to atone for their suffering and friends lost."

The GIs wanted victory, but Pyle admitted that the price of their tenacity was altered personalities that were darker and more complex than people on the home front might care to probe in-depth. According to Pyle, the typical combat soldier on the Italian front in 1944 is "rougher than when you knew him; his basic language has changed from mere profanity to obscenity. More than anything else, the soldiers miss women; their whole conduct shows their need for female companionship and the gentling effect of femininity. They have less regard for property than when you raised them; a home and money has [sic] little value. There is an appalling waste of everything at the front, but they are generous with strangers and each other. Many of our men, still thinking mainly of home, are impatient with the strange people and customs of the country they now inhabit; they say that if they ever get home, they never want to see a foreign country again but equally insist that once they do return home, 'Those bluenoses back home better not try to put prohibition over on us while we're away this time.'"

These obscene speaking, unshaven, homesick Americans were in the front lines of the first major ground battle of 1944, and they seemed to be literally inching toward an Italian capital fronted by looming mountains, swirling rivers, and an enemy determined not to allow them to move forward without paying an enormous toll in shattered or dead young men. Ernie Pyle was now leaving the war, although he would die a year later from a Japanese sniper bullet in the muddy hell of Okinawa. However, for the GIs who stayed, the most immediate goal was to somehow get past the looming monastery fortress of Cassino and to craft any chance to take that ancient Benedictine abbey. They had been told that it was necessary to cross a river called the Rapido, which the enemy was not about to voluntarily give them.

The Italian front in early 1944 was in some respects similar to an ongoing play in which the main stars had already left for a new production and their roles were assumed by lesser-known understudies. By January of 1944, the major luminaries of the Mediterranean conflict of the past year were now far away from this particular battle. General Bernard Montgomery, commander of the Eighth Army at El Alamein and Sicily, was now in England with a new title of Commander of Allied Ground Forces for Operation Overlord. Dwight Eisenhower, American Commander in the Mediterranean, was now Monty's superior: supreme commander of the looming invasion of mainland Europe. George Patton's star had gone in a different direction: he had left Italy in disgrace over slapping incidents in field hospitals and was essentially on ice in England until his superiors could determine how or whether to use this flawed genius.

Now, the highest-ranking officer in the Mediterranean was General Sir Henry Maitland "Jumbo" Wilson, with the main ground force, the Fifteenth Army Group, commanded by a fellow British general, Sir Harold Alexander. These two officers were overseeing an almost painfully slow dual drive up from the southern tip of Italy with Lieutenant General Sir Oliver Leese's Eighth Army assigned the right flank and American Lieutenant General Mark Clark tasked with the left side of the operation.

Mark Clark was a tall, handsome photogenic officer who had attained the notable feat of becoming the youngest three-star general in the American Army a year earlier at the age of forty-six, despite not fitting in with the largely white Anglo-Saxon Protestant cultural background of most senior

American commanders. Much of Clark's family was composed of Eastern European Jewish immigrants, and he ultimately married an Irish Catholic girl, but his tall stature, military bearing, good looks, and outstanding administrative ability drew increasing attention from superiors. Maurine Clark, probably the charter member of her husband's formidable public relations entourage and not necessarily the most dispassionate judge of him, insisted that when she met Clark for the first time on a blind date, he was "tall straight and handsome; poised and had exceptional qualities in his voice." On the other hand, his critics highlighted a less positive side, including his allowing photographs from only the "best" side of his face, his tendency toward leading an oversized entourage of public relations personnel, and his ruthlessness in absorbing casualties for relatively marginal military gains.

In January 1944, Mark Clark was in command of an army that would be pushed from the front pages of newspapers in a few months when Operation Overlord stole the headlines in the war against Germany. The most that the Americans and their multiple allies in Italy could hope for was that they could capture Rome and become the object of a media bonanza before the international spotlight shifted to the shores of France. Even though Clark was relatively solicitous of his men, he was also ruthless enough to take whatever risk might be necessary to lead armored columns into the Eternal City before the major spotlight shifted northward. For a commander who insisted that his name appear frequently in even minor press releases, capturing Rome after D-Day was an unbearable prospect. On the positive side for Clark, the commander of Fifth Army had a slightly unlikely ally in the person of Winston Spencer Churchill.

Unlike Franklin Roosevelt, who had served as Assistant Secretary of the Navy and always referred to the maritime service as "us" and the army as "them," and Adolf Hitler, who had served exclusively in the ground forces in the Great War and developed seasickness on virtually every foray onto running water, Winston Churchill had moved back-and-forth seamlessly during his career between naval and other military responsibilities. He had fought ground battles in the colonial and Boer wars of his youth, become First Lord of the Admiralty early in World War I, and then accepted a commission leading infantrymen in the trenches when his flawed Gallipoli amphibious expedition turned into a colossal failure. Now the Prime Minister was livid over the inability of the Allied Forces to push beyond Field Marshal Albrecht Kesserling's Gustav line that effectively kept his adversaries pinned down in the southern third of Italy. Churchill had been an adamant proponent of an Allied invasion of mainland Italy, and now the initial war of movement had congealed into the semi-trench warfare that Ernie Pyle had so vividly described.

Churchill had convinced Roosevelt and American military commanders that an invasion of the Italian mainland was a thrust into "the soft underbelly of Europe," but now that underbelly had stiffened into a series of successive German defense lines that were bleeding the Allied forces for little tangible gain. The prime minister proposed to catch the Germans in huge pincers by combining an attack across the Rapido River in the general vicinity of Monte Cassino Abbey with a presumably surprise amphibious landing at the port city of Anzio about sixty miles behind the Gustav line and only thirty miles from Rome. Ironically, while most of his own British admirals and generals were, at best, anywhere from cool to openly hostile to the plan, Mark Clark, who shared the prime minister's eagerness to capture the Eternal City, joined him in an alliance to formalize the plan. Thus, in one of the most closely interlinked twin assaults of World War II, the men who huddled in the windswept hills below Cassino would unleash a desperate assault as the invasion ships for newly departed Operation Shingle were transporting a second assault force to the beaches of Anzio and Nettuno.

The focal point in American participation on the lower part of the giant pincer that Churchill envisioned was the Rapido River, a fifty-foot-wide, roughly ten-foot-deep water barrier that gained its name from the currents that ran through a heavily wooded countryside at eight miles an hour against steep banks four feet above the water. Defense of the river at the ancient monastery of Cassino beyond its northern bank had been entrusted to General Frido von Senger, an aristocratic fifty-two-year-old officer who managed to demolish most of the stereotypes surrounding German Generals of World War II. Von Senger was an aristocrat who demonstrated none of the monocled arrogance of many of his class and was more a scholar who happened to be a general, rather than a mindless adherent to Nazi values. The general had been a Rhodes Scholar at Oxford University, spoke flawless English, and was a devout Catholic who was a lay brother in the Benedictine order that staffed Cassino Abbey. Von Senger had attained enormous honor for his motorized dash that captured the French port of Cherbourg in 1940 and had rapidly made friends among the French aristocracy in a rather light-handed occupation of the territory under his command. His transfer to Italy produced equally good relations with a wide segment of the Italian population, and he had disobeyed a direct order from Hitler to execute a large contingent of Italian soldiers after their 1943 surrender. Now, in early 1944, while he explicitly forbade any German occupation of Cassino Monastery, his scruples had caused no such impediment in turning the Rapido approaches into a potential death trap for any American troops unlucky enough to attempt to force a crossing.

First, von Senger ordered the demolition of a bridge north of the monastery and the construction of a dam with the bridge materials in order to flood the ground to the south of the dam. Then, German troops were dispatched along both banks of the river to cut down trees and branches in a mile-wide swath south of the Rapido so that the Americans would lack cover for their approach. Next, the swampy terrain that remained was liberally salted with mines. Finally, from the high ground on the German side of the river, the entire Rapido approach area was carefully targeted by Wehrmacht machine guns, mortars, and cannons.

Once the river banks were prepared, German construction crews searched for any local feature that could conceal troops or guns. A string of caves to the north side of the river was enlarged, while manmade versions were now appearing. The most significant population center on this part of the river was the town of Sant'Angelo, which, like a miniature Vicksburg that had sprawled on a bluff above the Mississippi River during the Civil War, created an instant fortification in its locale, forty feet above the Rapido. German engineers created a quilt-patterned urban defense system by alternately blowing up some of the Bermuda-like pastel houses for ready defense amid the rubble, while other buildings were fortified with reinforcing materials and filled with Landsers and their weapons. ("Landsers" are the German equivalent of "GIs.") Three miles north of Sant'Angelo, ensconced on high ground outside of the Cassino abbey, lay Benedictine brother Frido von Senger peered at the handiwork of his engineers and most likely fervently wished that the Americans on the far side of the river would attack his carefully crafted strong point.

The Allied officer who would bear the brunt of von Senger's engineering aptitude was General Fred L. Walker, commander of the 36th Army Division. Walker, who was four years younger than his German adversary, was an Ohio native who had an engineering degree from The Ohio State University. He had partially paid his college tuition by serving in the Ohio National Guard and was a sergeant at the time of his graduation. Walker passed a competitive examination to earn a commission and quickly logged significant time in danger zones, from the not completely pacified Philippines to the expedition to capture Pancho Villa, to the trenches of World War I France. At the Second Battle of the Marne in the summer of 1918, Walker was a battalion commander in the heavily engaged 3rd Division, where his men had the great good luck to be entrenched along the Marne River as successive waves of Germans broke against the fortifications.

By 1941, Walker was a Brigadier General and an assistant division commander and had taught Mark Clark at Command and General Staff School. Clark, who at that point was chief of staff to George Marshall, recommended the Ohioan for the command positions of the socially and ethnically diverse Texas National Guard unit.

While numerous outsiders had joined the unit between its initial wartime training in Camp Bowie, Texas, and its baptism in battle around the beaches of Palermo, this division, along with most of the National Guard divisions, still had a significant core of men who had grown up in Texas. Some companies featured a strong core of Latinos, including some for whom English was a second language. Others were Anglo ranch hands, oil well workers, and farmers; some teetotaling Baptists; and others veterans of seedy Texas saloons on wild Saturday nights. Unofficially, they were called the T-Patchers, and the spirit of the Alamo and San Jacinto was still an important element in their collective consciousness.

Walker's men had been a key component in the American assault on the heavily defended town of San Pietro in mid-December, a battle zone immortalized by the prose of Ernie Pyle and the film of director John Huston, who shocked American audiences with graphic carnage light-years more intense than the sanitized commercial films. The 36th Division had lost twenty-three hundred men in the battle for the rubble-strewn town, and now, a month later, the survivors were faced with a mission quite possibly more dangerous than that previous bloodbath.

Eighty years earlier, a Union Army that had suffered a carnage-ridden march south from the Wilderness Tavern to Spotsylvania Court House was deployed in yet another attack formation near a tiny tavern-centered hamlet named Cold Harbor. Tens of thousands of blue-coated soldiers had suffered death or injury in a bloody minuet between Ulysses S. Grant and Robert E. Lee. Finally, in a sort of emotionally driven reverse psychology, Grant at least half-believed that a single powerful thrust against a heavily fortified rebel position would send the Southerners packing and open the road for the Northern Army's Holy Grail, the rebel capital of Richmond.

Unfortunately, few of Grant's men had quite the same confidence in success as their commander, and the commander's senior officers gently attempted to dissuade their leader from a venture that seemed to have the same paltry chance of success as the army's mauling at Marye's Heights above Fredericksburg eighteen months earlier. While Grant's men did not desert their commander, they certainly demonstrated their lack of enthusiasm by almost ritualistically pinning pieces of paper with their names and other relevant personal information on their uniform coats, a thinly disguised statement that they did not expect to survive the day. Hours later, Grant watched impassively as successive units threw themselves against Lee's nearly perfect defense line in a battle in which the climax was measured more in minutes than in hours. Seven thousand blue-coated Americans fell dead or wounded at a cost to the Confederacy of perhaps one thousand casualties. A defeated Grant and a victorious Lee both devolved into immature spoiled school boys, as Grant would not request a truce to return his wounded men, and Lee would not grant one unless his adversary asked. For much of three days, wounded men writhing in pain gradually succumbed to the thirst, heat, and shock until Grant essentially "blinked" and asked for a truce that saved a handful of soldiers.

Now, eight decades later, the weather was equally miserable, but it was rain, snow, and wind, rather than heat, that swirled through the American camps as the GIs nervously eyed the menace that faced them on the far side of the Rapido. In one respect, the GIs had a psychological advantage, if a small one, over their Yankee predecessors. The lunge for the Rapido was only a single element in a massive Allied offensive that would deploy units, at one time or another, from Britain, New Zealand, India, France, Morocco, Algeria, Canada, South Africa, and Poland in the struggle to breach the Gustav line. Mark Clark had developed a bold plan that hoped to draw German forces away from Anzio to deal with the threat at Cassino along the Rapido and, in turn, withdraw many of those defenders to meet the thrust to their rear on the Anzio-Nettuno beaches. However, the huge problem for the American attackers near Sant'Angelo was that there was little prospect of the Germans weakening their defenses on the Rapido line when the battle had just begun. For the immediate future, the German defenders on the far side had no more concern for events at Anzio than they did for their comrades back-pedaling through Russia on the other side of Europe.

As the men of the "Texas division" prepared for their assault on the Rapido River, they could take some consolation that, unlike the ill-fated charges at Balaclava and Cold Harbor in the previous century, this attack would be at night. On the other hand, the men of the Light Brigade or the Army of the Potomac had not faced MG 1942 machine guns capable of firing twelve hundred bullets a minute or artillery that could fire a single shell that could annihilate much of a platoon. Given the potential fire-power of the German defenders, perhaps it was not unseemly that General Walker had come to the conclusion that the river assault had almost no chance of success.

While Walker said nothing to his men, he wrote in the privacy of his diary, "I do not know of a single case in military history where an attempt to cross an unfordable river that is incorporated into the enemy's main line of resistance has succeeded, so according to history, we may not succeed." Walker would not lead his division into battle from the front on a horse, as officers of earlier centuries had expected, but few men of any period would have entered battle with the combination of age and declining health that the "T-patchers'" commander faced. General Geoffrey Keyes, the II Corps commander who had been Patton's deputy in Sicily and took charge after Patton's public relations meltdown, had chosen Walker and his division for this most vital of missions, but he did have some concern that at age fifty-six, the Ohioan was the oldest division commander in the army. If Keyes had shadowed Walker closely, he would have been shocked to discover that the division leader was dealing with migraine headaches, shortness of breath, a dangerously high pulse, arthritis, impaired memory, and bouts of blindness in one eye. Luckily for Walker, he could largely dodge physical exams in this God-forsaken battle area, and somehow he pulled himself together for the big push to cross the Rapido.

At first full darkness on the evening of January 20, 1944, sixteen battalions of American artillery let loose in a thirty-minute barrage that seemed at least visually impressive as the assault force personnel remarked that they could have read a newspaper by the light of the barrage. Minutes later, the Texans began dragging assault boats across a marshy soup that turned the rush into a painful-to-watch, slow-motion waddle. While the American artillery had targeted relatively well-protected defenders, the German response caught far too many GIs slogging across a gooey mire with darkness their only partially effective cover. The men who were theoretically lucky enough to actually reach the river's edge in one piece packed four-hundred-pound assault boats into the water, climbed aboard if they were not hit first, and then started drifting downstream on River Rapido that was, unfortunately, accurately named.

The men of the 36th Division were now increasingly divided into three groups: GIs who were sprawled dead or wounded at the approach site; soldiers who were drifting on a river that was carrying them away from their designated landing site, and the smallest group, men who had actually reached the far shore and were now at least engaged in battle. The situation was expected to improve somewhat when engineers managed to push a bridge across the river, but that span was quickly peppered by German artillery fire and soon dangled just enough intact to tempt the men who thought that they were born lucky.

Somehow, senior American commanders could simply not envision the volume of fire that a modern, well-equipped defense could throw at attackers largely unsupported by air power or armor. For example, one entire battalion of the 143rd Regiment was not able to get one single soldier across the Rapido but still suffered heavy casualties from cleverly deployed mines and German artillery fire. In some respects, the Texans were taking on the role of the Japanese forces at Guadalcanal, in which their lunges across rivers defended by well-armed American Marines turned the battle into a nocturnal shooting gallery. On the far side of the river, General von Senger, in an unintended insult to the Americans, began suspecting that the crossing was nothing more than an elaborate feint designed to focus German attention on a location that was actually not the real crossing point.

On the morning of January 21, General Geoffrey Keyes arrived at Walker's headquarters and gave orders for the attack to be renewed promptly. As the conversation quickly devolved into two monologues at cross-purposes, Walker kept pleading for a delay, and Keyes kept insisting on an almost immediate follow-up attack. As the argument heightened, a few of the small number of men who had actually made it across the Rapido crossed back to their own lines and regaled GIs and officers with the disastrous situation on the other side. Finally, at some time after 3:00 p.m., as Keyes turned more belligerent and Walker's many ailments grew more severe, the renewed attack gradually jerked into motion. By some extraordinary luck, a reasonably large number of GIs managed to find torn seams in the German defense belt, but this initial success simply meant that, while the day before, dozens of men were trapped on the wrong side of the Rapido, by today it was hundreds.

At dawn on January 22, the Americans who had somehow crossed the Rapido and were still capable of functioning as combat soldiers hunkered down along a shaky defense line that emerged four hundred yards inland from the Rapido. Behind them, fragments of bridges dangled along the river, and ahead of them were powerful German units enjoying the emotional high that came with an almost absolute victory. Radio conversation between American forces on the two sides of the river was now nonexistent, with contact limited to the occasional messenger who was able to swim from one bank to the other.

Meanwhile, German units were gradually sidling behind the American positions and cutting off egress to the river bank. In essence, the survivors were now trapped in a rapidly contracting pocket and would soon be forced to fire in four directions at once.

On the other side of the Rapido, General Geoffrey Keyes, normally a reasonably competent commander, was now flirting with a fantasy world in which he insisted that the survivors on the far bank should be able to hold out long enough to allow new bridges to be constructed, and he mused that the one-sided battle had somehow sapped the morale of the Germans more than it had that of the attack force. As stunned officers began organizing the units that had not yet had their chance to be shredded to ribbons, Fifth Army Commander Mark Clark provided an unexpected reprieve. The men on the south side of the Rapido would live to fight another day. Stunned GIs received word that their comrades were at that moment landing at the twin beach towns of Anzio and Nettune, roughly fifty miles to the north, and the Rapido assault had at least accomplished one of its missions—the distraction of the German Army away from the northern landing beaches.

On the north side of the river, those survivors who had not yet managed to swim back to the south side of the Rapido gradually bowed to the inevitable and raised their hands, marched into the open, and trusted in some level of German chivalry that their lives would be spared. Given the intensity of the battle and the size of the operation, the Germans had suffered remarkably few casualties: just over sixty killed and less than two hundred wounded. The defenders had the right to feel euphoric; they had inflicted ten times as many casualties as they had suffered. Slightly over twenty-one hundred Americans were sprawled in either death or injury over the battlefield or were being marched to the rear to POW holding pens. Two American regiments had been essentially removed from the chessboard of war.

The Germans had clearly won an extremely one-sided battle and at that point could afford to be magnanimous. Soon an American medic who had been captured during the battle returned with a note from the German headquarters to Colonel Aaron Wyatt, commander of the decimated 141st Regiment, proposing a several-hour truce to retrieve dead and wounded GIs. Wyatt initially turned down the proposal, but when news of the offer reached General Walker, the German proposition was accepted.

In the aftermath of a grisly battle, an atmosphere much like the famous 1914 Christmas truce on the Western Front in World War I seemed to emerge. Soon, an American medical officer and a support staff of medics crossed the river in eerie silence. Accompanied by German-speaking GIs, several dozen personnel combed the battlefield for wounded Americans or carefully removed the bodies of the fallen. German medical personnel and more than a few regular soldiers left their defense positions to help their adversaries, and often found time to shake hands, exchange pictures of loved ones, share cigarettes, and even meet enemy soldiers who had lived or studied in the United States. For a few hours in this little corner of Italy, deadly enemies offered sincere hope that their newfound companions would survive the war. However, several dozen miles to the north, a whole new battle front was just emerging in a seasonal resort town. An American division had been largely sacrificed to shift enemy attentions away from the Allied landing at Anzio. For better or worse, Mark Clark's gambit had, more or less, succeeded, even if the Rapido assault itself had been a total disaster. Now, newsmen and cameramen would hurry northward and chronicle a rather different kind of battle as Operation Shingle lurched into motion.

CHAPTER III

The Anzio Gambit

On the frigid night of January 21–22, 1944, as American commanders along the Rapido River debated whether to reinforce their 36th Division lodgment on the north bank or pull back the survivors, a flotilla of nearly two hundred forty assorted landing craft and transport ships, escorted by five cruisers and twenty-four destroyers, steamed northward off the west coast of Italy. Their very presence in these seas was a direct result of the implacable will of Winston Spencer Churchill.

The British prime minister had largely cajoled a reluctant President Franklin Delano Roosevelt and his senior military commanders to complement their primary mission of an invasion of Northern Europe with a lunge against an Italian peninsula that he considered to be "the soft underbelly of Europe." Yet now, in the winter of 1944, the Allied invasion of southern Italy had congealed into a World War I–era stalemate along the Rapido-Cassino front, which the Germans had designated the "Gustav line." Churchill had managed to contradict every American objection to an admittedly risky amphibious landing in the general vicinity of the major prize of Rome, and now an Anglo-American invasion force was streaming toward the coastal resort towns of Anzio and Nettuno.

This daring venture, code-named "Operation Shingle," was commanded by a graying, slightly stooped, bespectacled American officer who looked and moved like a man a decade older than his fifty-four years. Major General John Lucas was a highly regarded but not particularly physically robust World War I combat veteran who had served as Dwight Eisenhower's liaison to George Patton's Seventh Army during the Sicily campaign. Then he assumed command of the VI Corps after the initial setbacks in the Salerno invasion cost senior officers their commands. Now, Lucas commanded a diverse Allied Force centered on the U.S. 3rd Infantry division, the British 1st division, a regiment of the U.S. 45th Infantry Division, most of the U.S. 1st Armored Division, a regiment of American paratroopers, an independent battalion of parachute infantry, two British commando battalions, three American Ranger battalions and a combined American-Canadian special forces brigade.

John Lucas now commanded an invasion force that, while smaller than the assault strength of the D-Day landings, was still roughly the size of the army commanded by Ulysses S. Grant when the Army of the Potomac began its march toward Richmond eighty years earlier. However, while Grant had a fairly accurate estimate of the Army of Northern Virginia, which confronted him in his drive southward, Lucas had little idea how many enemy troops would contest the Allied landings or confront the landing force a week or a month later. Luckily for Lucas's career prospects, his commander, General Mark Clark, and other superior officers did not have access to his diary, which revealed more the backbone and ardor of an assistant manager of a department store than the commander of a massive invasion force. Lucas admitted to his diary that he was simply little more than "a poor working girl trying to get ahead" and "far too tenderhearted ever to be a success at my chosen profession." He then equated the Shingle operation to George Armstrong Custer's ill-fated expedition against the Sioux nation, insisting that "Battles of the Little Big Horn are not much fun."

Now, in the predawn hours of January 22, the less-than-cocky John Lucas stared toward a shoreline of a beachfront that had been a major summer resort in the age of Imperial Rome, faded into insignificance during the Middle Ages, and then expanded again during the Benito Mussolini experiment with fascism. The area that encompassed Anzio included both the town and neighboring Nettuno, both of which centered on beach resort economies; an inland fascist "model community," designated to introduce a manufacturing economy to the area; and a manmade watercourse, the Mussolini Canal that had been part of the Duce's attempt to drain the malarial Pontine Marshes and reclaim swampy wastelands into arable farmland. If nothing else, much of the battlefield bore the impact of Mussolini's reign, yet now the defenders wore the field gray of the German forces, and those men were not prone to surrender or retreat at the first sign of an enemy lurking.

Despite his misgivings about the risk of landing an expeditionary force sixty miles behind the front lines, Lucas had developed clearly defined assignments for this enormously diverse landing force, and when the invaders realized to their enormous relief that the beachfront was only minimally defended, spirits rose throughout the army. After a few shore batteries were silenced by overwhelming naval gunfire, the main initial threat was from the air. At one point, a half-dozen ME-109 fighters broke through the Allied air cover to destroy a few newly landed supply trucks, while a covey of FW-109 fighter bombers carrying bombs on their undercarriages sank one American landing craft. Approximately fifty Luftwaffe raiders managed to penetrate Allied air cover on the invasion day, but at least seven of them were shot down in exchange for three destroyed Allied planes.

Utilizing their control of the sea and their new control of the air, the invaders pushed through the Padiglione Woods, secured the Anzio-Albono Road, occupied the Nettuno dockyard, and, by lunchtime, established a perimeter between two and three miles inland from the sea. As the sun set on the short winter day, Lucas tallied a casualty list of a dozen Allied combat deaths and roughly one hundred wounded in exchange for two hundred German defenders now sitting in POW enclosures. As the professorial-looking commander settled into his command post and planned upcoming operations, the controversy that would plague Operation Shingle began to germinate in the new headquarters.

One of the glaring omissions of Allied planning for Shingle was the inability to clearly define exactly what the invasion of Anzio was supposed to accomplish. The high command—from Churchill to Mediterranean Commander Sir Henry Maitland Wilson to Fifth Army Commander Mark Clark—seemed unsure whether the men of the Anzio invasion were going to distract enough German units to allow the Allied Army on the Rapido-Cassino line to lunge forward to Rome or whether the Allied Forces astride the Gustav line would distract their adversaries enough to allow the forces at Anzio to lunge toward the Eternal City. Thus, Lucas, who, as previously mentioned, was certainly not plagued with overconfidence, almost immediately devolved alternately into euphoria or dread that colored the whole venture. Lucas's orders from his superiors were a parser's delight; he was expected to "advance" on the Alban Hills looming between his invasion force and Rome, but the general admitted that he was not sure exactly what "advance" really meant. In turn, General Mark Clark, his immediate superior and, at least theoretically, Lucas's close friend, advised the Shingle commander to avoid "stretching his neck out" in a way that had almost cost the Fifth Army commander his job several months earlier at Salerno when a bold attack almost ended in disaster.

While Allied intelligence gathering was not incompetent, it was often contradictory, with so much information that some appraisals canceled others out. Now, German units could be detected moving in numerous directions, but to where were they moving? For a while on the morning of January 22 and at least a short time afterward, Rome *was* nearly undefended, as German combat units were gathering both north and south of the city proper, while the critical city environs were so depleted that rumors were already circulating on both sides that a Jeep that was full of GI scouts had actually moved into Rome's suburbs undisturbed by defenders. A very aggressive commander might have seized on such information and organized an armored column to land a *coup de main* before the enemy could respond, but a very aggressive commander might also be ordering his men into a trap, much like Custer had done at Little Big Horn. Lucas commanded what was, in essence, a reinforced army corps, but the Germans still fielded a full army north of Rome and another army further south that could theoretically trap the Anzio invasion force in the middle if the Allies ventured too far from maximum naval and air support. Therefore, to a cautious, physically tired, and emotionally drained, late-middle-aged commander, an order to move "on" the Alban Hills clearly meant "toward," not over and beyond, those looming heights. The Allied forward line that now stretched nearly three miles beyond the beach seemed like a very good place to be on that cold winter day, especially considering the capabilities of the German enemy.

On the other side of those Alban heights looming in the distance, German decision makers were beginning to respond to an enemy gambit that might be anything from a feint to a serious thrust toward Rome. The officer ultimately responsible for the defense of the Italian capital was, somewhat ironically, an air force officer who had spent much of the first part of the war commanding tactical air fleets in support of army operations. Field Marshal Albert Kesselring was a study in contradictions, a flier who was well-liked by both Air Commander Hermann Goering and several senior army leaders. He was a German who generally liked and admired the Italian people and their culture, yet occasionally ordered antiterrorist reprisals that resulted in the grisly executions of hundreds of Romans, and, though a man of iron will, his humor and photogenic smile led to his nickname, "Smiling Albert."

At the time of Operation Shingle, Kesselring was supreme commander of Italy, with two field armies, the 10th and 14th, under his command. Colonel General Heinrich von Vietinghoff commanded Tenth Army, the organization that was tasked with holding the Allies at bay between the Gustav line and the area immediately north of Rome. Von Vietinghoff was a much-decorated infantry officer in World War I who remained in the postwar army and commanded a Panzer division in the invasion of Poland, an army corps in the defeat of France, and the 9th Army on the Eastern Front. His counterpart, Colonel General Eberhard Mackensen, experienced much less front-line duty than his colleague in 10th Army but still won an Iron Cross and appointment as chief of staff of the 12th Army before leading the 1st Panzer Army in the battles of Stalingrad and Kursk. Now, in early 1944, Mackensen was tasked with defending everything in Italy, from the northern outskirts of Rome to the German border, as a counterweight of any possible Allied amphibious invasion in the area of the industrial heart of the Italian peninsula. Kesselring and his two principal field commanders could deploy in Italy a ground force roughly equivalent in divisions to the multinational Allied force gradually advancing up the peninsula. However, the enormous terrain advantage in a mountainous country was considerably nullified by a lack of almost any offensive naval capacity and reliance on a Luftwaffe that still had plenty of fighters but almost no real strategic bombing capability and only enough medium bombers to score victories in tactical, local spoiling attacks. The Germans still had command of many of the mountains, but the Allies held control of the sea and the skies above the battlefields.

The Italo-phile Kesselring genuinely seemed to believe in the joint destiny of Germany and Italy. And, while capable of occasional brutal reprisals against perceived "unsporting" Italian resistance spectaculars—such as for the murder of a formation of German soldiers marching relatively inoffensively down a Roman street—the German leader often known unofficially as "smiling Albert" was an excellent strategist and tactician. He genuinely seemed to make efforts to keep the war in Italy closer to the conflict in the Great War or the battle of North Africa instead of the brutal death struggle that was raging on the Eastern Front.

Kesselring's initial response to the Allied landing at Anzio was energetic and rapid. The field marshal immediately contacted General von Vietinghoff at 10th Army headquarters and ordered him to rush a corps-sized response force into immediate movement toward the beachhead. Within hours, 71st Infantry Division and much of Hermann Goering's Panzer Division were on the move, with 26th Panzer Division and 1st Fallschirmjager Division contributing their most battle-ready units. At this moment, one of the significant elements of Operation Shingle—the expectation that German units would be pulled from the Gustav line to confront the new threat from the sea—was essentially thrown out of the equation when Kesselring kept his nerve and insisted that the Anzio landings were not a direct threat to Rome. For the time being, the Rapido garrison would not be raided to confront Shingle.

Only a few dozen miles from Rome, General John Lucas was already confirming Kesselring's faith in the caution of his adversary. A George

Patton, Stonewall Jackson, or William Sherman most likely would have jumped at the opportunity to at least probe the enemy defenses and possibly score a dramatic coup by entering a still poorly defended Italian capital. On the other hand, Lucas had the sometimes excessive conviction of Joseph Johnston or George McClellan, who both always believed there were far more enemy troops facing them than their own army could safely confront. Lucas now became increasingly convinced that his directive to move "on" the Alban Heights meant no more than a cautious probe somewhere between the beachfront and the hills.

At nightfall on January 24, 1944, roughly sixty hours into the operation, the Allied front lines extended about three miles outward from the invasion beaches. The major problem with this ultracautious advance was that the only prizes that held any defensive value were the towns of Anzio and Nettuno themselves, and they had been captured almost immediately. In a flat, extended beachfront, almost any natural or manmade variation from the prevailing sand flats was a possible piece of valuable real estate, and the Germans still held almost all of them. The inland town of Aprilia and its factory complex; the Campoleone and Cisterna railroad stations; the main railway line to Rome and the Mussolini Canal—all remained in Axis hands and offered excellent launch points for counterattacks. These points would soon become battle sites, but the first organized German response to Shingle would come from the sky and utilize one of Adolf Hitler's vaunted arsenals of "wonder weapons."

As dusk descended on the bleak winter landscape of the Shingle beachhead, several squadrons of state-of-the-art Luftwaffe bombers roared over the Anglo-American positions and headed for the invasion fleet offshore. The planes were new HE-177A bombers capable of night operations, and they carried onboard weapons systems much more advanced than those of their Allied counterparts. Two Luftwaffe raiders were equipped with tiny, deadly, precision-guided weapons: the Fritz-X–guided bombs and the Henschel HS-293 guided missile. Here was a hint of twenty-first-century warfare, as each plane carried a weapons officer in the nose section who maneuvered a futuristic-looking joystick as he controlled the path of the missile toward an intended target, often more than a mile away. While Allied personnel attempted to counter the attack with radio-jamming devices on the ships below, Luftwaffe counterparts dropped parachute flares to illuminate the attack zone. While the new weapons systems were still too primitive to decimate the Allied naval flotilla, there were some stunning individual kills, such as when British cruiser, HMS *Spartan,* American supply ship *Samuel Huntingdon,* and British hospital ship *St. David* all went to the bottom in an eerie preview of electronic warfare. The Germans actions scored a moral victory in this "tech war" premiere, as those sinkings, combined with nonfatal damage to a number of other vessels, encouraged naval officials to repeatedly insist on pulling support ships away from the beachhead when enemy attacks seemed most likely. Then, as Allied ships fought for their lives in the missile attacks, Kesselring's land forces began to intervene decisively in the cautious Allied advance toward the looming Alban Hills.

The first Allied offensive in the Shingle operation centered on a primarily British operation to seize the town and factory complex of Aprilia, the rail stations of Campoleone, and the Anzio–Anziate road, while American forces would seize the town of Cisterna and the Cisterna–Rome highway. The basic idea was to push the front lines well away from the beaches and hopefully create a solid jumping-off point for a follow-up lunge toward the Alban Hills and, finally, to Rome itself. However, Allied commanders were not fully aware that Kesselring was shifting forces to the threatened area faster than the Allies were landing their own reinforcements, so that within a week of the first landings, the sixty-one thousand Allied troops were actually going to launch an attack on seventy-two thousand defenders, hardly an inviting prospect when assault forces were generally expected to outnumber their adversaries by a three-to-one margin.

Eighty-one years earlier, in one of the bloodiest actions of the Civil War, Union General William Rosecrans and Confederate Commander Braxton Bragg had each planned an almost identical assault on enemy lines for the wintry morning of December 31, 1862, near the city of Murfreesboro, Tennessee. Men in blue and gray were shocked to see a deadly minuet in which men who expected to be attackers were themselves being attacked. The deadly confrontations ceased on New Year's Eve night, reignited on

January 2, and left an astounding 40 percent of both armies as casualties in the very technical Union victory achieved when Bragg pulled away from the battlefield.

Now, in an almost as frigid central Italian battlefield, John Lucas's Anglo-American Army managed to push toward German lines just as General Mackensen sent his Landsers in the exactly opposite direction. However, while their Civil War predecessors at least had the opportunity to see their adversaries in daylight, this new battle was waged under the stars.

On the left side of the battlefield, the Sherwood Foresters of the British 1st Division were teamed up with General Ernie Harmon's American tankers of the 1st Armored Division in a drive up the Anzio Road through Aprilia and toward Campoleone Station. The chilly night was filled with the sounds of the throaty motors of Shermans forming a blocking wedge for the Foresters between the German 65th Infantry Division and the 3rd Panzergrenadier Division. Even with the major advantage of dozens of American tanks swirling around the wintry landscape, almost six hundred of the eight hundred British infantrymen went down with wounds, including every company commander in the battle. By the time the Nottinghamshire Tommies reached the outskirts of the Campoleone train station, one one-hundred-sixteen-man company had only sixteen unwounded survivors as the sun rose. One of the most famous British regiments in history had been nearly annihilated and had failed to capture the vital train station in the bargain. However, the monumental British casualties in this part of the battle would appear almost tolerable compared to what was happening to an equally distinguished American unit about eight miles away.

In the early days of World War II, when Britain stood virtually alone against Hitler, American movie audiences thrilled to British war films that highlighted elite units which prevailed against great odds against Nazi hordes. One of those formations was the Royal Commandos, an elite, hard-hitting force trained in stealth and diversion, and with almost absolute disregard for personal survival. While General George Marshall openly frowned on "special units" in the American Army, insisting that in essence, *every* soldier was both brave and important, public pressure forced him to bow to the creation of an American equivalent of the Commandos. A popular term for *special forces* in early America was the title *Ranger,* which encompassed such notable units as Rogers' Rangers in the French and Indian War and the Texas Rangers, who defended the Lone Star State against everything from Santa Anna's Mexican Army to notorious outlaws and train robbers. Rogers' Rangers had recently been hugely popularized by the lush, big-budget Technicolor spectacular *Northwest Passage,* starring Hollywood icon Spencer Tracy as Colonel Richard Rogers, while the Texas Rangers were a staple of Western films, featuring box office draws such as Errol Flynn.

Marshall's reservations gave way to reluctant consent, and part of the Shingle invasion force consisted of three battalions of Rangers under the command of photogenic, high-strung, young Colonel William Darby, who was to the modern Rangers what Richard Rogers was to their colonial counterparts. Luckily, generational links between Rogers and Darby were promoted by the American news media, and few Americans knew about the unpleasant reality that Colonel Rogers retained such affection for the British Crown that when the American Revolution began, he reintroduced the Rangers into the war as a crack loyalist regiment that killed large numbers of Patriot fighting men. Darby was faced with no such mixed emotions in 1944 and so hated the Germans that the Rangers commander discouraged taking any prisoners. Unfortunately, the paradox in this stance was shortly to become tragically evident on a cold winter night near Cisterna.

Now, at just past 1:00 a.m. on January 30, in a nocturnal operation on a particularly bitter winter night, the Rangers moved out toward their goal of capturing the town and train station at Cisterna. Soldiers quietly cursed the irony of shivering in "sunny Italy" and cursed the choice of approach: a meandering irrigation ditch, where they slogged ankle deep through frigid water. As the Rangers slogged northward, German troops marched above them at ground level, also cursing the cold and damp. Ironically, Darby's Rangers were not led by their young colonel; he was back at headquarters nervously awaiting confirmation that their mission had succeeded.

In a scene that would have been appropriate for a comedy if the stakes were not so high, men in olive drabs trudged northward in a ditch while men in field gray pushed southward in the frozen mud of farmers' fields. Then, only one thousand yards from the outskirts of Cisterna, the two forces discovered one another, and a disastrously one-sided battle began.

By the time the Rangers closed in on the town, the icy water was nearly knee deep, and footsteps had become splashes as forward progress was reduced to a person walking knee-deep in the ocean. Suddenly, flares arched into the night sky, tracer bullets created a deadly light show, and more than seven hundred men found themselves trapped in a mile-and-a half-long column with enemy volleys pouring down on them. Eight decades earlier, in a desperate ploy to break the stalemate in the Union siege of Petersburg, Pennsylvania mining engineers and coal miners created an extensive tunnel under the Confederate lines. The resulting explosion shattered a portion of the rebel works and allowed a mixed force of white and black regiments to storm into the heart of the enemy defenses. Then, stunned and entranced by the sheer scope of the explosion, Union troops clambered down into the crater floor, often hunting for souvenirs among the stunned, wounded, or dead Confederates. A division commanded by William Malone rapidly moved to seal the breach, and soon the top of the crater was lined with gray-clad riflemen firing furiously on the trapped Yankees. The one-sided battle was a classic case of the more fortunate side "shooting fish in a barrel," and now, eight decades later, this role was taken by the fully alerted Germans.

The few radios that still worked sent increasingly panic-stricken messages back to American headquarters, as the Germans quickly cut off advance or retreat in the waterlogged ditch. Colonel Darby, an emotional man at the best of times, cried, cursed, and pleaded with his superiors for permission to leave headquarters and join his men in their moment of crisis. While two battalions were trapped in Cisterna, a third was still in reserve, and Darby insisted that these approximately three hundred fifty men might yet turn the tide. The colonel was nearly physically restrained from attempting the rescue, as the firing gradually devolved from a crescendo to scattered gunfire.

In a military culture where the order to "take the high ground" was now nearly impossible for the Rangers, the trapped Americans were often reduced to simply attempting to take as many Germans with them in death. The Rangers certainly went down fighting, as a few men somehow scrambled out of the ditch and even captured two German tanks, which they turned on their tormentors. Some American survivors later insisted that some Germans threatened to kill the prisoners they had already taken if the survivors refused to surrender, but, as dawn revealed the bloody scene, there was little evidence that the enemy had the same aversion to taking prisoners as Darby had hinted for his men. The battle of Cisterna was certainly a massacre on the level of the Alamo or Custer's Last Stand, in that of the seven hundred sixty-seven Rangers assigned to the operation, only six men staggered back to headquarters to report the disaster. However, unlike the Mexicans at the Alamo or the Sioux at Little Big Horn, the victorious Germans did readily accept surrender, and four hundred fifty Americans survived the night, if only to spend the rest of the war as unwilling guests of the Third Reich. William Darby was only emotionally wounded by the battle but, unlike his surrendered men, would not survive the war, meeting death at another time and another battle. Now, as the men of Darby's Rangers marched toward Rome and captivity, and the men of Sherwood Foresters grieved over their losses, General Eberhard Mackensen arrived from Verona to take charge of what he expected to be a decisive counterattack that would drive the Anglo-Americans back into the sea.

Now, in the wake of the Allied landings and the German checkmate of the Allied attempt to gain the Alban Hills, the Anzio campaign began to take on a life of its own far beyond what Churchill had initially envisioned. The Allied offensive toward Campoleone Station and the town of Cisterna had pushed the front lines farther from the sea but left a dangerous bulge in the lines between the outskirts of Campoleone and the town of Aprilia, which now appeared on the maps as protruding thumbs that seemed to invite a German attempt to eliminate the Allied salient.

This six-square-mile portion of the Allied beachhead was about to become a focal point of the Italian campaign, as General Mackensen supported his infantry assault force with nearly twenty state-of-the-art Hornisse, self-propelled, 88 mm tank destroyers.

Just before midnight on February 4, the German infantry and tank forces moved southward under cover of heavy rain and successively overran British defense units that were too scattered to match the enemy threat. Soon, nearly one thousand Tommies were being led off the battlefield as prisoners, while almost five hundred more men were sprawled around the muddy battlefield, wounded or dead. Each successive British defense position was able to slow, but not stop, the relentless German drives, as the Landsers utilized the long winter nights and the seemingly endless rain to help infiltrate fallback positions until British 1st Division Commander William Penney was forced to abandon Aprilia and attempt to form a new line at the base of the Thumb.

At this point, General Lucas was compelled to commit his main reserve force, the American 45th Division, in the hope of preventing Mackensen's forces from penetrating all the way to the sea. On the morning of February 11, the 1st Battalion of the 179th Infantry Regiment, supported by the 191st Tank Battalion, surged back into the streets of the model community that was a showpiece of Benito Mussolini's fascist state. By now, both American and British soldiers were calling the town "the Factory," because of the huge smokestack protruding from the center of the complex, and in an all-day battle, the GIs and their supporting Shermans managed to take the lower half of the town. Then General Mackensen, who saw Aprilia as the vital launch point for a renewed German general offensive, poured every available tank and assault gun into the upper part of the now ravaged community and turned the battle into a grisly example of urban warfare. By dawn of February 12, the American battalion was reduced to only 30 percent unwounded personnel, and the GIs reluctantly pulled back to a more defensible position.

On Valentine's Day 1944, an Allied garrison of twenty-three American and twelve British battalions was deployed along a series of highways and railroad lines on a ten-mile front between the Mussolini Canal and the sea about ten miles inland from Anzio and Nettuno. While General Lucas's

Shingle invasion force had excellent artillery support, a fleet of bombardment vessels on call, and reasonably good air support, the major weakness
of the Allied position was that most of the beachhead consisted of open
ground that contained few natural defense points such as hills or buildings. If a German offensive really got rolling, there was almost no natural
stopping point between the front lines and the sea.

General Mackensen could see the battlefield as well as his American
counterpart could, and he assured Adolf Hitler that with two additional
assault divisions, he could most likely push the invaders back into the
water. Hitler insisted that Mackensen already enjoyed numerical superiority, and, although Hitler refused to provide more troops for a new
offensive, now codenamed *Fischfang*, he offered a consolation prize of
some of the Fuehrer's favorite new "secret weapons." Mackensen soon
received a battalion of the new Panther tanks that had been tested on the
Eastern Front and had never been used against the Western Allies. The
Panthers outperformed any Allied tank in Lucas's armored inventory, but
it remained to be seen if a battalion was a true game changer. The tanks
were accompanied by a formation of Borgward B-IV demolition vehicles,
which looked like small tanks. The tanks carried a driver close to a chosen
target and then allowed him to exit the vehicle and ram the explosive-
laden marauder into an enemy target by remote control. Mackensen
would probably have preferred a generous reinforcement of traditional
infantry units, but on February 16, the men in field gray, supported by
the experimental weapons, initiated a "final push" to throw the Allies into
the sea.

As a welcome late-winter sun glinted off the swampy fields, Wehrmacht
troops poured down the main road from Campoleone to the town of
Anzio, with the 3rd Panzergrenadier Division and the 715th Infantry
Division threatening to overwhelm the American battalions. Meanwhile,
the 452 heavy guns that Mackensen had assembled in his artillery park
sent hundreds of shells into the Anglo-American main defense lines
south of Aprilia. German soldiers, from the teenagers who filled many
of the companies of the Panzer Lehr Infantry Regiment to the veteran
paratroopers of the Fallschirmjager Lehr battalion, gained a new level of

courage and excitement as they watched the new Borgwards and Panthers roar ahead of them with their deadly mix of remote-control demolition capabilities and long-range turret guns on the new tanks. Then, in a sight akin to watching a film in slow motion, the scene gradually transformed from elated victory to the grim reality of stalemate.

First, as the Borgward operators frantically manipulated their remote control joysticks, the explosions ignited in a swampy mud that muffled both sound and impact of the 450-kilogram charges that, in turn, inflicted minimal damage on the Allied defenders. Then the Panthers, which would eventually emerge as probably the best World War II tank under "normal" battle conditions, began to show signs that they had not yet worked out their "teething problems" of mechanical unreliability. Senior Panzer unit commanders, terrified at the thought of allowing their superb new weapon to fall into enemy hands, kept a tight leash on their prized vehicles and would not allow them to mix it up with the Anglo-American Shermans. Soon, more mobile Shermans and assorted tank destroyers were roaming the battlefield far more freely than their enemy counterparts and, even if less technically advanced, were still game changers along the swampy battle sites.

The Germans may have had more cannons, more technically advanced tanks, and the fighting skills of a core of elite units, but the Allies knew the ground far better than their tormentors and often turned the enemy's blunt force against itself. For example, one of the highest-profile German units, the Fallschirmjager Lehr battalion, was a favorite formation of Hermann Goering; it was forced to show other German paratroopers the latest tactics in airborne warfare. In the opening hours of Fischfang, the paratroopers, supported by a company of Panzer IV tanks from the Hermann Goering Division, were ecstatic as they scattered a retreating American unit in multiple directions in front of the paratroopers' advance. Then, as they moved directly forward toward the seemingly crumbling enemy formation, they realized that they had been lured into a stretch of marshy ground that virtually halted them in their tracks. Minutes later, a well-placed American artillery barrage sent paratroopers and tanks flying in pieces just as the Germans realized that they had been duped into an ambush. Now, the only audience for which these young elite troops would be "demonstrating" was their POW camp guards, for those lucky enough to survive the encounter.

The most optimistic members of Mackensen's assault force believed that they would be relaxing on the beaches of Anzio by nightfall of February 16; instead, sunset found the German forces short by almost five hundred killed or missing and twelve hundred more in medical facilities with no significant or permanent gains to compensate for the bloodshed. Mackensen now began to envision Fischfang as a multiple-day operation and initiated a rotation of units in and out of the battle zone, as each task force lunged forward in the late-winter mudscape. However, whenever the attackers pushed closer to the sea, the powerful Allied offshore fleet promptly sent many of them fleeing back to their own lines. Then, as units regrouped, XII Air Support command joined the fray with seven hundred Allied planes committed to aerial support for the landing zone.

As Mackensen received the grim news that some of his best assault battalions could field little more than one hundred men for renewed attacks, he simply combined fractured units into provisional assault forces and continued the massive offensive. Lucas responded to his adversary's gambit by backstopping the badly mauled 45th Division with the equally depleted British 1st Division, which was in the middle of a command organization when its commander, General Penny, was seriously wounded by an artillery barrage.

Operation Fischfang had now devolved into a desperate brawl between two exhausted boxers, but Mackensen was under more pressure than Lucas, as he now faced increasingly shrill commands from Hitler to excise the Anglo-American "boil" on German-occupied Italy. More and more, unbloodied German units were folded into the assault regiments that had faced the greatest fury of the Allied defenders, while on the other side of the line, Colonel William Darby, who had lost most of his Ranger command at Cisterna, was shifted into the command position of the badly mauled 179th Regiment, and 1st Armored Division Commander Ernie Harmon was ordered to meld an armored infantry regiment, a tank battalion, and a standard infantry regiment into a force that would be coiled to strike at any perceived weak point in the German line.

While Mackensen increasingly exhorted his unit commands to throw the enemy back to the landing beaches so that they could "Dunkirk the Allies," the defenders started assigning colorful names to battlefield positions that would soon pepper newspaper reports. For example, a road connecting the Aprilia "Factory" complex to the edge of the Padiglione Woods was now called the "Bombing Alley," while a heavily contested railroad overpass was designated "The Flyover."

After a brief pause to reorganize his forces, Mackensen ordered a maximum-effort assault for February 19, which pushed even further through a sagging Allied middle but could never eliminate the still strong Anglo-American flank positions. The German line was now badly overstretched at the center, and one assault regiment pushed too far ahead of its support forces. An Allied spotter plane detected the danger the enemy had created for itself, and within minutes, over two hundred cannons roared in unison and turned the marshy landscape into an enormous killing ground.

The multiday Fischfang offensive had pushed the Allied front lines back a short distance but still nowhere near the need for a final stand at the beachfront. The operation had cost Mackensen more than six thousand casualties, with some divisions losing 90 percent of their combat strength. While only about 10 percent of the German casualties were now prisoners in Allied POW cages, the thirty-five hundred Allied casualties included a much steeper loss in captured men that topped out at just over thirteen hundred, which meant that the killed and wounded ratio was more than twice as high for the German defenders as for the Allied side.

Probably the final casualty of Operation Fischfang was not the clearly unsuccessful Mackensen but the technically victorious commander of the Allies, General John Lucas. Two days after the German offensive fizzled, Lucas was not officially fired but given a transfer "without prejudice" to the newly created position of deputy commander of Fifth Army. Lucas was a canny enough soldier to know a relief order when he saw one and insisted to Clark, "I thought I was winning something of a victory." Mark Clark had repeatedly encouraged Lucas to be cautious and avoid any overly risky moves, and the Shingle commander had done precisely that. While Churchill had a vision of a game-changing amphibious victory, Clark saw Shingle as a dangerous gamble. None of the senior Allied leaders had foreseen the speed with which Kesselring could cobble together a huge attack force, while the Allies had to depend on a still-inadequate naval transport force to dribble reinforcements ashore more slowly than their adversaries could truck them in by land.

As late winter gave way to the promise of early spring in central Italy, the opposing armies counted their losses so far in Shingle, and the tally for each side topped out at about nineteen thousand men, with about two thousand killed on each side. John Lucas would be replaced by the more dynamic, more abrasive Lucian Truscott, while the relieved general was partially rewarded for his "team spirit" in maintaining silence over his relief by being returned to the United States and promoted to command of the Fourth Army, which technically existed to repel an unlikely German or Japanese invasion of America. The war around Anzio and along the Gustav line would settle into a temporary late-winter stalemate, but a vast new battle was about to open on another front, in the frigid skies that formed the roof of Hitler's northern Europe.

CHAPTER IV

The Rise of the Sky Knights

On Thursday, October 14, 1943, two hundred ninety-one American Army Air Force bombers took off from bases in East Anglia on a mission to destroy three vital German ball-bearing factories. These factories were a vital component in the rapidly expanding Luftwaffe presence in the skies over Northwest Europe, and their destruction would be a major blow to the Reich air defense network. As the four-engine bombers crossed the English Channel into the airspace above occupied Europe, each member of the ten-man crews double-checked his oxygen systems, confirmed that his machine guns were operational, and checked for any open spots in the multilayered clothing he wore to protect himself against forty-below-zero air temperatures. Pilots and gunners swung their heads in a choreographed rhythm, constantly watching for a telltale dark spark that was an enemy fighter launching an attack run.

This sky armada, escorted by one hundred fifty fighters, flew over the border of occupied Holland and then, with only minimal warning, found themselves flying parallel to their adversaries, carefully deployed just out of range of the American bombers' array of guns.

The American pilots flying state-of-the-art heavy bombers—B-17 Flying Fortresses and B-24 Liberators—were from almost every one of the forty-eight states but shared the common trait of being generally quite young, mostly in their early to mid-twenties and yet in command of enlisted crew members who were likely to be in their late teens. Now, equally young men wearing similar clothes and gear but decked out in Luftwaffe blue began their deadly attack runs, determined to break up the multiple "boxes" of American intruders. One large formation of German fighters turned majestically in an almost ballet-like synchronization and unleashed dozens of deadly rockets on four formations of sixteen of the Allied intruders. In perhaps two minutes, thirteen of these American bombers exploded in fireballs and simply disappeared from tracking radar screens. These ME-110 and 210 "destroyers" were quickly joined by faster, single-engine ME-109 fighters that ripped through neighboring squadrons with equal intensity. Finally, far above the American bomber stream, Stuka dive bombers crossed over the American formation and began dropping bombs as if the Fortresses were French or Russian tanks in the great land battles of 1940 and 1941.

As dozens of American bombers and a smaller number of German fighter planes filled the autumn sky with the impending destruction of a final drive, the swirling mass of planes passed over the pleasant German community of Schweinfurt as puffs of black, cotton-like smoke rose in a deadly challenge from the city's antiaircraft batteries. All three aircraft factories and dozens of less important buildings were hit by the aerial deluge, but, despite the apparent spectacular damage, none of these planes was substantially put out of action.

The intruders, lightened by the release of their bomb loads, gained welcome altitude and speed, and even the Luftwaffe pilots sometimes pursued them all the way back to their air bases. Sixty of the planes were now flaming wrecks on German soil, eight crashed somewhere on the way back to England, seven landed as irreparable wrecks, and almost two-thirds of the survivors suffered significant damage. Of the roughly three thousand men who had eaten or attempted to eat the powdered eggs, bacon, and toast at breakfast that morning, six hundred forty-two of them were now dead, wounded, or reluctant guests of the Luftwaffe for the remainder of the war. By dinnertime back in England, an increasing number of pilots were referring to their adventure as simply "Black Thursday" and silently calculating how many missions remained on their tours of duty.

Three months later, the calendar had been turned to 1944, and almost every senior officer in the Allied Air Forces knew that in five months the largest armada in history would set sail from Britain and attempt to land an invasion force somewhere on the coastline of Adolf Hitler's massive empire. Given the recent fates of armies that had attempted to fight a battle under skies controlled by the planes of the enemy, it soon became apparent that there simply could be no Operation Overlord without Allied control of a significant amount of the airspace over whichever Northern European beaches the allies chose to land these invasion forces.

The Allied response to this conundrum was a plan to effectively remove the Luftwaffe from the chessboard of Overlord by destroying the factories that manufactured the Axis planes, which in turn, would force enemy fighters to challenge the intruders and leave them open for destruction. If the Anglo-Americans could control the sea adjoining the invasion beaches and the skies above the landing areas, it seemed that the odds of a successful invasion would suddenly swing substantially in the Allies' favor. A single raid like Schweinfurt had demonstrated some interesting possibilities, but even more exciting things might happen if the Luftwaffe fighter-construction industry could be hammered for an entire week.

For the youngish and often iconoclastic men who commanded the increasingly autonomous portion of the United States Army, designated as the Army Air Forces, the Japanese attack on Pearl Harbor was probably more a providential gift than an aerial disaster. The Nipponese raiders *had* nearly annihilated the Air Force's combat power in Hawaii, but much of the destruction was perpetrated on obsolete or obsolescent planes that would have been retired soon anyway, and the two planes that had actually managed to get into combat at Pearl Harbor had brought down seven of the Japanese raiders. Now, two years later, the AAF had erased much of that day with spectacular missions such as the bombing of Tokyo, the ambush of Admiral Yamamoto, and the aerial destruction of a Japanese destroyer and transport fleet in the South Pacific. However, the air commanders knew that the single most decisive moment of the coming year would be the invasion of Northwest Europe, and control of the skies above the battlefield would go a long way toward negating the reality that the Allies would be invading without a very large numerical advantage in ground forces.

In early 1944, the Army Air Force was an organization that featured a mindset somewhere between a late adolescent waiting to be released from parental authority by leaving for college and a spouse in an unromantic partnership craving a divorce. For almost three decades, the Air Service of the United States Army had clamored for autonomy from the ground-bound elements of the military service and had watched with envy as German and British counterparts had engineered total breaks with their respective armies.

Now, brash Henry Harley "Hap" Arnold was in the process of engineering a similar split from the American ground forces. The fifty-six-year-old senior American airman's nickname stood for the vaguely smiling face he used when posing for most photographers, but inside was a roiling, nervous energy displayed externally by an intensity that manifested itself in a chain-smoking habit even more intense than Franklin Roosevelt's four-pack-a-day regimen, which, in turn, was a major factor in a series of heart attacks that would consign Arnold to a relatively early grave.

Arnold's career was, in fact, the embodiment of the service that he commanded. He was taught to fly an airplane by the Wright brothers and then jumped into army aviation on the ground floor of a service that was determined to squeeze in between the army and navy by promoting airmail delivery, the future of aerial bombing, and the defense of the American shoreline. Now, decades later, Henry Arnold had mobilized public fascination with flying; the perceived glamour of aerial combat; and the public relations support of film producers, authors, and the news media to gain significant concessions from its parent, the ground army. One key concession was the right of AAF's recruitment office to skim a substantial percentage of the high-end scorers on the intelligence test given to new inductees as they entered the service. This ensured a "best and brightest" mentality within the aerial component of the army. Second, Arnold now held a seat at the all-important Joint Chiefs of Staff meetings, with full equality to George Marshall and Ernest King. Finally, he had secured assurance from Franklin Roosevelt that a move to full independence from the army would be considered after the end of the war.

However, in the early days of 1944, the future independence of the Army Air Force clearly had to take a backseat to the major problem at hand: could the Air Force create conditions in which the Overlord invasion force could land on enemy beaches and proceed inland with little or no interference from the vaunted Luftwaffe? In a clash of arms where the attacking army had little or no numerical advantage over the defenders, control of the skies over the battlefield could well be the crucial determining factor in defeat or victory for the Allied cause.

The officer entrusted with this Herculean task was General Carl "Tooey" Spaatz, the commander of United States Strategic Air Forces in Europe. Spaatz had followed a career path relatively similar to that of his Air Force commander but had spent the period before Pearl Harbor working with the British Air staff in London, creating the foundations of Anglo-American air war cooperation. Now, along with a rapidly growing staff in his headquarters at Park House in the London suburbs, Spaatz began to generate a plan to deal a death blow to Luftwaffe hopes to annihilate the expected invasion force from the air. Rather than launching sporadic attacks on the enemy aircraft industry, Spaatz insisted that a full week of maximum-effort bombings would provide a double threat against the enemy by decimating their production facilities while forcing the Luftwaffe fighter arm to risk planes and pilots when they rose to challenge the intruders.

At the beginning of 1944, the most significant challenge to successful air strikes against the Third Reich's industrial core was the simple fact that most fighter escort planes did not have enough range to stay with the bombers for their entire, dangerous mission. The AAF had begun bombing operations in Northwest Europe in 1942, with the capable but not outstanding P-40 Tomahawk as the primary escort fighter. While that aircraft was sturdy and relatively easy to fly, it was not quite as good a fighter as the ME-109 and FW-190, which challenged control of the skies. As the American Air Force commanders began the massive air raids of early 1944, the Tomahawk was being phased out in favor of more recent additions to the American fighter arsenal.

The two primary escort planes in the winter aerial battles were the P-38 Lightning and the P-47 Thunderbolt. The Lightning was unusual for an air-to-air combat fighter in that it had two engines, a fact that could make the plane a bit more awkward to handle in the rapid turns of an aerial dogfight. However, flying the P-38 in combat certainly had compensations. The Lightning featured an awesome array of firepower built around four machine guns and supported by a fast-firing cannon that could rip apart enemy challengers. The plane was both large and sturdy, which allowed it to absorb more punishment than most of the other fighters, while the availability of two engines was particularly gratifying if one engine was destroyed in a dogfight. The Lightning was designed with above-average range, which allowed for a deeper penetration into enemy airspace, at least partially compensating for its slightly lower-than-average maneuverability, especially at low altitudes.

The other workhorse American escort in the winter air battles was almost as unusual looking as the Lightning—the P-47 Thunderbolt, more commonly called "the Jug" by its pilots. The Thunderbolt was one of the heaviest fighters designed in World War II and featured a weapons array of eight machine guns that could inflict enormous damage in aerial combat. The Thunderbolt's weight allowed the plane to keep flying after relatively significant punishment in a dogfight and allowed the plane to become an offensive threat with its capability of carrying three thousand pounds of bombs, as well.

The escort capabilities of the Lightnings and the Thunderbolts, coupled with the massive defensive firepower of the B-17 Flying Fortresses and the B-24 Liberator, had finally allowed the AAF to stage massive air attacks on the outer edge of the Third Reich with acceptable, if not exactly light, losses. Raids on Abbeville in France and Bremen near the North Sea or on German bases in Holland were moderately successful, and the fighters kept the Luftwaffe at bay to some extent. However, the German aircraft industry was much further inland and protected by a state-of-the-art system of interlocking antiaircraft batteries. Thus, fighter operations far into the heart of Hitler's empire would require enormous risks and at least some technological upgrades in the assault force.

The first significant technological advance that reduced long-range penetration of the Reich from a nearly suicidal mission to merely a risky venture was an enormous boost in the rate of production of the newly developed auxiliary fuel tanks for American escort fighters. In preparation for the attack on the German aircraft industry, P-47 Thunderbolts began to be retrofitted with seventy-five-gallon metal belly tanks, which would allow the planes to finally accompany the bombers for most or even all of a long-range mission. Now, for the first time, the "little friends" would not be forced to leave the bombers just as a tidal wave of interceptors was about to pounce.

The second crucial addition to the AAF escort arsenal emerged from one of the most classic "Ugly Duckling" tales of World War II. At the outbreak of the war, the North American Aviation Company, a firm primarily involved in designing bombers, developed a prototype fighter, the NA-73, which was a plane without an engine. The aircraft, which had a revolutionary airfoil design, was eventually mated with an underpowered Allison engine that had little potential to bring out the real power of the airframe. Meanwhile, British aircraft designers had produced a powerful new engine, the Merlin, which would not fit into their available array of airframes. Ultimately, a British test pilot openly wondered what might happen if the more successful half of each project was mated, and the "Cadillac of the skies," the P-51 Mustang, emerged in small numbers for the impending operation that was now increasingly labeled "The Big Week." The Mustang could fly and dive as fast as or faster than all non-jet-propelled Luftwaffe fighters and could function superbly, even encumbered with supersized, 108-gallon auxiliary fuel tanks. As 1944 progressed, the Mustang would become the new Thoroughbred in the American stable of fighters, but, even in small numbers, the plane would be a major asset in the developing air offensive.

What was essentially the opening round of Operation Overlord was, ironically, now dependent on the authorization of a science professor at California Institute of Technology. While operating from his home base in the Pasadena's branch Department of Meteorology, Dr. Irving Krick had developed a successful side business in utilizing past weather patterns to predict future conditions. While more traditional weather experts dismissed Krick as a smug self-promoter, General Hap Arnold was intrigued by his level of success and commissioned the professor as a major in the Air Force. This appointment may or may not have been as exciting to Krick as his work with David O. Selznick, when Krick had been employed to predict the weather for the burning of Atlanta scenes in *Gone with the Wind,* but now the meteorologist was in England, literally trying to find a patch of blue in the dreary winter landscape.

Now, as thousands of air personnel waited for the initiation of an air campaign currently code-named "Operation Argument," Krick huddled over weather data going back a half century, working on seemingly incomprehensible calculations. Then he majestically announced that beginning on Sunday, February 20, 1944, the skies over Germany would be clear for three or more days. Army Air Force weather personnel scoffed at his February 18 predictions, insisting that predicting three days of weather conditions in a European winter was a losing venture. On the other hand, once the predictions reached Hap Arnold, Operation Argument was well on the way to reality.

On the morning of Sunday, February 20, early risers in the aircrews' Quonset hut barracks may have glanced at the heavy overcast above their base and assumed that there was a good chance this actually would be a day of rest. However, reconnaissance aircraft reported that the weather over Germany was largely clear, and Krick had at least been accurate for Day One of the Big Week. The men who would be the aircrew for Operation Argument were all volunteers who ranged from actor Jimmy Stewart and recent college graduates to gawky teenagers who were sometimes just adolescent enough not to know the real meaning of fear and death. While they generally spent far less time in full-scale combat, they were actually far more likely to die than the average rifleman in a foxhole, and, once their plane was targeted by an enemy fighter or hit by an antiaircraft blast, there was simply nowhere to run, and even jumping out the door and engaging a parachute often took a few more seconds than the fates of air warfare allowed. The men who would crew the Fortresses and Liberators designed to turn the industrial heartland of Germany into the set of a later postapocalyptic film were almost never below the rank of sergeant, even if they were still teenagers.

In many respects, these men, on average younger than their ground army equivalent, generated initial envy from their land-forces counter-parts. They slept every night in clean, well-lit, at least tolerably warm quarters with little or no exposure to the elements. They ate cooked meals in relatively comfortable mess halls, often had access to local pubs and entertainment, and even had regular dances that featured ample supplies of liquor and opportunities to form social connections with British females. Above all, unlike most ground troops, their encounters with deadly force had a clearcut termination. Depending on the period of the war and the type of missions flown, most aircrew were rotated home after somewhere between twenty-five and forty missions, with the clear understanding that only if they volunteered would they be returning to combat missions. However, what the ground forces did not particularly understand but the aircrews knew intimately was that the calculus of death versus survival in early 1944 still clearly favored the Grim Reaper. Even if only 10 percent of planes failed to return after a single mission, that mission was only one of perhaps thirty flown by an airman, and, by that calculation, very few would survive death or capture. Much of 1944 and most of the war, for that matter, would be spent in a grim comparison among American fight-ing men as to which particular service "had it better" or alternatively "had it worse." The problem was that the discussion was an apples-and-oranges comparison. During the upcoming summer, only a tiny percentage of naval crew died in the highly important Battle of the Philippine Sea, but only a few months later, GIs who envied the "swabbies" began to change their tunes when the Japanese shifted tactics to suicide bombings and vir-tually the entire complement of a destroyer could die with an unlucky hit from the men of the Divine Wind. In turn, the marines and soldiers who would be fighting in the Pacific island battles of the year often took very heavy casualties for each day of fighting, but once the island was secured, there would be a lengthy hiatus until the next assault. On the other hand, ground battles in Europe often had relatively few casualties in any single day, but, as would be seen later in the Hüertgen and Ardennes forest battles, they could drag on for days or even weeks.

Now, perhaps with those thoughts in mind, the aircrews of the "Big Week" offensive clambered aboard their Fortresses and Liberators and prepared for their war in the sky.

The youngest segments of the crew were usually teenagers or early-twenty-somethings, all of whom had at least some responsibility for one of the machine guns deployed to defend the plane from all possible angles. The interior of their planes was often compared to an aluminum cigar tube that lacked central heating and would turn into a largely frozen tube once the mission was fully underway. A typical B-17 Flying Fortress was defended by a crew of designated gunners that included a tail gunner ensconced in a tiny rear compartment; left and right waist gunners who stood back-to-back, peering out of open doors; a usually rather short crew member crouched in a rotating ball turret on the bottom of the plane; a slightly more comfortable upper gun turret operator who rotated in a plastic ball on the top of the plane; and a radio operator who kept in communication with the lead plane and often manned another machine gun on the side.

Unlike British and German bomber crews that might have only one commissioned officer, the pilot, on board, the AAF was far more generous with officer rank for the four-man contingents who were the technical brains of the missions. Officers' insignia went to the navigator, who was responsible for plotting a correct course to the target and home again; the bombardier, who actually armed the bombs, decided the moment to drop them, and then released his lethal cargo; the copilot, who flew the plane for part of the mission; and, most important, the "captain" of the "ship," the master and commander who had been designated the lead pilot. The pilot was often just a bit older than the other crew members, part surrogate father and part big brother to the younger crew and ultimately responsible for the welfare of nine other men. Pilots could theoretically cancel a mission at any time, but, in reality, too many "turn back" orders might also land the pilot in a permanent grounding condition, so each "abort" call had to be carefully considered.

Now, on this cloudy, cold Sunday morning, hundreds of these ten-man "teams" joked, cursed, bantered, and probably often secretly prayed as their planes coughed to life, rolled down the runway, and suddenly defied gravity and were airborne. Aircrews had been extensively briefed earlier that morning, and, despite skepticism from numerous sources that Operation Argument would be a "fiasco," Big Week got its start.

The man immediately responsible for the Eighth Air Force planes taking off from England was one of the most recognizable personalities in 1944, General James Harold "Jimmy" Doolittle, the new commander of bombardment forces stationed in Britain. "Jimmy" Doolittle had missed out on World War I but in compensation had earned one of the first doctorates at MIT awarded in aeronautical engineering and had gained some fame for making the first "blind" flight, flying and landing entirely on instruments while covered with a black hood. Doolittle had spent much of the interwar period as an executive for the Shell Oil Company but had returned to the service in time to land the supremely risky, and ultimately legendary, air raid on Tokyo from the carrier *Enterprise* in the dark days of April 1942. Now, in 1944, a household name, Doolittle was in command of the highest-profile unit of the Army Air Forces, the "Mighty Eighth." Just over nine hundred Liberators and Fortresses of that Eighth Air Force were flying toward the heart of the Luftwaffe aircraft construction empire.

This pulsating, olive drab armada was being escorted on this frigid Sunday morning by almost six hundred seventy P-47 Thunderbolts that formed the main obstacle to enemy fighter attacks. Unfortunately, the target areas were still beyond the combat range of these burly war planes, and they would simply fly cover as long as possible, return to base for refueling, and then escort the bombers home as they drew near their exit points along the coast. Thus, when the bombers actually arrived over their targets, their survival would depend on the workmanship of their own gunners: ninety-four long-range P-38 Lightnings and seventy-three extended-mission P-51 Mustangs, a fighter escort that might deter but certainly couldn't totally deflect the Luftwaffe fighters now climbing to intercept them.

Within the Third Reich, over which the American intruders were now flying, few individuals were as lauded, pampered, idolized, or cheered as the Luftwaffe's almost legendary fighter pilots. They were commanded by Hermann Goering, who had spent much of World War I as a highly decorated member of Baron von Richthofen's "Flying Circus" and had become, in essence, the second most powerful man in the Third Reich. Unlike American or British equivalents, the Luftwaffe controlled every aspect of aerial warfare, including the paratroop formations and naval support planes. Yet in 1944, as Luftwaffe bombers could launch only token raids against Britain, and the paratroopers were gradually being turned into ground-bound infantry, the fighter pilots were darlings of the Reich's enormous media empire. The fighters were the major barrier to an Allied bombing campaign that was now progressively turning German cities into rubble, and one of the few consolations that bombed-out German civilians still had was seeing what they now called the Anglo-American "Luftegangsters" shot out of the sky by marauding Messerschmitts and Focke-Wulf planes.

Now, on what was a clear, bright Sunday in much of Germany, the "flying gangsters" had clearly returned, and the cities they threatened shared something in common: they all housed major aircraft factories. The American intruders were gradually breaking off into smaller groups heading for targets as diverse as the Junkers aircraft factory in Leipzig to Luftwaffe manufacturing centers in far away Stetten and Rostock. However, wherever they flew, the raiders eventually encountered a German defensive array that had been developed with Prussian-like precision.

The first German gambit in this enormous aerial chess match was to challenge the American bomber formations with quadroons of robust, powerful ME-110 fighters. These aircraft were twin-engine, radar-equipped planes that were originally designed primarily as night fighters, but now roamed the skies in search of Allied daylight intruders. The ME-110s were not intended to engage in a plane-to-plane dogfight with

American raiders but instead operated in tightly controlled aerial phalanxes of six to two dozen planes. American bomber pilots would see a formation appear either in front of or at the side of their bomber stream, and then, a moment later, a barrage of deadly air-to-air rockets was unleashed in a stupendous aerial volley. The bombers were fortunate only to the extent that their tormentors did not have the heat-seeking capabilities of future generations of missiles, but even one hit could demolish a bomber, and more than one hit left virtually no evidence that the aircraft had ever existed.

Then, as the ME-110s turned sharply and headed to base to resupply their rocket tubes, a new danger often appeared from above. In their desperation to deflect the Allied bomber menace, the Luftwaffe defense command had begun converting their own primary bombers into an aerial assault weapon. The twin-engine JU-88 was the workhorse bomber in the Luftwaffe aerial assault against embattled Britain in the 1940–41 Blitz. Now, Junkers air crews were retrained to fly over American bomber formation and actually conduct a bomb run over the Yankee intruders. This form of attack was far more difficult than attacking a stationary block of British houses, but the success rate was just high enough to begin to turn the bomber offensive into an even more multidimensional battle and add a new threat to an already deadly bombing mission.

The danger that American bomber crews experienced from this varied array of conventional fighters was enhanced still further by a new technique just emerging from the Luftwaffe playbook. Unlike the Bushido sprint of the Reich's Japanese ally, which encouraged the frequent use of suicidal activities if a battle could not be won by ordinary measures, Nazi Germany still had just enough of a link to Western culture to make personal, willful, self-destruction a rare occurrence. On the other hand, the Luftwaffe was now at a point where there were more planes available than there were experienced pilots. One outcome of this dilemma was an increasing call for volunteers who would essentially move into position, aim their planes at an American bomber, and bail out at the last minute before the aircrafts collided. This strategy was viewed at headquarters as an advantageous trade of a single-engine plane for a much more expensive multiengine bomber and the removal of ten highly trained American crew members from the chessboard of war.

Once the bombers and their escorts had gone through the gauntlet of enemy interceptors, they passed into a new zone of danger of multiple rings of German antiaircraft batteries. When American heavy bombers began to appear in daylight operations and the British Bomber Command switched to nighttime attacks, Luftwaffe ordnance engineers developed the FLAK 41 antiaircraft gun, an eighty-eight-millimeter cannon designed to shoot down Flying Fortresses and Liberators flying as high as twenty-nine thousand feet. Beyond their stationary batteries, the Germans utilized "flak trains" of a powerful locomotive and a string of flat cars, each equipped with an antiaircraft gun and specially designed to engage in a running duel with any American bombers that conducted their bomb runs from low altitudes. Yet, while flak fire was terrifying to crew members as near misses jolted and shook the planes incessantly, relatively few planes actually exploded in midair as the antiaircraft fire was still widely dispersed.

In essence, the first day of Big Week was actually hundreds of individual battles between American bomber crews and fighter pilots and German fighters and antiaircraft crews. Given the carnage over Regensburg and Schweinfurt the previous year, Eighth Air Force staff officers expected a loss of approximately two hundred bombers and two thousand crew men, which would still have been a reasonable price to destroy a significant portion of Luftwaffe air power. As planes returned and went through debriefing, it became apparent that the German aircraft industry had been badly mauled. One pilot insisted to debriefers, "We had the most perfect bombing conditions we've ever seen. There was a big hole in the clouds for a twenty mile radius around the target. If we didn't shake that place today, we'll never hit anything." At the key aircraft-construction sites around the city of Leipzig, six plants suffered serious structural damage, while factories around Braunschweig, Gotha, and Rostock were battered.

The other pleasant surprise for the mission planners was that losses were barely one-tenth of what they had expected. The relatively small numbers of Mustangs and Lightnings over the target and the much larger gaggle of Thunderbolts that had escorted the bombers part of the way in and out had run up an amazing, largely verified total of sixty-one Luftwaffe fighters destroyed at an incredibly small loss of only four of their own ranks. The multidimensional Luftwaffe defense plan had worked to an extent; twenty-one American bombers were shot down, but, in turn, surviving crews reported a most likely exaggerated sixty-five enemy fighters down.

More than two hundred American airmen died or were taken as POWs on that Sunday night, but operation Argument had gotten off to a spectacular start.

The next day, Monday, February 21, 1944, nearly nine hundred bombers began their choreographed takeoffs and began flying to a very different set of targets from the day before. Now, instead of flying toward enemy aircraft factories, they were targeting the finished planes on the Luftwaffe air bases. Key targets included Bromsche, Hopsten, Quakenburch, Rheine, and especially a huge, multi-field complex called Fliegerhorst Diepholz.

As the American air fleet roared over multiple airfield targets, Luftwaffe interceptors rose like angry hornets to protect their home bases. On the ground, German schoolchildren ran out of their classrooms and cheered their heroes of the sky as plane after plane roared down runways and formed for combat. One American bomber crew member insisted, "This was the fiercest engagement I ever saw in the skies; clusters of German fighters, six twelve, then thirty and forty dove at the bombers behind smoke screens laid by other Nazi aircraft." One group of Fortresses encountered a formation of eighteen ME-110s "in such tight formation that we thought they were also Fortresses; then they all got into a tight line, swinging right and let go a broadside of rockets. The rockets approached like a string of long-range torpedoes as several bombers burst into flames and hurtled earthward while damaged planes dropped out of formation, trying haltingly and desperately to climb back into the group as ME-110s circled around, fired another barrage of rockets and then came barreling in, firing 20 mm. cannons."

On this late-winter Monday, some American units encountered enemy "wolf packs" of forty to fifty FW 190s, attacking in massive extended lines, often without their usual tactics of rolling on their backs to take advantage of their belly armor plate. Using sheer strength of numbers, Germans bullied their way into tightly packed bomber formations to split them open, despite the Americans' advantage of combined defensive firepower.

Some of the attacking squadrons faced the threat of another newly emerging German defense tactic: "balloon mines," which were aerial bombs fastened to the end of a cable towed by an advance fighter plane that would pull the mines into American formations, release them, and let them explode automatically. American bombers would then become entangled in the steel cables, trapped within the explosive radius of the mines or, at the very least, thrown badly off course. Damaged Fortresses and Liberators, slowed by the cables, often became a prime target for predatory German fighters that would enjoy an enormous speed advantage in this risky game of aerial bumper cars.

Just as on the day before, by the time the bombardment divisions reached their main targets, the Thunderbolts that formed the bulk of their escort contingent had been forced to return to England to refuel, leaving the escort duties to a thin screen of Lightnings and Mustangs. However, mission commanders had managed to scour the whole string of fighter bases in England and cobble together another strike force of P-51s that was just reaching the attack force as it bombed the Luftwaffe airfields. What followed was one of the most spectacular series of aerial dogfights of World War II. One bomber crew gasped in astonishment as a single Mustang dove through "a gaggle of nearly thirty German fighters" and broke up a potentially devastating attack. The purpose of these P-51s was more to frustrate enemy attacks than run up a large personal victory tally, so the swirling melee ultimately shot down only fourteen enemy fighters in return for a loss of three Mustangs, but, more importantly, many German fighters were deflected from even more deadly attacks on the American bomber stream.

The results of the second day of Big Week began to demonstrate how even a generally successful mission could not effectively annihilate a major segment of the Luftwaffe in a single day. The irony of a mass assault on German air bases was that, by the time the raiders arrived, most of the enemy planes were already in the air, attacking the raiders as advanced German radar equipment ensured that a truly surprise attack was increasingly impossible in this type of air war. The cost of relatively heavily damaging a fairly impressive string of enemy air bases had been a loss of twenty-three bombers and seven fighters in return for a claim, though probably exaggerated, that forty-three Luftwaffe fighters were destroyed.

The next day, Krick's forecast of three successive clear days over Germany proved only partially correct, as so many targets were under total cloud cover that the main air battles of the day were over a relatively limited number of airfields and aircraft factories, allowing the Luftwaffe to concentrate their fighters in a relatively small battlefield. The result of the operation was "Bloody Tuesday," in which a staggering fifty-three American bombers were shot down, along with eleven escort fighters, in return for a possibly inflated number of sixty enemy planes lost.

The Big Week was essentially reduced to the "big six days" when, at least for a day, most of Northern Europe returned to its usual winter overcast, but the Caltech weather wizard's prediction of another seventy-two-hour "patch of blue" proved accurate, and on Thursday, February 24, 1944, the sometimes overused AAF term, "maximum effort," was back in force. When fighter crews filed into ready rooms and saw the curtain over operations maps go up, the red and blue strings of yarn used as markers pointed once again to the heart of the Third Reich. Once again, German fighters swarmed aloft to protect the ball-bearings works at Schweinenfurt, the Messerchmitt factory at Gotha, and the numerous other centers of the German aircraft industry. One bomber pilot marveled at the starkness of the winter landscape, "a white, snow-covered landscape four miles below looking cold and lifeless; only large communities, rail lines and an autobahn stood out in relief." Another bomber crew member noted "a countryside of dark forests and white fields dotted with cities and villages, all connect[ed] by road and rail lines . . . where I know air raid sirens blow and people hurry to hide in underground shelters."

The one-sided successes of the previous Sunday were now slipping back into a series of bloody tradeoffs; the gunners on the bombers and the escorting fighters claimed thirty-seven enemy planes shot down over the targets. However, at least ten American fighters joined them in a death spiral, and forty-four bombers were also lost.

By Friday, February 25, the Big Week was about to shrink to six days, only five of which actually featured significant missions. The seven hundred fifty bombers leaving British air space now had more than nine hundred escort fighters accompanying them with a substantially enhanced contingent of nearly one hundred forty of the invaluable long-range Mustangs. The main targets centered on production of the main first-line fighters of the German Air Force—the Messerschmitt BF (or ME) 109, which by now had achieved nearly iconic status with an industrial production run of thirty-five thousand planes. From Augsburg to Regensburg, fighter-construction plants were severely damaged in an aerial bombardment that at least temporarily knocked out more than one-third of the construction capability of this iconic fighter. Meanwhile, between the Eighth Air Bombers and Fifth Air Force raiders from Italy, seventy-two American bombers spiraled into the wintry landscape, leaving more than seven hundred Americans dead or imprisoned. Yet, despite the appalling losses, the Reich had paid even more dearly with losses of nearly one hundred fighters in the air and many hundreds more under construction on the ground. The main beneficiaries of this costly, but successful, operation were the thousands of American soldiers who were now arriving daily in Britain on a seemingly unending stream on transport ship convoys. These were the men who would land on the beaches of Normandy on D-Day and beyond, and much of their ultimate survival would depend on the ability of their Air Force counterparts to ensure that it would be the Allied Air Forces, not the Luftwaffe, that ruled the skies over Operation Overlord. For the moment, these GI ground troops, their Air Force counterparts, and even a growing contingent of sailors were peacefully "invading" their temporary host country, which was ultimately a relatively small island, already inhabited by forty million Britons linked together in a world of chronic shortages and "make-do and mend."

CHAPTER V

The Last Invasion of Britain

During the early weeks of 1944, *Life* magazine featured a lengthy article and photo spread about two of the thousands of British subjects who had "invaded" the United States since the beginning of World War II. Michael and Venise Harninden, by then ages fourteen and eleven, were sent by their British parents to stay with close friends on Long Island in an attempt to escape the dangers of the German aerial assault on England after the fall of France. As the *Life* correspondent noted, "Spending their formative years in the United States has really made them children of two countries." The children were described as having a mix of British and American accents and "are quite at home in the mannerisms of normal American teenagers." Michael was photographed in his uniform as a baseball pitcher for his high school and now had a keen interest in "football, cowboys and motorcycles." Venise, who had gained eleven inches and forty pounds since arriving, was an active Girl Scout and hoped someday to "marry a cowboy."

These two photogenic children were a tiny microcosm of the seventeen thousand children who had been evacuated to North America by often frantic parents who took advantage of the generosity of American and Canadian sponsors to allow their children to escape a besieged Great

Britain that was beginning to undergo a blitz that would kill sixty thousand civilians, including thousands of children, and turn entire neighborhoods into unrecognizable heaps of rubble. As evacuated children wrote alternately plaintive and reassuring letters to their parents that "we see the same moon and stars as you do," those same kids reveled in huge amounts of ice cream and candy bars and complained about the absence of really greasy fish and chips, and a new bond was forming between Britain and America that cemented the potential alliance that had been initiated by Winston Churchill and Franklin Roosevelt.

However, while these thousands of British children attempted to adapt to living on a huge continent quite capable of absorbing this stream of newcomers, a torrent of Americans only a bit older than some of those "seavacuees" were now heading in the opposite direction, alternately welcomed for their contribution to final victory and derided by many of the English locals as "overpaid, oversexed and over here." Britain had not undergone a full-scale, successful invasion since Duke William of Normandy had destroyed a British Army under King Harold almost a millennium earlier. In the great war, a generation earlier, Britain had largely escaped an inundation of Americans since the doughboys were able to land in the Atlantic ports of a France that was still largely unoccupied by the enemy. Now, in this second round of world war, France was an occupied nation, and Britain was a relatively small island in a sea of nations either occupied by the Nazis or carefully neutral to the point of bending over backwards in their attempts to escape the wrath of Adolf Hitler's roaming gaze. On their own, the British were (barely) capable of preventing the Germans from invading and occupying their nation, but if Hitler were ever to be defeated, an enormous supply of Yanks would have to arrive in Britain for the war to be returned to the Continent. Unfortunately for both the natives and the friendly "invaders," their two cultures were a volatile brew of shared beliefs enormously complicated by different backgrounds and different dreams.

Seven decades after the end of World War II, the United Kingdom is one of the premier foreign destinations for Americans interested in traveling beyond the United States and its adjacent neighbors. Over the past half-century, with the advent of communication satellites, computer linkups, and global phone service, British imports to American popular culture from the Beatles to Harry Potter and *Downton Abbey* have triggered an excitement to visit a nation just different enough to seem mildly exotic, but not so alien as to turn a vacation into a challenge. However, the Britain that American visitors encounter after an only moderately long and uncomfortable jet flight is not the Britain that hundreds of thousands of GIs encountered after a long, dangerous, cramped, and seasick-dominated ocean voyage.

When the GIs landed in Britain, their most prominent first instinct was that the island, unlike the deck of the transport ship, was not rolling and pitching. This sensation was an immediate bonus to the development of cordial Anglo-American relations. However, once the Americans were acclimatized to the fact that seasickness was not endemic to the British landscape, the disadvantages of Britain over the American homeland quickly became readily apparent. The first revelation that overtook many Americans was that this strategically invaluable portal to the invasion of Hitler's Europe was enormously overcrowded to almost everyone, with the possible exception of the residents of the possibly even more crowded streets of New York City. An island roughly the size of Oregon was jam-packed with more than forty million people, while back home only a little more than three times this number of Americans sprawled around a landscape that contained much of the habitable landmass of an entire continent. Now, as servicemen and -women recovered from the rigors of a supremely uncomfortable and sometimes dangerous Atlantic crossing, they began to encounter and explore a land invitingly similar to and yet at times unbelievably alien to their own lives in the United States.

Initially, every American who landed in Great Britain was issued a tan-covered booklet with the innocuous title *Instructions for American Servicemen in Britain*. This manual included a handy table of comparative values of British and American money; a brief history of the British people, including their customs and manners; and general guidelines on why the British behaved as they did, with a not very subtle warning to the GIs: "It is always impolite to criticize your hosts; it is militarily stupid to criticize your allies." One of the major stereotypes this booklet attempted to correct was the perceived over-politeness, bordering on foppishness, which permeated Hollywood features about upper-class British lifestyles. One of the most common stereotypes emerged from the hugely popular film *The Scarlet Pimpernel,* which featured Leslie Howard as a lazy, snuff-imbibing rake, Sir Percy Blakeny, who was so effete that he needed servants to draw his bath and dress him before transforming into a swashbuckling swordsman saving French nobles from Madame Guillotine. British characters in American films, and in British films as well, usually tended to be soft-spoken, polite, and less inclined to verbal or physical showdowns than their American counterparts, but the tan booklet insisted that the GIs needed to view their hosts as more multidimensional than their film depiction. The authors insisted, "The British can be plenty tough when they need to be. The English language didn't spread across the oceans and over the mountains and jungles and swamps of the world because these people were panty-waists. Sixty thousand British citizens—men, women and children—have died under bombs, and yet the morale of the British is unbreakable and high. A nation doesn't come through that if it doesn't have plain, common guts. The British are tough, strong people and good allies. They are not particularly interested in 'taking it' anymore. They are far more interested in getting together in friendship with you, so that we can all start dishing it out to Hitler."

While most of the newly arriving GIs had no particular reason to doubt that the British were as eager as they were to defeat Hitler, the Britain in which they landed somewhat shocked these Americans in its contrast to the United Kingdom that they had encountered on the silver screen while growing up. Hollywood producers and directors of the 1930s and 1940s were very much unlike their twenty-first-century counterparts in their determination to avoid filming on authentic locations when their own back lot could stand in for almost any time period or any locale. Therefore, the Britain of the exciting new world of Technicolor typically appeared as a sunny, pleasant, almost achingly colorful environment as depicted in such blockbuster films as the Errol Flynn-Olivia De Havilland spectacle, *The Adventures of Robin Hood.* Even lower-budget contemporary black-and-white films, shot in Hollywood, still supplied an impression of a climate not that much different from that of Los Angeles, with the exception of an occasionally clearly fake downpour.

Now the Americans clambered down from the gangplanks of troop ships and often entered a murky, dreary world that always seemed to hang somewhere between downpours and sunshine. There was never the biting cold of either the northern states in winter or the humid sunshine of much of America in summer. Instead, at best, there were "sunny spells" and "bright in patches" and "clear intervals" interspersed much of the year with some damp concoction between fog, mist, and drizzle that the British largely ignored and Americans made the centerpiece of letters home.

Most Americans with a more dispassionate view of the circumstances would probably have realized that while Britain was cool and overcast much of the time, their home states, depending on geographical location, were plagued by tornadoes, hurricanes, blizzards, droughts, earthquakes, and other meteorological calamities that their temporary home was generally spared. Instead, letters to and from home generally evoked sparkling, snow-covered Christmas mornings, lazy summer afternoons, the startling colors of autumnal foliage, or the first really warm day of spring. Armed with this selective memory, the GIs essentially believed they had been subjected to a reverse experience of Dorothy Gale in *The Wizard of Oz*, when she left a black-and-white, featureless Kansas landscape for the stunning Technicolor of Oz. Now, the American personnel who would assault Hitler's occupied Europe had left the partially real and partially fantasized "Technicolor" of an America blessed with a combination of a booming wartime economy and immunity from the destruction of war and were entering a semi-besieged nation that seemed to offer the same monochrome backdrop as that remembered but unlamented America of the Depression era.

The United Kingdom that these peaceful invaders were now entering was a nation that had valiantly deflected the power of Hitler's wrath but had paid the price for its valor by being reduced to a frayed "make do and mend" existence that in many ways was less comfortable than life in Nazi Germany and in some reports more austere than occupied France,

Holland, or Denmark. The world the Yanks now entered was a jumble of bomb-damaged buildings in a variety of stages of reconstruction or neglect, badly overcrowded transportation systems in which each square inch of space was a personal battleground in a determined but polite confrontation, and food establishments that had more notices of "items not currently available" than more positive notification of what was actually "on offer." While America was ablaze with propaganda posters exhorting citizens to do their bit for the war effort, Britain was positively awash in propaganda notices depicting Hitler overhearing the conversation between two mothers on a bus as a continued reminder to always wear gas masks, since "Hitler will send no warning."

Most cities from the north to the midlands to the southern ports confronting occupied Europe had the gap-toothed look that indifferent dental care had inflicted on the denizens who routinely wore dentures and bridges in their twenties. Impressive homes sprawled next to vacant lots that had once held the abodes of neighbors but were now either submerged in weeds or given over to a victory garden to supplement a diet that made American rationing look like a banquet. Food was always on the minds of the British hosts of this new American Expeditionary Force, although some people were too polite to the Yanks to admit it. This was not the near starvation of besieged Vicksburg in 1863 or of Hitler's concentration camps, but it was the dull sensation that, while there was enough food available to prevent growing hunger, most of the enjoyment of meals had disappeared with the onset of war. First of all, rationing seemed endless in duration; in 1944, the system was four years old, and, before it ended, Elvis Presley would be famous and children born after the war was over would be entering their second or third year of school. Orange juice and milk were largely reserved for children; there was enough butter for perhaps one slice of bread or one baked potato a week; bread was always semistale with artificial additives such as sawdust that added bulk but little nourishment.

On the other hand, British citizens seldom asked the American "invaders" for much of anything if a visitor did not count the sexual favors that occupying military forces experienced throughout history. Alcohol seemed more plentiful than food, and music, singing, and dancing seemed more plentiful than drinks everywhere from Piccadilly Circus to a thatched roof of the pub, or to the moors, even if most of these cultural attractions never made it back in soldiers' letters or reporters' articles. Most of all, in the months leading up to Operation Overlord, the last invasion of Britain was an intercourse between equals. The British may have needed the Americans to chase Hitler across Europe and corner him in his lair, but the Battle of Britain, when that island nation's people were virtually alone, had demonstrated that Britain could at least probably throw the enemy back into the sea if Sea Lion, Hitler's plan for invading Britain, ever morphed from paper plan to actual battle. In some respects, the Yanks landing in Britain in 1944 were like the doughboys disembarking in France in 1917 and 1918. They were coming to the aid of a people fighting to maintain their freedom from an oppressor but fighting well enough that they did not have to beg for outside help.

As thousands of American military personnel streamed into "Fortress Britannica," they began to adopt multiple personas, adapting to their new environment. Most of the time, they were warriors in training, not to occupy Britain but actually in preparation to leave that island for the war that would be won or lost on the far side of the English Channel. The GIs who would form the core of the American assault on Normandy trained hard under increasingly realistic conditions that some of them would not survive; they tramped across endless miles of countryside in mock engagements that were expected to replicate the approaching battle. On the other hand, the aircrews of American combat bombers and fighters were spending more time fighting than training; their war was already fully underway, and many of their families would be exchanging the blue service stars hanging in their front windows for the gold stars representing supreme sacrifice well before such an exchange would be required of most of the families of the ground forces.

The second part of the American experience in Britain occurred most often at night when servicemen and some servicewomen gathered in small groups to attempt to decode their experiences in this strange new environment, share opinions of Britain with others, and write letters home to friends and family, attempting to explain their strange world to Americans who were sitting in parlors or front porches in the world that the Yanks had left behind. Like explorers to distant lands in earlier times, they deciphered, decoded, exaggerated, and bragged about their role in this new world setting in what they had learned as children was defined to Americans as the "Old World." Britain was often described as a place where it "rained all the time" but somehow seldom flooded; it was hugely overcrowded by American standards but contained desolate moors and hills scarier than anything in their own home states; the food was bland and the beer was warm, but servicemen would sneak out of their barracks at night to imbibe in both if they were offered at a pub.

The third American experience in 1944 Britain—beyond training in Britain and discussing, evaluating, and writing of Britain—was to participate in British life in a unique role reversal where the voyagers to the new world now had an opportunity to return to the old world and interact with its denizens. This was the part of the "last invasion of Britain" that would be most remembered on both sides of the Atlantic long after the war had ended.

Perhaps the most effective guide for Americans making the transition from the barracks and training fields of their bases to the much larger world of Britain beyond the limits of a GI camp was a person born in Britain but one of the most popular icons of Hollywood. As the transport ships filled the harbors of Britain, American military leaders asked Hollywood to produce a big-budget film that would aid American service personnel in their transition to a new environment. The film, *Welcome to Britain*, featured first-tier film comedian Bob Hope as the star of a slick, professional, entertaining feature codeveloped by British and American screenwriters and featuring a supporting cast ranging from emerging star Burgess Meredith, as a "typical GI," to General Jacob Devers providing the "big picture" of why the Americans were needed in Britain.

The film was a hugely entertaining comedy of manners that encouraged American service personnel to laugh collectively at themselves as the cinematic GIs managed to bumble into an endless stream of social mistakes. Since most of the American "invaders" found much of their social energy in an environment of maximizing supplies of alcohol and female companionship, much of the film action occurred in a classic British pub with not very subtle, frequent reminders that the pub was essentially a "combination of American taverns and social clubs" and that "like any club, there are certain rules."

The most common "rules" that Americans seemed to break were dramatized in a comic backdrop that included touching barmaids; displaying English currency as "play money," asking, "Is this stuff any good?"; complaining about warm beer; making sarcastic remarks about dart games and players; and failing to understand that the patter of common American "friendly insult" humor genuinely hurt British people who had no experience with this type of interaction.

Bob Hope's humorous trademark patter in *Welcome to Britain* hinted at but did not specifically discuss the social demographics that marked the American "invasion" of Britain. In this enormous influx, young, sometimes socially immature, servicemen were pouring into a nation in which the majority of its own young men were in some other part of the world, fighting the common enemy. In essence, the Yanks were pouring into Britain and filling a missing piece of the native population: its young or relatively young male subsets. Just as in a missing piece of a mostly complete jigsaw puzzle, the arriving Americans were a near-fit to the piece that was missing in 1944 Britain. The nation had a large populace of young children, adolescent and young adult women, and middle-aged and older subsets of both genders, but the unique, and sometimes exasperating and dangerous, spark created by energetic, daring, and sometimes socially dangerous young men was now being filled by homesick residents of a foreign but not quite alien society, and authority figures from both nations were not exactly sure how to cope with the side effects of this amalgamation.

Much of the debate by generally middle-aged and older British citizens about the "invasion" of the Yanks usually missed one of the most obvious yet not particularly clearly discussed elements of frustration between natives and foreigners. That was the simple fact that by 1944, there was a substantial shortage of eligible British young men in the country, and the American servicemen offered an exciting alternative to young British girls and women who had been spending most of their time in either each other's company or with older, and far less adventurous, adults. Despite the official hand-wringing about the Yanks being overpaid, oversexed, and over here, a major portion of young adult and adolescent girls and children of both genders believed that the American "invasion" was the most exciting thing that ever happened to them. A brief glance at the assets the Yanks brought across the Atlantic with them quickly explained why this was the case.

First, British teens and children of the 1944 era had spent much of the 1930s and early 1940s growing up on American films that stressed character attributes such as generosity, self-confidence, flamboyance, and exaggeration that were far more appealing to young people than the relatively quiet, reserved, stoic personas often displayed in the British film industry. Being young in America just seemed to be much more fun than growing up in a highly stratified society with little room to climb substantially higher than their parents' often mundane existence. American cinema's emphasis on crime, violence, rapid solution of problems and unexpected crises, and falls in status seemed much more of a real adventure than the British concept of just "getting by."

Second, in a clearly unfair but unavoidable context, the average American enlisted man in England made triple or quadruple his British counterpart's income, wore a uniform that was at least as stylish as, if not more so than, that of a British officer. He also tended to be bigger, stronger, and more photogenic than his age-equivalent British counterparts. However, the aspect of the "overpaid, oversexed, and over here" mantra of a strange alliance of British intellectuals and hungry young men was that so many young British men were now stationed overseas that there was plenty of opportunity for social connections with friends for both the GIs *and* the residue of physically unfit, vocationally exempt, and home service-stationed young men combined. The ongoing lament about the great number of young British girls being "stolen" by the Yanks was hugely exaggerated; what *was* accurate was the dissatisfaction of at least some British lads who lost out to a Yank in a competition for their first choice of female companionship and then had to settle for what they considered less desirable matches in consolation.

Finally, American GIs were noticeably successful in their pursuit of new relationships because there was a major difference in educational theories between British and American educators. Britain in 1944 featured an educational system where virtually all schooling beyond the age of twelve was single sex, and even classrooms at lower grade levels were strictly separated by gender. On the other hand, the vast majority of American servicemen had attended a public school system that was coeducational from kindergarten through college. In that environment, boys and girls developed an easy familiarity unknown in Britain and most other countries. American boys and girls shifted in and out of relationships, had multiple friends of the opposite sex, and exhibited a social openness that British officials, educators, and parents often found shocking. What should have been a happy hunting ground for British males too young, too unhealthy, or too lucky to have been sent overseas was now not quite so attractive, when hundreds of thousands of mildly exotic and socially assured young men from the other side of the Atlantic suddenly descended into the British relationship game. As parents tactfully encouraged their young daughters not to get too involved with the GIs, huge numbers of them almost literally voted with their feet as they frequented dance clubs sponsored by the various American services and reveled in dance contests; in live music from American music superstars, such as Major Glenn Miller; and in the adulation of lonely boys and young men who generally were far better behaved than the British press described them.

The other major demographic group in 1944 Britain that rivaled the adolescent and young adult girls for their enthusiasm at the arrival of the Yanks were the children of this war-threatened nation. Unlike British adult attitudes toward the proper behavior of children, which tended to be stricter and more demanding than those of their American counterparts, the onset of the Blitz and a possible invasion had tended to mellow older Britons a bit in their expectations for the next generation of their society. In a society seemingly short of almost every commodity, children were pushed to the front of the national queue for access to milk, orange juice, meat, fish, fruits, and even sweets. In both a figurative and a literal sense, adult Britons sacrificed the sugar they adored in their tea so that a youngster could have a weekly ration of a Lion Bar or Mars Bar candy.

However, when the Americans arrived with their endless cornucopia of consumer goods, optimism, and sense of humor, sometimes parents and grandparents had to take a backseat in their role of candy provider to children, as the GIs seemed to have arrived with both the means and the will to brighten the dull experience of wartime Britain for its youngest generation. A friendly alliance emerged between late-adolescent and young-adult American service personnel and the youngest Britons who eagerly followed formations of GIs moving along roadways with exuberant requests of "Got any gum, chum?" This was in essence verbal shorthand for an offer to run errands or put in a good word with their older sister in return for the American treasure trove of Hershey Bars, Life-Savers, Baby Ruth bars, Coca Cola, and other treats that seemed to be bulging from the Aladdin's treasure trove known as the U.S. military commissary.

A fascinating symbiosis began to develop in wartime Britain as both younger children and adolescent girls convinced their parents to invite homesick American servicemen to their homes for tea or dinner. In many respects, parents were making a substantial sacrifice, for anything approaching a tempting meal often devoured a huge supply of family food-ration coupons, a reality that the GIs may or may not have fully appreciated. Yet, in return for a small piece of a normal family occasion, many servicemen reciprocated by arriving at the host's door with sacks of candy, cigarettes, fresh fruits, and meat that the British civilians saw only sparingly in wartime society. In this optimal relationship, it was often either children or slightly older girls who emerged as the intermediaries between slightly suspicious British adults and somewhat socially unaware American visitors. If all went well, "adopted" servicemen could find a second home with a British family where shared festivities such as Christmas, Easter, and New Year's Day; British celebrations such as Guy Fawkes Day; and the distinctively American experience of Independence Day could be spent in a diverse selection of venues from private homes to American bases to somewhere in between.

Many British towns used public buildings to welcome a mixture of residents and American service personnel to jointly celebrate Christmas. A heavily sandbagged entrance might become the gateway to huge rooms adorned with both British and American flags and huge stockpiles of army-donated candy, cakes, pies, and cookies featuring a transatlantic "jolly old elf," who was part Santa Claus and part Father Christmas, and distribution of what one British child insisted was "'an Aladdin's Cave' of toys delivered from a Jeep instead of a sleigh."

As much of 1944 slowly gave way to early spring, and the American military presence in Britain climbed toward the two million mark, both the "invaders" and the "invaded" shared a moment of tacit acceptance of each other as the long-awaited invasion of Europe loomed even larger. Organizations such as the American Red Cross and *Stars and Stripes* magazine collected huge donations to support British children who had been orphaned or suffered the loss of a father through death or capture. Military units routinely "adopted" specific children for a donation of five hundred or a thousand dollars a year, while also individually sending extra clothes, toys, and invitations for parties at the unit's bases.

New American magazines routinely published articles, photographs, and even paintings depicting the now relatively congenial cultural accommodations being made by both sides. One correspondent focused on a single Sunday afternoon in Hyde Park, basking in what passed for nearly hot weather in London. Photos depicted a huge crowd of British civilians and American servicemen seated and standing around a cricket pitch that had been converted to a baseball field for the day. As the Americans laughingly screamed, "Kill the Umpire!" with gusto, fascinated Londoners attempted to understand the reason for the outrage. Another photo essay focused on the popular Serpentine section of the park, where "on 364 acres boats are rowed by boys from Connecticut and Kansas for girls from Surrey and Yorkshire. At any grand moment in the park there were probably more boys in the park from the states than the Shires. American boys and British girls sit in rented chairs on green lawns under elms before the boys turn to the stern tasks of war."

While some fortunate American servicemen were able to enjoy baseball or boating in a sun-splashed park, as the countdown toward invasion day wound down toward zero, much of the interaction with nature would be on windswept fields where GIs prepared for their destiny on the far side of the English Channel. More and more American soldiers spent long hours tramping the lonely, stark English Downs, eating a cold, doughy mixture called a meat pie, and collapsing into a bunk in a cramped barracks room where four men shared fourteen square feet of living space filled with an austere array of four bunks, two straight chairs, and a small fireplace that periodically provided warmth; four walls were often covered with maps, hometown newspaper clippings, greeting cards from wives, girlfriends, and other family members. In this cramped antechamber to the battlefield, a private first class would exert rank over buck privates, and corporals would edge out PFCs for the most shelf space or the best bunk location.

These olive drab versions of collegiate dormitories were tiny American islands in the bleak landscape of wartime Britain, and here the "invaders" talked incessantly about girls, cars, sports, movies, and music, often comparing British and American versions of each. In a youth culture now teetering on the brink of the rock and roll era, the men who would hold the future of America in their hands prepared for combat while still finding time for jam sessions with guitars and banjos, comparing the performance and looks of British and American cars, and writing to old girlfriends at home or new girlfriends in London.

One magazine correspondent equated these young warriors in a semi-strange land to "a boxer in a corner just before the bell rings; getting last minute instructions about how to hit the guy in the other corner."

Soldiers insisted that their training in the British countryside was so real that "it is probably just like fighting," as company commanders outlined a daily problem or mission. These men waiting to enter combat on the other side of the Channel were taught to use TNT to become familiar with the noise and chaos of explosives; how to get natural protection from underbrush or woods; and how to locate a handy escape route if the battle turned sour.

Yet, in the midst of their preview of death and killing, many of these young Americans had experienced just enough classical history to understand that in many cases, they were marching on Roman roads, bivouacked near Roman campsites, and digging foxholes on Roman training grounds. They also had received enough classroom background on British literature that they wrote letters home filled with allusions to *David Copperfield* and *Ivanhoe* and admitted that the castles and cathedrals had no real equivalent in their American world.

Also, unlike many previous invaders of Britain, and contrary to some British pundits' assumptions, many American soldiers admitted to correspondents from their own country that they were mostly interested in meeting British girls to take to dances or movies and were worried about the complications of falling in love so close to possibly imminent death. Behind the facade of self-confidence and exuberance, many GIs proved at heart to be shy and cautious in social relationships and seemed to take up half of their free time getting up the nerve to ask girls to dance and the other half keeping other soldiers away from the girls. Far from being ferocious invaders, these outsiders frequently married British girls to ensure that someone would be thinking of them when they entered combat, while others insisted that they would give up several months' pay just to see their American girlfriends for thirty minutes. However, while those young servicemen were training for combat in an environment only moderately different from the world in which they grew up, other Americans much like them were fighting on the other side of the world in a battle zone so exotic that those warriors might very well have been willing to give up several months' pay just for thirty minutes in Britain.

CHAPTER VI

Storming a Stolen Empire

In January of 1944, as men of the Fifth Army were attempting to breach the Gustav line, and GIs clambered down the gangplanks in the mist-covered parts of Britain, a young-looking naval officer with distinctive blond/gray hair and a weathered face stood at the edge of a municipal park in downtown Honolulu, Hawaii, and patiently watched as exuberant servicemen rallied to his side. The solitary figure was Admiral Chester Nimitz, the senior naval commander of the Pacific Ocean theater, and he knew instinctively that he would not be alone for very long.

Nimitz had recently issued an invitation to a "Texas barbeque" in this park to any soldier, airman, sailor, or Marine who hailed from Texas or at least boasted some tie to the Lone Star State, a relationship that did not promise to be scrutinized very closely. As military police and shore patrol units stood in groups along the wide boulevards of Honolulu, not particularly certain what to expect, thousands of service personnel thronged the streets and entered the gate of the park, forming an ever-widening circle around the admiral who stood at ease as his entourage began to swell the enormous proportions of the event. Then, naval personnel began to uncover huge cases of bottled beer and ignited roaring barbeque fires for steak and burgers. An eclectic mob of hardened combat veterans, neophyte recruits who had never served in battle, and desk-bound personnel who would never see a shot fired in anger interacted freely on the spacious park lawns, a sea of white, denim, khaki, and green, united only by their decorative leis and their utter delight with their slightly smiling host.

Unlike many taproom venues in any town that catered to military personnel, few tempers exploded, and, for one day, interservice rivalries gave way to eating, drinking, and bragging, and the park pathways seemed to sink under beer bottles that soon passed the one hundred twenty thousand mark. Then, as something between forty thousand and fifty thousand revelers polished off anything edible or potable, Nimitz strode to the center of the park, shook hands with his Army counterpart, Lieutenant General Robert Richardson, and the men began to walk through the park at a brisk pace. As these twin Pied Pipers marched through the grounds, a huge buzz began to emerge in the crowd, and the whole mob formed an interservice entourage and followed their leaders, "whooping it up like a pack of Comanches." Chester Nimitz, the "founder of the feast" on this balmy, tropical winter day, was fully at ease, obviously enjoying himself hugely, laughing, waving, and signing autographs as the revelers marched behind him at an ever-increasing pace that "nearly winded the merry melee."

If the Japanese attack on Pearl Harbor had forced the military and civilian denizens of Hawaii into an immediate fear of the vulnerability of their islands to Nipponese invasion, the sheer mass of imposing-looking, confident American military personnel at the soon-to-be legendary Texas picnic two years later demonstrated that now it was the turn of Japanese civilians to worry about their safety as a huge military tidal wave was forming in Hawaii and would begin sweeping toward the empire as soon as American commanders finalized their campaign plans. Pearl Harbor and its environs were no longer a fortress under semisiege but a powerful bastion that was the springboard for a transpacific offensive designed to stop only at the shores of Tokyo Bay.

When Undersecretary of the Navy James Forrestal arrived in Pearl Harbor from an inspection tour shortly after the Texas barbeque, he was astounded by the size of the armada that now seemingly squeezed into every nook and cranny of the Honolulu coast. The American Fifth Fleet, which did not include either Hawaii defense flotillas or ships currently on sea duty, could deploy three hundred seventy-five ships and seven hundred aircraft with eighty-six thousand soldiers and Marines available for the next planned offensive. This powerful assemblage of men, ships, and planes would have welcomed a second Japanese attack on Hawaii as an opportunity to annihilate the enemy without the bother of another ocean voyage.

The person most responsible for the deployment of this Olympian display of air, sea, and military power was the same Texan who had recently sauntered through the friendly gauntlet at the recent picnic and who had grown up in a community where the only nearby body of water dried up during the summer. Chester Nimitz was now emerging as one of the most famous admirals in the history of naval warfare.

A national news magazine described the commander of the most powerful aggregation of naval power in history as a "tall, lean man, rigidly straight with a shock of bleached hair, like a whitecap over his bright sea blue eyes. He looks like a perfect picture of an admiral whose mild demeanor does not lessen his drive or force and whose geniality might be a part of his stern self-discipline." This genial yet driven man was a fifty-nine-year-old mariner who was preparing the most massive maritime offensive in history from an office filled with canvas chairs and a desk "almost as untidy as President Roosevelt's as it is piled high with greeting cards, souvenir ashtrays, souvenir photos of other leaders, and half-empty coffee containers."

In a war replete with prickly, self-centered temperamental leaders, Chester Nimitz routinely piped radio music from his office intercom to subordinate officers; enlisted anyone from the lowest seamen to join him in horseshoe matches and long walks; and regularly organized outdoor cookouts for all ranks as he wandered through the festivities sharing pleasantries. In a war of distant and haughty officers, this was a commander who on at least one occasion accommodated a seaman joining his walking activities who admitted to the admiral that he had bet a bunk mate that he could have his picture taken with the admiral. Nimitz promptly summoned a photographer and laughingly asked the semishocked sailor what he intended to do with his winnings.

Two years earlier, the Hawaiian naval base to which Chester Nimitz arrived after Pearl Harbor was far more focused on a possible Japanese invasion than picnics, barbeques, and cheeky sailors' wagers. Days after the Day of Infamy, President Roosevelt issued a sharp command to a stunned Chester Nimitz: "Get the hell out to Pearl Harbor and don't come back till you've won." The new commander of the Pacific Fleet had to gently nullify his wife's exultation at the new command by reminding her that most of his fleet was now sitting at the bottom of the harbor.

Nimitz's ability to rationalize and contain unpleasant news or events was largely based on an almost movie-like childhood in the very unnautical community of Fredericksburg, Texas. When the future admiral's father died before the birth of his son, his mother moved in with her father-in-law's family, which owned a local hotel designed to look like a ship plowing through the rolling hills of Central Texas. Growing up in a tourist attraction that lodged an impressive array of Confederate officers, including several generals, Nimitz dreamed of a West Point appointment and only somewhat reluctantly accepted an alternate route to commission by attending the United States Naval Academy. Nimitz survived a routinely career-ending gaffe of running his first ship aground but went on to emerge as an expert on the new branch of submarine service and demonstrate his extraordinary personnel skills by openly sympathizing with his predecessor at Pearl Harbor, Admiral Husband Kimmel. He emphasized that all of the former commander's staff would still be welcome under the new command structure.

At least partially because of Army-Navy wrangling over Pacific War turf, the Pacific War of 1944 was being conducted along two roughly parallel routes to the heart of the Japanese Empire, which, it was assumed, must be pierced before there was any thought of bombing, storming, or invading Japan into surrender. By January of 1944, Chester Nimitz served as a co-equal theater commander with General Douglas MacArthur, with the admiral's bailiwick designation as Pacific Ocean Command, while his Army counterpart was charged with directing the war in the Southwest Pacific theater. Luckily for the American war effort, the rather laid back Nimitz had established good working relations with the dramatic, driven

MacArthur, and it was hoped in Washington that the dual drive "whip-saw" approach to the Pacific War would constantly keep the Imperial high command off guard, unsure which was the "genuine" thrust toward their inner sanctum.

Unfortunately, the combined Army-Marine thrust against the Tarawa atoll a few weeks earlier had threatened to upset the equilibrium of the American offensive plans, as the severe Marine losses in the capture of Betio Island had launched Douglas MacArthur on a public relations cam-paign centered on the high cost of losses of American men in the process of capturing a tiny island, while the general's parallel campaign across the northern coast of New Guinea was gobbling up huge swaths of Japanese-occupied territory in a series of bold hops along the coast that left large enemy garrisons bypassed and useless.

Now it was time for the next stage of the Pacific Ocean theater offensive, and Nimitz and his naval, air, and ground commanders were attempting to locate a weak spot in the outer bulwarks of the Nipponese empire. American strategists largely agreed that a thrust deep into enemy terri-tory had little chance of success unless the two major fortresses of the outer Empire were either captured or neutralized. American newspapers, magazines, and movie newsreels were now constantly focusing on the twin citadels of Nipponese air and naval power—Truk and Rabaul. These two otherwise placid tropical islands were like porcupines, bristling with ships and planes that would challenge any American intrusion beyond their current positions in the Solomons-Gilberts axis. While none of the new Japanese command team in the area was as hated, feared, or publicized as the relatively recently killed author of the Pearl Harbor attack, the heirs to Admiral Yamamoto still seemed to hold considerable pieces in this mari-time chess match.

Meetings between Nimitz; his superior, Admiral Ernest King; and his Army, Army Air Force, and Marine personnel produced a cunning new plan to essentially neutralize Truk and Rabaul, while avoiding a ground assault on either Imperial bastion. The first major Pacific Ocean theater campaign of 1944 would be codenamed Operation Flintlock, and it envi-sioned an amphibious invasion in which it would leapfrog well beyond

Truk and Rabaul at the Marshall Islands, on Kwajalein six hundred miles north of Tarawa, and well beyond the Truk-Rabaul axis, where the enemy expected the next American attack.

This was a bold attempt to catch the enemy off guard while avoiding the mistakes of "bloody Tarawa." Unlike other armed forces at other times and other places, Chester Nimitz had no intention of sweeping under the rug the mistakes made in the attack on Betio Island, and his amphibious assault commander, Admiral Richmond Kelly ("Terrible") Turner, had completed an extensive critique of Operation Galvanic titled "Lessons Learned at Tarawa," which would be the new handbook for this next venture. Turner insisted on a long list of changes for the new operation: more air reconnaissance, better use of submarines for scouting duties, more operational destroyers, and at least triple the bombardment power inflicted on Betio, with special emphasis on more use of landing craft.

The siege of the Marshalls began when the growing and robust fleet commanded by Raymond Spruance sortied from Pearl Harbor and set sail for a target that was technically inside the massive defense perimeter that Imperial Japan had constructed to deter an enemy assault on the homeland.

Admiral Raymond Spruance was a fifty-eight-year-old Baltimore native who had replaced the ill Admiral William Halsey just in time to make the covers of virtually every newsmagazine or newspaper in America after the resounding victory at the Battle of Midway. Spruance's demeanor and personality were almost polar opposites of those of his mentor and friend "Bull" Halsey. The Fifth Fleet commander was polite, quiet, thoughtful, and controlled, and in a nonflamboyant way solicitous of his officers and men. Like Nimitz, one of Spruance's favorite menus of exercise were brisk walks, and he regularly paced dozens of times around the deck of his flag-ship as he often invited one or two junior officers to join him for far-flung conversations.

Spruance would be rated highly by army and Marine assault troops in Operation Flintlock, as, unlike the early debacle at Guadalcanal, when the fleet commander pulled his ships far from the island in fear of enemy air attacks, the Fifth Fleet commander envisioned his main charge as protection and support of the ground forces, even if it meant passing on an attempt to gain more glory by destroying the enemy fleet further out to sea.

Now, in February of 1944, the courtly, quiet Spruance was closing on an atoll that was defended by twelve thousand Imperial troops, roughly twice the size of the garrison at Tarawa and sprinkled with a covey of airfields that were now receiving significant aerial assets from Rabaul and Truk. On the other hand, the Army-Marine invasion force for Flintlock had been bulked up to over fifty thousand men, and the onboard fire-power of the invasion fleet was also significantly enhanced as the ghosts of Tarawa pervaded the cramped quarters of the joint assault force.

Kwajalein Atoll was discovered by Spanish adventurers, originally named for the daughter of a British captain, renamed by later arriving Germans, and inhabited by natives for whom modernity was an infringe-ment on their idyllic lifestyle. While Marines and soldiers on vessels clos-ing on Guadalcanal believed they were landing on a tropical paradise only to discover that they had entered a tropical hell of which the Japanese defenders were only one of their deadly enemies, Kwajalein really was a genuine tropical haven, one of the largest of a string of ninety-seven islands that, combined, equaled only six square miles of land dominated by an eight-hundred-square-mile lagoon looming offshore.

After the American capture of Tarawa, much of the Japanese military and naval command continued to focus on the primary naval and air bases of Rabaul and Truk as the next logical enemy target, and Tarawa was assigned secondary importance to the Marshall Islands. Thus, when the Fifth Fleet suddenly loomed over the horizon of Kwajalein, Imperial offic-ers expended more energy on reminding their men of the glorious stand on Betio Island and encouraging them with the reality that the garrison on the Marshalls was larger and better equipped than the Gilbert defenses. However, the Imperial high command holding this latest battleground still faced two significant challenges. First, while they fielded nearly an entire division across a relatively small landmass of six square miles, the Marshall Islands were scattered over an enormous area that would allow the enemy to choose from a wide array of landing sites, none of which would feature a particularly large number of defenders. Second, they were facing American naval and ground force commanders who had been studying the shortcomings of the Tarawa operation from almost *every* perspective, and these men were determined to avoid a second Central Pacific bloodbath.

The American officer most responsible for landing Marines and soldiers ashore within acceptable casualty limits was a member of a relatively small circle of high-ranking officers who held important command positions in both the European and Pacific theaters. Admiral Richard Connolly had developed one of the most ambitious command resumes in the American Navy of 1943, when he followed outstanding service as a task force commander in the invasion of Sicily with a new senior posting with V Amphibious Corps in the wake of the Gilberts campaign. The fifty-two-year-old admiral, soon to acquire the nickname of "Close-In Connolly" for his willingness to deploy support ships far closer to the invasion beaches than his counterparts were willing to, quickly set up an office at the Marine base at Camp Pendleton, California, and worked intensely with the 4th Marine Division leader, Major General Harry Schmidt, in incorporating the lessons of the Gilberts campaign in ship-to-shore maneuvers at San Clemente Island. Connolly was one "old salt" who did not mind risking his naval vessels if their fire support could save ground troops' lives in their dangerous transition from sea to invasion beach.

If "Close-in" Connolly had a personality and nickname made for fascinating press release, the "Flintlock" ground commander would prove to be an even greater correspondent's dream news personality. An early 1944 cover of *Time* magazine depicts a scowling white-haired Marine general staring in the foreground of a tropical bay full of American ships and personnel with an accompanying caption, "Old Man of the Atolls." "Howling Mad" Smith was described as an "explosive, spectacled, mustached general, with a visage that spelled trouble for both the Japanese and any Americans who got in his way."

Holland McTyeire Smith was a member of a prosperous Alabama family who as a young man was fixated on his goal of obtaining a commission in the United States Army. After graduating from the University of

Alabama Law School, Smith quickly found jurisprudence too boring for his action-oriented temperament, and he soon queried a local congressman and family friend about earning a commission in the army. The politician admitted that he had better connections with the Marine Corps than with the Army, and the young lawyer quickly coupled his significant career change with marriage to a young woman from suburban Philadelphia, despite his family's notorious "anti-Yankee demeanor."

Now, "Howling Mad" Smith was commanding a combined invasion force of soldiers and Marines in the first significant island invasion since Tarawa, a fact of which virtually everyone in the entire task force was acutely aware. Yet, as long as the Nipponese high command was not yet committed to a decisive showdown with the American Pacific Fleet, the Nipponese defenders instinctively knew that their personal gift to the emperor was simply to fight as long and hard as possible and sell their lives dearly before going to their honored place in the afterlife.

The basic American assault plan for Flintlock was to land Major General Charles Corlett's 7th Infantry Division as a southern attack force on the island of Kwajalein, the atoll's main port, while the 4th Marine Division would constitute the northern assault force tasked with securing the atoll's airfield facilities at the twin islands of Roi and Namur.

The last two days of January and the early morning of February 1 became a numbing marathon of fear for the Imperial defenders as they were subjected to a nonstop bombardment by American destroyers, cruisers, and battleships that alternated with carrier air attacks to turn much of the landing zone into a lunar landscape. Then, as dawn made its usual stunningly sudden appearance that was common in the region, the Amtracs of the 23rd Marine Regiment puttered toward shore, and a Japanese garrison that, desperate because it was already being badly mauled, eagerly awaited the opportunity to actively shoot back at its tormentors.

The "ground pounders" of the invasion force were not alone, as sixteen Sherman tanks accompanied them onto the coral sand, and, as one observer noted with satisfaction, they "roamed the fields like predatory dinosaurs." Of the two conjoined islands, Roi offered the more open ground, as it was the site of a major airfield flanked by open fields and an interlocking series of drainage ditches designed to prevent the landing areas from getting waterlogged. Whether by design or in desperation, as the Imperial troops grudgingly ceded the beaches to the leathernecks, the Japanese scrambled into the ditches and resorted to a form of trench warfare.

Meanwhile, on the adjoining beach that fronted the much more built-up island of Namur, the 24th Marine Regiment quickly found itself in a tropical version of urban warfare. Nipponese defenders sprinted from street to street and door to door in a battle zone dominated by warehouses, administrative buildings, barracks, and recreational facilities that produced an extended shoot-out much closer to battles in Italian or French towns in the "other theater" than the iconic jungle warfare of Pacific battles such as Guadalcanal. However, as the Marines engaged in a deadly game of blind man's bluff as they barged through front doors and clambered up stairs often featuring enemy soldiers shooting from the top, the most developed areas of the island gradually shifted into American-held territory.

Yet the Japanese had enjoyed several ways in which to fine-tune their defensive array on an island that they assumed might eventually be attacked, and no sooner did the leathernecks clear through a maze that had elements of both a frontier town and bootlegger gangster hideaway stills than they slammed against a new danger centered on an interlocking system of expertly engineered pillboxes and blockhouses not unlike the structures that had helped decimate the Marines in Betio. For example, when a team of combat engineers zeroed in on one of the largest block-houses on the island, threw satchel charges through the openings, and then signaled the supporting riflemen to rush the building, an enormous cache of Japanese ammunition suddenly ignited with an explosion that could be seen for miles.

The more fortunate Marines stared in shock and horror as they saw comrades hit with chunks of concrete, unexploded torpedoes, and pieces of cannons that had been stockpiled inside. A hundred or more leath-ernecks dropped like puppets with their strings cut. This tactic had the same devastating impact as when, eight decades earlier, General George Pickett's Confederate assault force at Cemetery Ridge came within range of the Union artillery. However, while Pickett's men were forced to retreat,

American tanks quickly clanked forward, opened fire with every gun, and surged ahead of the stunned friendly infantry in a phalanx of steel that relentlessly pushed forward.

During the fast-falling tropical night and the early morning that followed, Marine infantry, half-tracks, and tanks formed a tightening noose around a heavily wooded region near the end of the island that now formed the final rampart for the Imperial defenders. All during the night, groups of Nipponese troops would burst from the tree line, rush toward the American positions, and engage in a vicious shootout that always left more Japanese soldiers on the ground than their intended victims.

Then, just after daybreak, a mixed infantry, tank, and half-track column commanded by Lieutenant Colonel Aquilla Dyess moved along the beachfront near the water's edge and fought a running duel with the defenders of the pillboxes. As the surviving defenders retreated back to their final defense positions, Dyess jumped from his vehicle, clambered atop an enemy antitank ditch, and furiously directed a coordinated final rush as a Japanese fusillade made a statement in their tradition of no surrender. Dyess slumped to the ground with multiple wounds that quickly proved fatal.

Dyess was one of the last of nearly two hundred Marines to die in the battle of Roi-Namur, with an additional five hundred men wounded out of a total invasion force of nearly twenty thousand men. However, the number of fatalities was only one-fifth the toll at Tarawa, and, unlike in that bloodbath, at no point had the invaders been checked on the Roi-Namur battlefield. Roughly thirty-five hundred Imperial troops had died in this action, along with perhaps one hundred others, mainly conscripted Korean laborers, now sitting in POW cages. However, while Roi and Namur were now secured, the Marines' friendly rivals, the GIs of 7th Division, were still in mortal combat about sixty miles away on the southern end of the atoll in a battle for Kwajalein Island.

Only a few months earlier, the doughboys of the 7th Division had been caught in a deadly duel with the Japanese enemy in a world far removed from the tropical sands of the central Pacific. Instead of encountering heat, exhaustion, and dehydration, the fighting men had encountered frostbite

and numbing cold as they slogged through snow drifts in the only part of
the future fifty-state nation that was actually occupied by an enemy force
during World War II. This was the battle of Attu Island, a bleak outcropping
of a chain that extended outward from the Alaskan mainland and along
neighboring Kiska. Attu was now, at least temporarily, an occupied part of
the Japanese Empire. Embarking on a battle scheduled to last three days or
less, the American invasion force spent three weeks slogging through late-
May snowdrifts and losing more than three thousand casualties, including
more than five hundred dead, to return the island to United States control.

Now, with their snow boots and parkas stowed away far to the north,
the men commanded by Major General Charles Corlett were engaged in
a brutal shootout in a far different environment. Corlett would eventually belong to one of the more exclusive fraternities of senior American
military commanders; he would trade the palm trees of the Pacific theater
for the evergreens of Northwest Europe slightly later in the year. For the
moment, the former Colorado rancher nicknamed "Cowboy Pete" was
attempting to emulate the Marines in a sweep across Kwajalein Island.

Corlett faced a more difficult scenario than General Henry Schmidt,
his Marine counterpart sixty miles to the north. Kwajalein Island was
an almost perfect banana-shaped island that was so dominated by coral
reefs that only a narrow landing beach on the west end was of any use.
In an attempt to even the odds in the invasion, Corlett deployed one
of his three regiments in an attack on tiny Carlson Island, three miles
from Kwajalein, and then peppered the main island with five battalions of
powerful 155mm cannons that could pound Japanese emplacements on
the main island.

Kwajalein featured a somewhat larger garrison than Roi-Namur, with
five thousand Nipponese combat troops available, a significant force to
defend a "banana" only two miles long and five hundred yards wide. As
was now increasingly the case in American invasions, the combination of
tanks and heavily armed amphibian tractors tended to deflect much of the
enemy fire and then prove invaluable when the Imperial forces launched
their almost obligatory counterattacks that guaranteed that most of the
defenders would be dead before the culminating battle.

While Kwajalein had plenty of defenders and a significant array of pillboxes, the street fighting on Namur was largely replaced by the defenders using more primitive cover, ranging from stacks of cement bags to trees and bushes. Despite these tactical drawbacks, the Kwajalein garrison managed to outdo their Roi-Namur comrades by extending the struggle to four days and pushing the American Army casualty list to nearly one thousand, while the fatality list was actually 30 percent lower than the Marine losses.

In four days of intense fighting, a joint Army-Marine invasion force had essentially outflanked the invaluable Japanese naval bases of Rabaul and Truk. Imperial Navy strategists were forced to virtually strip the now almost-useless bases of their capital ships with the mighty battleships, carriers, and cruisers now redeployed to either the southern tip of the Philippines or the Inland Sea outside their homeland. Planes that were parked on their two citadels' multiple airfields were now almost impossible to utilize in combat as a curtain of American naval steel severed their vital fuel supply lines from north and west.

For a few months, as American forces prepared to dash for Rome and for land in France, the war in the Central Pacific would devolve temporarily into the sorties and scouting expeditions of an enormous siege. The Imperial fleet would sail majestically to battle again, but, as spring emerged in America and Europe, new battles were about to begin, and a nation's eyes would pivot toward two iconic names: Rome and Normandy.

CHAPTER VII

The Race for Rome

Shrouded by the predawn darkness of a chilly April morning, an attractive middle-aged woman slouched nearly out of sight in the backseat of an automobile parked near the landing strip of Bolling Field, the military airbase across the Potomac River from Washington. This wartime wife was in the car at the personal invitation of Army Chief of Staff George C. Marshall. She admitted that she had carefully chosen her most attractive outfit and was "as fluttering as a schoolgirl." The tall man she saw disembarking from the plane wore an army officer's uniform fitted out with a green scarf and combat boots and looked far more haggard, tense, and tired than the last time she saw him. As this tall soldier clambered in the backseat of the car with her, the cold blast of air that accompanied him was quickly warmed by a heated mutual embrace that would have done proud two teenagers' passionate embrace as they sat in the back row of a movie theater and largely ignored the film on the screen.

However, this couple did not have to cast a furtive glance for the appearance of an annoying usher or, in this case, military policeman, for the man was General Mark Clark, commander of Fifth United States Army, and his fellow passenger was his wife, Maurine. The car quickly whisked the couple to Fort Myers, Virginia, and the home of General Marshall so that the two generals could engage in one of the most important meetings of 1944.

While "Renie" Clark rested in a comfortable room and dreamed of the promised twenty-four-hour leave that the couple would share in their own apartment, the two generals consulted maps and tables of organizations supporting the plan for a massive double breakout from the stalemate at Anzio and along the Cassino-Rapido line. With the countdown to D-Day now well underway, the Allies desperately needed a successful offensive in Italy to prevent the Germans from moving massive reinforcements from their southern defense line up to the French coast, which would become the operational center of Overlord.

Thus, while the Clarks received their day and night together in their apartment, under Marshall's orders to not leave the unit or even answer the phone, the Fifth Army commander was also escorted to an exclusive Washington club and, after regular patrons were hustled out, gave an informal report on the war in Italy to a dozen national leaders. As the general and his companions quaffed beer and pitched empty oyster shells into a growing pyramid on the table, Clark held the attention of such luminaries as Vice President Henry Wallace and House Speaker Sam Rayburn, as he patiently explained the new operation that would hopefully trap much of the German armies in huge pincers and open the Eternal City up to Allied occupation.

The Roosevelt administration, now only months from a national election, was receiving unwanted international and national attention to a war front that at the moment seemed to present a no-win situation. A vast, multinational Allied army had been largely stuck on the south side of both the Rapido River and the nearby monastery town of Cassino for the entire winter, and the enormous sixth-century Benedictine structure was now the centerpiece of a roiling international outcry. Although senior German officials in Italy, most notably the lay Benedictine brother General Von Senger, had scrupulously forbidden their soldiers from occupying the monastery, Allied troops insisted that they saw gunfire coming from the monastery windows, and the complaints finally resulted in a massive American air attack that turned much of the building into a heap of rubble. Once the Allies had made the first move in this war of nerves, German commanders quickly deployed their men in the rubble, which turned into a virtually impregnable position. Now the Allies were facing the worst of two worlds. The air attacks had roused indignation in the world of neutral nations while, in turn, the monastery had morphed into an almost impenetrable salient in the heart of the Allied lines. Mark Clark, who was variously identified in the press as a High Anglican Church or a convert to Roman Catholicism, had vehemently opposed army bombing of the abbey as a continuation of a public relations disaster and an invitation for the Germans to turn the rubble into an invincible fortress. The general was absolutely right on both accounts, and now his army faced a miniature version of Stalingrad sitting in the middle of the enemy line. However, while the Fifth Army commander largely escaped the voice of the public outrage from American Catholics and members of some other denominations, by the time Clark returned from his brief interlude with Maurine, Marshall, and McCormick, the Italian campaign itself was undergoing a major shift in focus and direction.

When Dwight Eisenhower left the Mediterranean theater for command of Overlord, Clark was left subordinate to two senior British officers: General Sir Henry Maintland ("Jumbo") Wilson, supreme commander of the Mediterranean theater, and General Sir Harold Alexander, commander of Fifteenth Army Group, of which Clark's Fifth Army was one of the two constituent forces, along with the British Eighth Army. As the repeated assaults on the Gustav line fizzled in rapid succession, Alexander began to propose a radical redeployment of forces for an ambitious multinational offensive code-named Operation Diadem. Under these new plans, Fifth Army would be shifted westward toward the Tyrrhenian Sea, which, in effect, made the nightmarish terrain of Rapido-Cassino someone else's problem, a situation not unattractive to Clark and his lieutenants. As American forces were shunted northwest toward the sea, the Rapido-Cassino struggle became an "incomplete" grade for American commanders—neither a victory nor a defeat. Now, the real glory of battle lay in the capture of Rome, and that moment could occur only when and if the stalemate around Anzio could be broken. As Polish and French soldiers filed into American-built foxholes and trenches along the Rapido, a whole new battle near the sea awaited two still-separate American contingents.

By mid-April, the Anzio beachhead had settled into a defensive semi-circle about ten miles deep and ten miles wide, which, at the moment, Clark could neither abandon nor expand. The Germans had failed in every attempt to expunge the invaders and now contented themselves with shelling the beach with long-range 170mm guns that could cover every square foot of the Allied line. The Anglo-American garrison could fire back with equal ferocity, but they were firing at a much more dispersed enemy position. The visual embodiment of this stalemate looked startlingly similar to photos of the Western Front in 1917—a treeless, flat moonscape where one day seemed much the same as another, with the single minor consolation that Italy's cold, wet winter was gradually inching toward the sunny environment of countless travel posters.

This stalemate continued to produce a steady weekly casualty rate of about one thousand Allied soldiers, and, by April, the garrison had four thousand dead, eighteen thousand wounded, and seven thousand captured, a situation grotesquely enhanced by a staggering toll of thirty-seven thousand noncombat casualties from trench foot to venereal disease. However, if Operation Diadem actually worked, the Anzio garrison might be back in the thick of the war as they swarmed over the looming Alban Hills and swept downward into Rome.

Clark; Eighth Army commander Oliver Leese; and Army group commander General Alexander agreed on the opening of a massive offensive on May 11, with the Anzio garrison's role in the offensive code-named Operation Buffalo. The Anglo-American garrison would be reinforced from the sea, while a similarly upgraded contingent along the Gustav line would simultaneously push forward in a flying wedge that stretched from the Route 7 highway to the sea. Operation Diadem would soon rival the famous international effort to relieve the embassies in Peking during the Boxer Rebellion of 1900, as the attack force included not only the Anglo-American units that had crawled up the Italian peninsula but contingents from Italy, India, Canada, France, Poland, New Zealand, Morocco, Algeria, and South Africa. Since a number of first-rate British and American units had been transferred to the north for Overlord Operation, these multinational units were a welcome reinforcement, but they would complicate the nature of the fighting in Italy. Since the days of the battle for North Africa, the general absence of SS units had kept the fighting tolerably within the limits of the Geneva Convention, with a general mutual recognition of the rights and protections of medical personnel, prisoners, and innocent noncombatants. Now, with a combination of the introduction of soldiers from areas who had received cruel treatment from the German occupiers or from soldiers with a more liberal view of what constituted legitimate killing, the Allied drive for Rome would be on a teetering edge of descending into a wider dimension of violence.

At 11:00 p.m. on May 11, 1944, the most highly publicized campaign in the war for Italy began with an eruption of flames, from mountain crags to beach resorts. All along the Gustav line, a long line of Allied units from the American 85th Division in the west to the British Guards nearly forty miles to the east surged forward and began constructing British-designed Bailey Bridges across an assortment of water barriers. Their German adversaries were as formidable as ever, but their number had been reduced when their senior commanders fell for an Allied ruse, and desperately needed units were shunted northward to deflect an expected invasion north of Rome that was nothing more than a figment of clever intelligence operative imaginations.

Operation Diadem was both a brilliantly planned offensive and, concurrently, the epitome of war in slow motion. At Lexington, Massachusetts, British regulars had dispersed Captain John Parker's militiamen in less than five minutes; George Pickett's iconic assault on Cemetery Hill at Gettysburg devolved from formidable advance to agonizing retreat in less than an hour. Yet, in May, 1944, the Gustav line fractured incrementally, with no single attack decisively routing the enemy. Instead, while one German unit withstood an Allied charge, a neighboring party might be forced to withdraw and the successful defender obliged to join their defeated countrymen in retreat or be destroyed piecemeal.

On the Gustav line front, the main American forces belonged to U.S. II Corps, the "rookies" in the campaign, who had largely missed earlier action in the struggle for Italy. The corps commander was Major General Geoffrey Keyes, who had been Patton's deputy during the Sicilian campaign and had been at least partially responsible for the fiasco of the Rapido River assault. The relationship between Keyes and Clark was at times complex and unpredictable, as the technical advantage of both generals serving the same nation's Army veered between a surface cordiality and an intimation by Keyes that his commander was a micromanager who called the corps commander frequently and compared Keyes's leadership skills unfavorably to those of other Allied units, a tactic the Corps Commander ascribed to the personality of "a nervous fifteen year old kid."

Meanwhile, at Anzio, the approaching major offensive found General Lucian Truscott's VI Corps coiled and ready for their particular contribution to Operation Buffalo. While Clark and Keyes seemed to be engaged in a complex love-hate command relationship, Truscott saved much of his energy for scaring his men into taking risks to break out of the semisiege in which they were embroiled. Truscott was a forty-nine-year-old former Oklahoma school teacher who had accidentally swallowed carbolic acid as a toddler and was left with a raspy drawl that one news correspondent insisted was a "rock crusher" voice. Most soldiers could not fully comprehend whether his gravel voice meant approval or displeasure, but large numbers of GIs damned him for "trying to turn infantrymen into cowboy horses," although some men insisted he was "damning them with affection." In a tight-knit fraternity of senior generals who seemed to alternatively embrace mayhem and culture, Truscott turned from ferocious overseer to cultured gentleman as he insisted on the delivery of fresh flowers to his headquarters tent each day, had his meals prepared by a Chinese American cook, and prided himself on his ability as a polo player. Now, as the great breakout was about to begin, the gravel-voiced corps commander seemed to spend all of his waking hours dreaming up a meticulous battle plan that would spur the Anzio garrison on to Rome.

The concept that "all roads lead to Rome" was narrowed, in effect, to one road for the Anzio garrison: the German-controlled Highway 6, the main avenue between Cassino and the capital, winding north of the now blood-encrusted fields of enemy-controlled Cisterna. Truscott's garrison had been quietly reinforced since the winter battles, and he now commanded a powerful assault force grouped around five American divisions, two British divisions, and the brigade-sized Canadian-American Special Service Force, now deployed against five less-powerful German divisions.

Truscott quietly maneuvered three American infantry divisions, the powerful 1st U.S. Armored Division and the versatile Special Services Brigade, against a single German division garrisoning in Cisterna. Truscott was convinced, correctly, that the German high command was focused on an Allied lunge for Campoleone station that would be linked with an expected massive amphibious landing north of Rome and, therefore, garrisoned Cisterna with a single Reich division.

On May 11, after three disastrous Allied attempts to smash through the Cassino-Rapido defenses, a massive multinational offensive lurched into motion along a carefully chosen twenty-mile stretch of the Gustav line between Cassino and the sea. Most of the Fifth and Eighth armies, supported by massive artillery and air support, formed an operational sledgehammer that was designed to crush the defenders before they had time to scuttle back six miles to a newly constructed backup position—the Hitler Line.

The assault was bookended on the sea by Geoffrey Keyes II Corps, and in the vicinity of Cassino Abbey by Lieutenant General Wladyslav Anders II Polish Corps panting for revenge for the nineteen-day German blitz across their homeland when they fought alone with no directly available allies. Field Marshall Albert Kesserling expected some thrust along the Gustav line, but he had little idea where or when the blow would fall. Now, with one eye still on an amphibious landing north of Rome, the Luftwaffe-trained Marshall threw in infantry reserves while holding his mobile divisions in reserve, ready to move when the enemy plans were clarified. Somewhere between the Polish and American bookends, General Alphonse Juin's largely North African French Corps used their agility in mountain warfare to scramble up insurmountable heights and attack the startled German defenders in the rear.

Meanwhile, Keyes II Corps slowly pushed back the single German division assigned to protect the seacoast as the men of that 94th Division watched with growing alarm as a yawning gap appeared between themselves and their nearest friendly units. Even for an increasingly victorious army, crossing wide rivers and clambering up steep hills were far more demanding than rolling tanks through the desert or steppe, and this Allied "Blitzkrieg" was not quite at the pace of Desert Storm. However, as the attackers gained momentum, General Clark was poised to play his next trump card: Lucian Truscott's coiled VI Corps.

Just before dawn on May 23, the twelfth day of Diadem, Operation Buffalo surged into action, as tanks of the 1st Armored Division clanked toward the Cisterna-Campoleone railroad line. German mines, artillery, and antitank weapons promptly turned ninety of the assault vehicles into burning wrecks, but Truscott had plenty of reserves, and Eberhard von Mackensen watched in horror as his 362nd Division buckled under a tsunami of Allied attackers and then saw two regiments of the supporting 715th Division evaporate soon after.

Now, Mackensen was essentially faced with the grim prospect of parrying the assaults of the equivalent of seven Allied divisions with only three similar units of his own. The Germans could not hold everywhere, and the British 1st Division soon captured the important Carroceto train station, while the American 45th Division overran Campoleone station to effectively halt German use of the Anzio–Rome rail line. Then, General Ernie Harmon's rampaging 1st Armored Division discovered a rapidly expanding gap in the fraying enemy defense line at the key road junction of Velletri, which now threatened to cut off one of Mackensen's primary routes of retreat.

By May 25, 1944, two weeks into the Allied offensive, the German Army on both the Anzio and Cassino fronts was reeling from sledgehammer blows inflicted by two powerful armies. As Kesserling watched in horror as one stop line after another simply disintegrated before the Allied tidal wave, the field marshal asked Hitler for permission to blow up nearly twenty bridges that connected Rome to both its own far-flung neighborhoods and the rest of Italy. In a shocking reversal of the usual pattern in which the Fuehrer usually ordered his somewhat more reluctant generals to destroy cultural artifacts in a scorched-earth retreat, Hitler actually vetoed this measure, insisting that the intrinsic artistic and cultural value of these spans outweighed military necessity.

While Hitler and Kesserling feuded over the fate of the bridges, generals Mark Clark and Harold Alexander were engaged in an equally testy debate over which nation's army should enter Rome first. Alexander issued a diffident directive to 5th American and 8th British armies that their main objective should be the destruction of enemy forces, not the capture of militarily unimportant real estate. Both Mark Clark and Oliver Leese cheerfully ignored the order and ordered their strategic staffs to plan an attack that would put them in the Eternal City first.

Clark fumed that his instructions to block the retreating German Army east of the Alban Hills at Valmontone was nothing more than a directive to essentially use the American Army as football offensive linemen blocking for the British Army running backs who would score the winning touchdown of the capture of Rome. The result was a revised plan in which Clark directed one American task force to push from Valmontone to Rome along Highway 6 and a parallel task force to drive toward the Eternal City on a more southerly route of Highway 7 to find a way into the capital.

During the climactic period of Operation Diadem, the emerging rivalry between Clark and Alexander was not particularly publicized to the combat units for fear that GIs, Tommies, and the multiple other nationalities were not eager to die solely for the career advancement of senior commanders. Yet, by late May, Rome and its environs were clearly beginning to take on the appearance of a major prize about to be abandoned by the defenders. Important documents were finding their way to outdoor bonfires; thousands of wounded Germans were evacuated by hospital trains; Reich diplomats, functionaries, and their Italian collaborators headed north with as much booty as their relative status allowed. Roman civilians turned overnight from German allies to potential welcoming committees for the Anglo-American columns. German troops became more trigger-happy, as resistance groups became bolder and more violent.

Meanwhile, not too many miles to the south, supposedly "impenetrable" German lines began to buckle, cave in, and then disintegrate like the bulkheads of the *Titanic,* as an Allied sea swept over each stop point. In some respects, the German defense of Rome was beginning to mirror the

French experience in Paris during the Great Blitz of May and June 1940, as commanders insisted that the *next* line had already been breached by the enemy, and the invaders moved off the maps that supposedly represented the current state of that battle. Marshall Kesserling was now increasingly obliged to choose one among lesser evils, as Lucien Truscott's VI Corps burst on into the Alban Hills and the multinational assault force burst through the short-lived Hitler line with their eyes also on the prize of Rome.

At the height of this complex battle, Mark Clark initiated a bold but controversial gamble to move forward the date of arrival in the Eternal City. When he had returned home for his short interlude with his wife and the discussion with senior officials, the Fifth Army commander had been repeatedly queried whether he could capture Rome before the initiation of Operation Overlord. Civilian and military officials were convinced that the capture of Rome before D-Day would be a major morale booster to the citizens of occupied Europe and possibly negatively affect the morale of the German troops tasked with challenging the invasion of Normandy.

Mark Clark was a loving father and husband, and a personally brave commander, but he craved publicity for himself and his army at a point in which Overlord and the massively accelerating offensive in the Pacific threatened to turn the Mediterranean theater into a backwater. The capture of Rome was the single most important career enhancement the Fifth Army commander could currently expect, and he was now fighting a calendar as much as the Germans for this prize. Given this level of emotional intensity, it is not surprising that Clark quietly approved a proposal from II Corps commander Geoffrey Keys to seize the heights above Valmontone Gap and then execute a rapid turn westward over the Via Casilina, while America VI Corps and Eighth Army covered the exposed flanks of the onrushing assault force all the way to Rome. In essence, destruction of the German Army now took a backseat to the political and psychological bonanza of a pre-Overlord American capture of Rome, and Clark quickly signed on for the new plan.

Almost immediately, Keyes II Corps became in all but name essentially an operational army, as Clark gave his friend most of 3rd Division, a combat command from 1st Armored Division, and the Canadian-American Special Service force to double Keyes's offensive punch. Meanwhile, Clark encouraged Lucien Truscott to widen his own thrust toward the Alban Hills, and late on the evening of May 30, two American regiments began climbing the slopes toward the summit. By dawn, they found that they had dug into the flanks of two entire German corps. Engineers were quickly tasked to bulldoze a road to provide both infantry and tank support for the path-finding regiments, and by the morning of June 1, the entire German garrison at Valmontone had been cut off and surrendered.

As Marshall Kesserling gradually became aware that Clark seemed more interested in the capture of Rome than the annihilation of the German Army, the Luftwaffe general began to implement his own plan to at least save much of his army to fight another day and make defense of the Italian capital a secondary concern. While General von Vietinghoff's Tenth Army was given priority approval to evacuate to the north, General Mackensen's Fourteenth Army formed a gradually contracting cover force in a disciplined, step-by-step evacuation. Any vehicles that could be used for transportation were pressed into service for a northward evacuation. Kesserling was able to deploy just enough units at the right spots to at least slow the Allied advance. While some German units virtually mutinied and others carried out mass executions of Roman citizens who were now seen as turncoats, Clark officially insisted that bagging large numbers of enemy troops was the main priority, while spending much of his energy deploying American military police units to delay British and French units from arriving in Rome before his GIs could enter.

As Kesserling finally declared Rome an open city, the always resourceful Colonel Robert Frederick of the Canadian-American Special Service Force performed a particularly special service for Clark. When Frederick linked up with an armored column commanded by Colonel Hamilton Houze, they made a test run into the city in the early morning of June 4. As a forward echelon of sixty men in eighteen jeeps commanded by Captain Taylor Radcliffe dismounted and began snapping souvenir photos, a final fusillade of German machine gunfire encouraged a hurried fallback that, in turn, allowed other units entering on other roads to gain a share of the prize of entering Rome first. Then, General Keyes, flying in an observation plane over the city, dropped orders to Colonel Houze to lead his more heavily armed main force into town, which, in turn, was absorbed by General Frederick into a brigade-sized occupation force. Frederick, wounded in the thigh by a German sniper, managed to officially welcome his superiors, Keyes and Clark, to Rome, and the three officers posed in front of a "Roma" directional sign at the entrance to the city that would quickly become an iconic image in American news media.

Mark Clark and his Fifth Army would now gradually begin to take a backseat in newspapers, magazines, and newsreels to the more heavily publicized exploits of Americans in Northern Europe and the Pacific theater, but Clark would emerge again in the Korean War as commander-in-chief of all United Nations forces. Within twenty-four hours of the news of the American liberation of Rome, a new front would grab the headlines, and the nickname "Ike" would become familiar to almost everyone in a nation at war.

CHAPTER VIII

The Deadly Sands of Normandy

A few hours before dawn on Monday, June 5, 1944, a balding though impressively handsome man awoke in his trailer in southern England, shocked by the ferocity of the storm roaring through this Allied encampment. General Dwight David Eisenhower had responsibility for almost every individual in this vast bivouac, and he was deeply concerned because "the whole camp was shaking and shuddering under a wind of almost hurricane proportions with accompanying rain that seemed to be traveling in horizontal sheets." However, this four-star general who grew up in a Kansas home that featured a warm, affectionate mother and a father who exhibited the stern, physical discipline of a Dickensian patriarch, actually breathed a huge sigh of relief when he observed the impact of the weather. The reason for this relief was that this June 5 was scheduled to be the date of Overlord, the vast Allied expedition to Normandy with the ultimate object of ending Hitler's reign of terror over the European mainland.

However, Dwight Eisenhower was still faced with a decision, as he quickly dressed and walked over to the main building on the grounds, Southwick House. This mansion near Portsmouth Harbor was the headquarters of Admiral Bertram Ramsey, commander of naval operations for the planned invasion, and provided a spacious conference room where the senior commanders of the invasion of Normandy were about to convene for a discussion of a momentous decision. Shortly after 4:00 a.m., a dour Scottish Royal Air Force officer entered the room and quickly became the center of attention for men of far higher rank than his group captain status. J. M. Stagg was the senior meteorologist for the Allied Expeditionary Force, and he knew that his superiors would face him with only one question: would the current storm dissipate sufficiently in the next four hours to permit a Tuesday morning landing? Ramsey's answer, although replete with qualifications and warnings, was that minimally acceptable conditions would be available, a predication that prompted a simple response from Eisenhower: "Okay, let's go."

Three and a half centuries earlier, much of Queen Elizabeth's kingdom quaked at the threat presented by one hundred thirty Spanish galleons as that Armada closed in on British shores. Now, a fleet made up primarily of ships flying either the British naval insignia or the flag of Britain's progeny America was sailing in the opposite direction with nearly five thousand vessels. This fleet included ten battleships and monitors, twenty-three cruisers, over one hundred destroyers, and one hundred thirty thousand assault forces that would storm ashore along a fifty-mile beachfront that extended roughly from Cherbourg to Caen and included five designated landing points: Sword and Gold for British forces; Juno for Canadian units; and Omaha and Utah beaches for American troops.

Field Marshal Erwin Rommel, the German commander responsible for throwing any Allied invasion into the sea, had insisted that defeat or victory for either side would ride on a single twenty-four-hour period after the first invader touched ground, a "Longest Day" that might very well decide the outcome of World War II. However, while German observers peered intently with their binoculars at the dark Channel beyond, redoubtable British and American troops were falling from the sky and landing behind the vast network of German fortifications to add a new dimension to amphibious warfare.

While their British counterparts were landing in the vicinity of Caen, two divisions of American paratroopers were floating landward in a wide arc of territory in or near the Cherbourg peninsula. Within moments after they left their planes, most of these thirteen thousand men were lost, scared, dead, or wounded, but the survivors were now on the ground and immediately becoming a factor in the battle to throw the Germans out of Normandy. Once free of what seemed to be the flying coffins that had been their transportation to battle, the men of the 82nd and 101st Airborne divisions were turning their incredibly widely scattered presence into an Allied asset, as German response units surrendered much of their advantage of superior weapons as they tramped over the countryside trying to locate real and imagined threats. Hitler's "fortress Europe" had now been invaded by phantoms, but these phantoms were elite, resourceful soldiers who were deflecting large numbers of Germans from responding to the far greater threat that was now poised just offshore in the predawn darkness. However, this gift to the Allied assault strategy often came with a terrible price to the soldiers from the sky.

Probably the most iconic image of the American airborne assault occurred in the crossroads town of St. Mere Eglise. This town was important only to the extent that the main road from Paris to Cherbourg ran through the community, and both Americans and Germans would soon want to control that highway. Just as German antiaircraft gun tracer bullets fell back into the town and set fire to one of the homes in the town square, German guards supervising civilian firefighting activities and American paratroopers dropping to earth six miles from their intended target ignited the first battle of D-Day in the American operational sector. As the town church bell clanged a summons for additional individuals to join a bucket brigade, civilians and then soldiers glanced upward in amazement as the airborne invaders dropped into trees, wells, the church steeple, and even the burning house. One either very lucky or unlucky paratrooper, Private John Steele, dangled below the steeple, suspended by his parachute strings, and watched a battle unfold as if it were a model diorama with moving figures. The garrison either shot or took the surrender of the unluckiest Americans either dangling from trees or sprawled on the ground with broken limbs, while only a short distance away, luckier Americans who had hit firm ground took a toll of the enemy as the sky soldiers sought better cover. The town would remain in German hands for a few more hours, but, as single paratroopers joined into informal squads and squads turned into provisional companies, the Americans would be back in daylight, and St. Mere Eglise would become one of the first islands of liberated France in what, for a time, remained a sea of German occupation.

What was seen as "invasion eve" for the troops crammed on the ships crossing the Channel was in fact a night of terror, confusion, and some triumph for these aerial invaders. Division commander Maxwell Taylor started the battle for Normandy in the company of an "army" of exactly one private falling in behind him. German General Wilhelm Fallen, commander of the 91st Air Landing Division, entered the battle with exactly the same force—a single driver for his staff car—and, instead of arriving at the war game exercise for which he was headed, lost his life in a Wild West type of shootout where he alternately yelled his intention to surrender while he crawled toward his dropped pistol.

As paratroopers clicked five-cent "cricket" noisemakers, hoping for the proper recognition, with counterclicks from the blackness beyond them more than a few of them may have wondered whether their amphibious counterparts really would land the next morning or whether they were being reduced to "forlorn hope" status. Even a strange face from a rival company or the "other" airborne division dissolved animosity of training days and forged a new type of brotherhood. At the boundaries of the British and American landing zones, airborne Tommies and GIs linked up against a common enemy, the last vestiges of Bunker Hill or Bladensburg now forgotten.

Then, just as the first streaks of pink in the sky gave a small sign that dawn was near, the guns of the bombardment fleet proved to the paratroopers that D-Day was actually here, and those GIs who did not need jump boats or airborne patches were about to join them to prove that their night-long action was not just an elaborate raid.

The American (and British) airborne troops who had fought in the predawn hours of June 6 had been forced to contend with minimal heavy weapons support, the uncertainty of the location of both friendly and enemy forces, and nagging fears that the main invasion might still somehow be canceled. The men of the main assault force enjoyed the advantage of much more air and artillery support, an opportunity to fight in day-light, and the knowledge that they would soon be followed by additional support units. Yet, given all of these advantages, the men who landed on the Omaha beaches on this Tuesday morning might have gladly joined the airborne service just to avoid the welcoming reception that was now waiting for them.

During the several months leading up to D-Day, Field Marshall Erwin Rommel had most likely attempted to compensate for the humiliating climax to his great North African desert war adventure that had concluded with the Desert Fox in a German hospital and most of his African Corps marching into Allied POW camps in a humiliating surrender much of the Anglo-American press dubbed "Tunisgrad." Now, the German hero who seemed to engage in a love-hate relationship with the Fuehrer, who provided him with unsurpassed honors but little tangible support in the desert war climax, had been appointed to create an "Atlantic Wall" to throw the prospective Anglo-American invasion of Northwest Europe into the sea. Rommel had been given thousands of German soldiers and both volunteer- and press-ganged French civilians to construct an almost impenetrable defense system along possible invasion sites, and he pro-posed to entangle and decimate the invaders in these fortifications and then annihilate the survivors with ten of his best armored divisions.

At 5:50 a.m., twenty minutes after the initial British bombardment to the east, a fleet of U.S. battleships and cruisers began to bombard an Omaha landing zone that Rommel had fortified with eight concrete bunkers, thirty-five pillboxes, eighty-five machine gun nests, and thirty-five rocket launcher sites. As dozens of the ingeniously designed "Higgins Boat" landing craft started inland from their mother ships, nearly five hundred heavy bombers droned overhead at twenty thousand feet, ten thousand feet below normal bombing altitude, with each plane crammed with one-hundred-pound bombs designed to tear through enemy beach defenses.

The battleships, cruisers, fighter bombers, and heavy bombers were crucial for any chance of Allied success, and despite far more hits on apple orchards and grazing cattle than on enemy fortifications, this air-sea combination was able to silence some cannons, blow up some machine guns, and kill or injure some defenders. However, hopes for a successful landing on Omaha Beach actually rode on the sheer willpower of about four thousand first-wave assault troops that belonged to the eighteen companies that would attempt to clamber alive from the pitching and weaving landing craft. Each Higgins boat carried a miniature society of thirty generally young American men, about the size of an average high school or college class back home, which they might be now attending if the legacy of World War I was anything but a World War II. Most landing craft had no officer higher than a lieutenant or captain who was probably of an age such that he could have been their teacher back home. While they all faced the same sort of looming cannons that the men of George Pickett's division faced eight decades earlier on Cemetery Ridge at Gettysburg, at least the men of that Confederate charge could always turn around and run back to safety if the enemy barrage seemed to promise annihilation; the GIs landing here had no direction to go but forward.

Yet, just as much of the carnage of Pickett's charge was caused by Confederate assumptions that the Union position on Cemetery Ridge was far weaker than was actually the case, the American assault on Omaha Beach was more perilous because Allied intelligence had severely undercounted the manpower that faced the GIs. The men of the assault companies of the 1st and 24th divisions had been briefed that their most likely opposition would be a single regiment of the 716th Coastal Defense Division, which fielded roughly two thousand men evenly divided between Polish and Slavic "Ost" troops, largely recruited from a pool of starving Soviet Army prisoners and German draftees limited by moderate health problems. This single regiment was believed to be holding a front of fifteen miles so that only a fraction of them would be actively contesting the invasion. Unfortunately, this information was badly out of date, as Rommel had recently reinforced the Omaha Beach defenses with a regiment of the first-line 352nd and Infantry Division that doubled or tripled the defensive capability of the garrison.

The initial American landing on Omaha Beach has been depicted in countless books, films, and television documentaries and is one of those moments where the course of World War II might have substantially changed if Dwight Eisenhower's already penned statement of failure and personal responsibility had ever gone to a printer rather than remaining in his uniform pocket. While the four thousand men coming ashore were only a small fraction of the invasion force, the tyranny of Omaha Beach was that success at all of the other four beaches was useless without the Omaha linchpin. In a cruel twist of fate, once senior commanders had chosen Normandy as a landing site, possession of Omaha was not negotiable; no other more compact landing zone in Western Europe held as much promise as Normandy. Omaha had to be taken, but none of the early auguries were particularly positive. Ten landing craft carrying three hundred men were quickly turned into flaming wrecks by enemy artillery before even one man in the group fired a shot at the defenders. An initially promising plan to backstop the attackers with three dozen cleverly designed "dual drive" amphibious tanks largely disintegrated when most of them sank to the bottom of the channel as they were launched from their mother ships at too great a depth of water. The enormous destructive powers of the heavy bomber assaults were initially negated when a succession of relatively innocuous changes in the target area destroyed more of the Norman apple orchard assets than German defenders. If the string of unforeseen setbacks had continued further into the day, the whole invasion plan just might have begun to unravel, and the "Longest Day" would have ended in German celebration. Yet, D-Day did not turn into a Gallipoli or Dieppe with a permanent aura of disaster and mutual accusations.

The most positive news of the early morning was that, despite steep casualties, the Americans had secured a shallow beachhead on Omaha, but a new crisis immediately emerged as soon as the invaders tried to push toward the line of bluffs that formed the main defense perimeter for the German Army. Unlike the war in the Pacific and North Africa, the beachfront buildings in Normandy seemed to the Americans like a return to familiar things, as they almost could have been landing at the Jersey Shore, Nantucket, Virginia Beach, or Malibu. Yet every building, from the shore cottages to the much newer pillboxes, seemed to house one or more of the notorious MG-42 Spandau machine guns poking out of a window or slit, and their firing capability of twelve hundred bullets a minute sounded like nothing more than a deadly version of paper ripping. The initial attempt to rush these guns produced near annihilation for some of the units who were caught in their deadly sights, as Company A of the 29th Division was whittled down to only eight unwounded men before any of the invaders even saw a German soldier.

Caught between the lapping waves behind them and the arcs of fire coming from the buildings in the front, the men of the Big Red One and the Blue and Gray divisions rushed through a giant shooting gallery that somehow had to be endured and navigated. Men of the Blue and Gray Division who often had ancestors who had fought one another in the Civil War were now forever linked together in their new version of Cemetery Ridge and Cold Harbor an ocean away from those iconic battlefields. Just as a moment of extreme crisis in those earlier battles produced a leader who changed the course of the struggle, a relatively junior commander on the Overlord organizational table rose to this ultimate challenge.

Brigadier General Norman "Dutch" Cota was assistant division commander of the 29th Division, and, although he was not permitted to land in the first wave, he followed soon afterward to find himself the senior officer on a nearly collapsing invasion beach. Cota dodged bullets, exhorted men to keep advancing, and gently encouraged men who were on the verge of retreating. In one of the iconic pronouncements of D-Day, Cota bellowed in his best command voice, "There are two kinds of soldiers on the beach—those who are dead and those who are about to die. So let's get the hell off the damned beach."

Cota was able to turn a scene of chaotic indecision into a textbook infantry school exercise solution by creating a fire-and-maneuver advance, in which assault forces alternated between firing, running inland under cover from men in the rear, and then firing again to cover the advance of the next formation. The soldiers were drawn almost magnetically to the two passes between the dunes that led to the town of Vierville and St. Laurent, as they found to their surprise and relief that many of the enemy guns could not swivel far enough to be fully effective at those two points.

It was at this critical point for the battle of Omaha Beach that the Allied ability to substantially convince the enemy that their *real* invasion would take place at the Pas de Calais started to pay significant dividends. The German garrison at Omaha was large enough to at least temporarily checkmate a direct frontal assault on their positions, but the defenders were spread too thinly to parry any invaders who managed to get around the flank or rear. Norman Cota quickly realized that the key to the battle was seizure of the passes at Vierville and St. Laurent, and he soon had significant help from the fleet offshore.

Captain Harry Sanders, commander of Destroyer Squadron 18, closed his ships only a few feet short of grounding them and then ordered every gun in his squadron to let loose on the German lines. When his superior, Admiral C. J. Bryant, realized what the "tin cans" were doing, he shouted over the radio, "Get on them men! They are raising hell with the men on the beach, and we can't have any more of that!" A spectacular duel now ensued between the destroyer and the German artillery batteries, and, although the American ships took hits, the fire support created just enough cover for Cota's men to push through the passes and then swing behind to hit the defenders in their far more vulnerable rear. The landing at Omaha Beach was one of the costlier short-term battles that America faced in the European theater, as more than twenty-five hundred assault troopers sprawled dead, dying, or injured on the beach or in the nearby water. On the other hand, the landing had partially distracted the German focus on the main American landing point, Utah Beach.

This pleasant strand west of the Omaha environs sector was actually even more strategically important than its sister objective, as the roads beyond a wide string of sand dunes led directly to the interior of the Cotentin Peninsula and its key port of Cherbourg. That city, one of the last stops of the *Titanic* as it made its maiden voyage across the Atlantic, was the first major objective of the American invasion force in concert with a simultaneous British Canadian lunge toward Caen at the eastern end of the Allied target areas. While the paratroopers fought their nocturnal battle against the enemy in the interior, Rear Admiral Don Moon and VII Corps Commander General "Lightning Joe" Collins stood on the bridge of the U.S.S. *Bayfield* to watch the embarkation of the twenty-one thousand assault troops and seventeen hundred vehicles that would redeem the pledge to the isolated paratroopers that they would not be expected to fight indefinitely without support. Battleship *Nevada,* American cruisers *Quincy* and *Tuscaloosa,* and British cruisers *Black Prince* and *Enterprise* opened a predawn salvo that compared favorably with the Omaha counterpart, although Collins, a rare veteran in the present European theater of the Pacific War, believed that both the size of the bombardment force and the length of their operations were below the standards being set for the amphibious operations on the other side of the globe.

Collins's reservations were militarily valid but, luckily for the assault force, rather superfluous, as the moderately successful naval bombardment was quickly followed up by an air attack that, unlike its Omaha Beach counterpart, was a dazzling success. While the heavy bombers over Omaha had generally operated at twenty thousand feet, three hundred two-engine B-26 Marauders swept across the German defenses of Utah Beach at only five hundred feet above the tallest sand dune. Moments later, German cannons, machine guns, mortars, and vehicles sprawled over the landing zone like a giant junkyard, and the men of the 4th Division splashed ashore under surprisingly light enemy fire. The senior official accompanying them was, like Omaha Beach's "Dutch" Cota, a one-star general of relatively modest military accomplishment. However, where Cota's fame was just beginning to emerge, his counterpart on Utah was a household name. General Theodore Roosevelt, Jr., had actually surpassed his father's highest military rank of colonel, but his stay in the White House had been as a family member, not a president.

Much like his father, Theodore Roosevelt, Jr., had reached late middle age facing increasingly serious health crises, and, while his superiors overlooked his arthritis in their reluctant permission to allow him to land on Utah, they were clearly unaware of the serious coronary issues that would take his life very shortly. However, on this day, like his father at San Juan Hill, T. R. junior had a command in the middle of a major battle, and he pointed his cane like a sword as he deployed his forces to overrun enemy positions. When a glance at the map revealed the shocking news that the landing force was on the wrong beach, a mile from its designated landing spot, Roosevelt quickly realized that his men had disembarked at a seam in the enemy defenses, and he confidently declared, "We'll start the war from right here."

Thus, by 6:30 a.m. on D-Day, much of the 2nd battalion of the 3rd Infantry Regiment was pushing inland under the direction of Theodore Roosevelt's raised cane, and reinforcements were pouring onto the beach as Allied destroyers steamed dangerously close to the shoreline to provide a hail of covering fire. As the invaders closed on the German defense line centered on a seawall, a string of vacation homes were turned into newly made redoubts. While the Germans still proved to be tenacious fighters, fewer than two hundred Americans were killed or wounded on Utah Beach, one-tenth of the toll at neighboring Omaha. As the GIs fought a house-to-house battle just beyond the sand dunes, their comrades in the airborne forces were now using daylight to form cohesive units and began to trap German units in a pincer between airborne and seaborne threats. At a cost of 2,374 American casualties, Omaha and Utah beaches had been secured, and a secure right flank had been gained for the Anglo-Canadian forces on Gold Sword and Juno beaches in the Caen-Bayeux area to the east.

Midnight of June 7, 1944, brought the official end of Erwin Rommel's predicted "Longest Day." His long-planned counterattack had been launched, and German tanks actually closed to within sight of the sea on the left flank of the invasion. However, all five invasion beaches had been secured, and, if the Allied line was porous in places, the control of the air that began back in winter with Big Week and the presence of five thousand Allied ships as a nautical backstop to the soldiers ensured that there was little chance that the invasion force was going to be pushed back into the sea. Dwight Eisenhower, who had prudently composed a personal apology to be published if the invasion failed, now commanded a vast military juggernaut to carry out what he called "The Great Crusade" to liberate Europe from Hitler and his Nazi henchmen. However, as the

Allies moved inland and Allied supply ships dropped anchor off the invasion beaches, another vast fleet was steaming toward the outer edges of
what the Japanese government saw as their inner empire. The invasion of
Normandy had succeeded; the invasion of the Marianas was now about
to begin.

CHAPTER IX

The Gods of Sea and Sky

On June 6, 1944, as the Allies were landing in Normandy, the most powerful fleet in the history of naval warfare to that time was beginning to rendezvous on the other side of the world. Newly captured Eniwetok Island was now the staging point for Operation Forager, the first American attempt to pierce the boundaries of Japan's prewar empire while also reclaiming the first piece of American soil captured by the enemy in the wake of Pearl Harbor. The American target was the Marianas island chain and its two most important islands, Saipan and Guam.

Just as Anglo-American military leaders had spent much of the previous year discussing and debating the invasion point for Operation Overlord, American Army and Navy officials had engaged in intense deliberations to discover the most expedient method of penetrating the inner defense perimeter of the Nipponese Empire. While the choice of Normandy for Operation Overlord was based on relatively cordial discussions between American and British commanders, the debate over the best way to approach the Japanese homeland was far more vociferous and did not fall into the scope of traditional Army-Navy rivalry.

Four different senior American military commanders proposed four different "best" routes to a decisive confrontation with the enemy at the gateway to its home islands. General Henry "Hap" Arnold, commander of the Army Air Forces, was anxious to demonstrate the capabilities of the new aerial superweapon B-29 Super Fortress, which the "bomber barons" believed could incinerate Japan into surrender from operational bases near the coast of China. General Douglas MacArthur insisted that the springboard to the Nipponese homeland would be to recapture the now Japanese-occupied Philippine Islands, which, in turn, would be the base for a massive amphibious invasion of the enemy homeland. Admiral Chester Nimitz, commander of the Pacific Fleet, viewed the island of Formosa as the operational center for the final invasion. Finally Nimitz's superior, Admiral Ernest King, insisted that the collapse of Japan could be accomplished through severing the supply line between the home islands and their recently acquired empire through the capture of their geographic jugular vein, the Marianas Islands.

The prospect of a four-way free-for-all loomed for the ultimate arbiter of the dispute, the commander in chief of the armed forces. However, before Franklin Roosevelt was forced to make difficult choices that would leave at least some senior commanders disgruntled, a series of events occurred that allowed a relatively tolerable compromise to emerge before the president had to don his executive decision-maker persona. A massive early 1944 Japanese offensive in China quickly overran the prospective base sites intended for Arnold's superforts; Ernest King assured his naval colleague that, since Formosa was closer to Japan than the Marianas, an invasion of that island could remain on the operational list *after* the Marianas were captured; and, finally, the president assured Douglas MacArthur that his beloved Philippines were not forgotten and that their liberation could be addressed after the Marianas were safely under the American flag. Therefore, Ernest King emerged as the short-term victor in the "battle" of the Pacific strategies, but his three friendly rivals would each receive most of their wish lists. Even the Air Force was not forgotten as new calculations revealed that the Marianas island of Tinian had airstrips that were in range of Japan for the new B-29s.

The American command structure in 1944 was a mix of relatively young officers and older personnel who had learned their trade in World War I. Here, General Joseph W. Stilwell talks with Major General Curtis E. LeMay of the 20th Bomber command, at a B-29 base in China, October 1944. (*Library of Congress*)

Government rationing authorities encouraged homemakers to "make do and mend" through activities such as preserving foods before they went bad and were discarded. (*Library of Congress*)

On the evening of June 5, 1944, General Dwight D. Eisenhower gives the order of the day, "Full victory—nothing else," to paratroopers somewhere in England, before they board their airplanes to participate in the first assault in the invasion of the continent of Europe. *(Library of Congress)*

News of D-Day was the biggest story since Pearl Harbor and filled theaters with people anxious to see the first film footage of "Overlord." Here, a crowd gathers in New York's Times Square. *(Library of Congress)*

Even the American home front in 1944 was populated by a huge number of service personnel either coming from war, going off to war, or filling coveted "stateside" positions. (*Library of Congress*)

President Roosevelt's announcements of the landings in Normandy encouraged places of worship to schedule multiple prayer services for the safety of participants in "Overlord." (*Library of Congress*)

General Dwight Eisenhower's concept of the liberation of Europe as the "Great Crusader" was reflected on the home front by demonstrations of religious faith and patriotism. The war was often presented as a struggle to ensure that American children could continue to grow up in a free society. (*Library of Congress*)

Retreating German forces attempted to slow the Allied power in Italy by massive destruction of port facilities. (*Library of Congress*)

Americans deployed to liberate Paris initially expected house-to-house fighting; instead, they became participants in the biggest celebration in modern French history. Here, crowds line the Champs Elysees as Allied tanks and half tracks pass through the Arc du Triomphe, after Paris was liberated on August 25, 1944. (*Library of Congress, via Wikimedia Commons*)

President Franklin D. Roosevelt in conference with General D. MacArthur, Admiral Chester Nimitz, and Admiral W. D. Leahy, while on tour in Hawaiian Islands in September 1944. (*US Navy, via Wikimedia Commons*)

FDR and Churchill in Quebec, Canada, on September 12, 1944. (*Franklin D. Roosevelt Library, via Wikimedia Commons*)

Allied air power was a key factor in permitting advances against a German army that was masterful in creating powerful defensive positions. (*Library of Congress*)

While Leyte featured a daunting terrain in which to fight a battle, the American landing reaffirmed Douglas MacArthur's pledge to the Filipinos that he would return to liberate their nation. (*Library of Congress*)

The 1944 presidential campaign was significant for several reasons. FDR was the first president to run for a fourth term, it was just the third U.S. presidential election in history to take place during wartime (up to that point), and the president was seriously ill—a fact that he and his staff concealed from the American people. (*Library of Congress*)

Thus, only one of four senior decision makers may have initially preferred a Marianas invasion, but by spring 1944, Operation Forager was well on its way to implementation.

The islands that would become the focal point for the Pacific war in summer 1944 were an extended chain of a dozen landmasses, of which three held significant value to both American and Japanese military planners: Saipan, Tinian, and Guam. Saipan was the Japanese administration center for this part of its Pacific empire, an important component of the Nipponese distillery and sugar cane industries, and a location of enough strategic value that it would force the Imperial Navy out of its relatively protected anchorages into a climactic battle with the American Fleet. Tinian, nearly an appendage to Saipan across a narrow bay was, in effect, Saipan's airport, as Tinian featured a substantial complex of airfields and facilities. Guam had been annexed from Spain in the 1898 war between America and Spain and featured a native population who were considered American citizens forced to live under the subjugation of the Nipponese Empire. Those would be the trio of American targets in the summer of 1944, and, once the Yanks landed, the largest sea battle since Midway was almost certain to occur.

On June 15, 1944, as will be discussed in detail in the following chapter, a mixed Army and Marine assault force stormed ashore on the beaches of Saipan and became a trip wire for a carefully planned Imperial Navy response. On the far side of the Philippine Sea, Vice Admiral Jisaburo Ozawa ordered his powerful Mobile Fleet into action for a planned decisive battle that would largely determine the land battle for the Marianas. Sprawled around the former American naval base at Tawi Tawi, at the extreme southern tip of the Philippine Islands was the embodiment of Japanese might as a seafaring nation. The enemy landing on Saipan was the trip wire for Operation A-GO, the deployment of virtually the entire naval combat strength of Japan in a winner-take-all duel with Admiral Raymond Spruance's Fifth Fleet.

Admiral Ozawa would command a battle fleet considerably larger than Isoruku Yamamoto's Midway expeditionary force, with nine aircraft carriers present for action compared to the four "flattops" under his predecessor's direct command two years earlier. The four hundred thirty combat planes on the carrier flight decks were essentially the entire front-line combat naval aircraft strength of Japan, and it was hoped and expected that these naval aviators would be joined in combat by at least as many ground-based planes scattered among the airfields of the Central Pacific islands. Ozawa's "A-GO" plan had all the audacity of a Mississippi river-boat gambler desperate to recoup his initial winnings in one final draw of the cards. Unlike the Midway confrontation, in which the Imperial Fleet had a theoretical edge of ten carriers to only three for the Americans (if all the Imperial carriers had been concentrated as one force), Ozawa knew that the enemy now could deploy fifteen carriers to his nine. Therefore, when the enemy invaded the Marianas, the great equalizer would be the hundreds of land-based planes stationed in the Marianas chain and other islands within flight range. Theoretically, the fleet carriers and planes would not fully engage the Americans until the land-based aircraft had already whittled the enemy down to manageable size.

Ozawa's adversary on the opposite end of the maritime chessboard was Admiral Raymond Spruance, commander of the Fifth Fleet and primary architect of the victory at Midway. Ray Spruance never received the media attention of his counterpart, William "Bull" Halsey, who was a correspondent's dream interview, as he exhibited his combination of gruff camaraderie and off-color humor. Spruance was a less attractive target for newsmen but, like Chester Nimitz, a "sailor's admiral," who often spent the long hours at sea in vigorous strolls around the deck, often dragooning young officers to accompany him in both exercise and conversation.

Spruance had the quiet confidence of the commander of the largest fleet of aircraft carriers ever assembled, also knowing that his fifteen flat-tops and more than one thousand planes would be gradually expanding as new ships left the numerous naval yards back in the United States. Yet Spruance had to deal with one possibly significant disadvantage compared to his Nipponese adversary. Ozawa could essentially play the role of buc-caneer, with no territory, ground troops, or vulnerable noncombat ships to protect; he was free to focus on an all-out offensive with no thought of shepherding vulnerable assets. On the other hand, Spruance was under explicit orders from Ernest King and Chester Nimitz that his primary mission was to protect and support the invasion forces and should not engage in any action that allowed the enemy to slip between Fifth Fleet and the all-too-vulnerable transport and hospital ships and the assault force battling for Saipan. In essence, Ozawa would play the role of a swashbuckling pirate; Spruance was more of a shepherd to a vulnerable fleet.

The fifty-seven-year-old Ozawa now held the title of commander-in-chief of First Mobile Fleet, which was effectively almost all of the surface vessels of the Japanese Navy. His only direct superior was Admiral Soemu Toyoda, who was commander-in-chief of Combined Fleet, which was essentially Ozawa's fleet with the addition of submarines and some supply ships. In his capacity as the Empire's senior naval officer, Toyoda sent his subordinate to battle with a charge befitting Admiral Nelson before Trafalgar, as Toyoda insisted that "the rise and fall of Imperial Japan depends on this one battle. Every man shall do his utmost."

However, while Toyoda was sending out his spirit-lifting directive, a far more strategically important message was being transmitted to the Fifth Fleet by the submarine *Flying Fish*. That boat was on patrol near the entrance to the San Bernardino Straits as the Imperial Fleet sailed into the open sea, and the captain dispatched a terse message to Spruance, who was on the cruiser *Indianapolis,* that the enemy was now clearly steaming in Spruance's direction. Almost immediately messages streamed out to the American flagships ordering supply ships to unload as much cargo as possible onto the now American-held Saipan invasion beaches within the next forty-eight hours and then retire two hundred miles eastward to stay clear of the Imperial Fleet. Meanwhile, Admiral Jesse Oldendorf was instructed to use his fleet of older battleships to form a protective screen twenty-five miles north of Saipan to serve as a backstop for both the beachhead and the invasion fleet. Finally, the two dozen escort carriers that supported the larger flattops were given primary responsibility for close air support for the Army and Marine units battling on Saipan in order to free up the larger carriers to concentrate on Ozawa's approaching threat.

While the quiet, courtly Raymond Spruance had overall responsibility for the deployment of Fifth Fleet, a leathery, crusty, chain-smoking incarnation of a swashbuckling pirate had the task of checkmating Ozawa's obviously imminent air attack on the heart of the American Fleet. Vice-admiral Marc Mitscher was commander of Task Force 58, the official title of what was known as the Fast Carrier Task Force. Sitting on a specially designed perch on the flight deck of the carrier *Lexington,* the leather-skinned, perpetually tan incarnation of a New England lobsterman sat chain-smoking on a backward-facing chair, frequently pulling the visor of his long-billed baseball cap over his eyes as he squinted into the sky and sea. Mitscher's nautical empire was now the beating heart of the American Navy—fifteen aircraft carriers, divided into four task groups that collectively could launch more than one thousand planes into aerial battles the pilots now fully expected to win.

Mitscher, like Chester Nimitz, grew up in a decidedly nonmaritime atmosphere, in this case, Hillsboro, Missouri; became a pilot at the relatively advanced age of twenty-nine; and commanded the carrier *Hornet* on its spectacular, morale-boosting 1942 Doolittle raid on Tokyo. While that exploit was a dangerous raid with the possibility of being discovered and overwhelmed by the much larger Japanese home fleet, Mitscher now commanded a task force so large and powerful that most crew members were eagerly anticipating a showdown with the enemy, with the confident feeling that the Americans would win a spectacular victory. The narrative for the anticipated showdown would be this weather-beaten admiral who delighted officers, crews, and new correspondents alike with a constant running commentary about almost any event, conducted in an almost inaudible growl laced with that special saltiness of maritime profanity.

One correspondent for a national newsweekly who, by modern terminology, was "embedded" on the *Lexington* for the coming battle, viewed Mitscher as the centerpiece of a theatrical production of a potentially bloody, decisive battle. "Narrating the sights and sounds of a carrier in combat would tax the talents of Herman Melville as they are a cacophony of noise and a bewildering montage of sights as deck crews work in a noisy drama to launch and return planes decked out in linen helmets, gloves and coveralls ducking in and out of snack compartments where sandwiches and coffee are available 24 hours a day. Their world is the carrier hangar deck, a dim area stuffed with planes with folded wings, filled with the odor of rope, canvas and oil and with an odd contrast between some crewmen working at a frenzied pace while other men doze fitfully between assignments."

Because the two contending fleets were essentially operating from opposite ends of a vast body of water, the battle could not begin until air scouts from one of both fleets sighted the enemy and set an attack plan in motion. On paper, Raymond Spruance's three-to-two advantage in carriers and aircraft seemed to give him an initial advantage, but Admiral Ozawa's ace in the hole was Admiral Kakuji Kakuta's formidable array of land-based aircraft scattered over airfields across the Marianas. Ozawa hoped to catch the Americans in a giant pincer of carrier and land-based aircraft, which would initiate a deadly shuttle operation between carrier decks and island airfields, which could in turn create a significant force multiplier. Thus, the leaders of the two primary opposing forces waited eagerly for dawn on June 19 to initiate a battle that dwarfed Midway in size and scope.

At 7:30 a.m. on that Sunday morning, a Japanese reconnaissance floatplane sighted two American carriers one hundred sixty miles west of Saipan, which put the vessels three hundred eighty miles from Ozawa's flagship. However, as the fleet commander decided to close to a more comfortable distance, Rear Admiral Sueo Obayashi, commander of the third carrier division, largely ignored his commander's wishes and sent sixty-nine planes aloft on an attack mission before Ozawa could even begin to coordinate a larger attack. Now, the mass attack that the Admiral Ozawa craved was already divided into two unsupported sorties.

As the aerial chess match lurched into action, Admiral Marc Mitscher countered the opening Japanese move with a scramble of his own fighters, and soon 222 dark blue Hellcats began settling into defensive formations to await the enemy arrival.

The American pilots already enjoyed the advantage of both better planes and better training, but now Obayashi had added the additional gift of a divided attack force. As the enemy first wave approached the outer edges of the American Fleet, the Hellcat pilots carefully counted how many of the raiders were actually fighters and came to a satisfying total of only sixteen Zeroes. These "Zekes" were outnumbered by fourteen to one, and, while they doggedly guarded their vulnerable dive-bomber and torpedo-plane charges, American planes were diving from every possible direction. For example, Commander Charles Brewer of *Essex* led a formation of eight Hellcats into a wave of sixteen Japanese fighters that had been retrofitted to carry bombs. As the Zekes frantically attempted to gain altitude while shackled to their payloads, Bremer quickly shot down four of them, while another Hellcat pilot splashed five more. Moments later, virtually the entire Japanese escort force was scattered around the sea below. As similar battles swirled across the blue Pacific sky, the Nipponese formations began to simply fall apart, as it became every pilot for himself as other formations joined Brewer's interceptors. A few raiders managed to briefly penetrate the American fighter screen, and one Nipponese bomber managed a direct hit on *South Dakota,* inflicting fifty casualties on the battlewagon waters, their main hope now being a certainty that a larger second strike force would accomplish much more.

Only a short time later, radar sets on the American Fleet flickered with even more impressive readings that represented a second strike force of fifty-three dive bombers, twenty-seven torpedo planes, and forty-eight escort fighters. On the U.S.S. *Lexington,* Admiral Marc Mitscher temporarily left his rear-facing deck chair for a seat on a couch in an adjacent conference room. As radio reports pieced together the nature of the new threat, Mitscher, Chief of Staff Burke, other senior officers, and one or two "embedded" correspondents sat on leather sofas and chairs, munched on a huge pile of sandwiches, drank endless cups of coffee, and created a smoky haze from cigarettes and cigars as they listened to the incessant radio chatter while a yeoman stenographer sat quietly at a corner desk, calmly recording the conversations between other ships and pilots in the air.

At 11:39 a.m. on that tropical summer morning, Commander David McCampbell, leading a dozen Hellcats from *Essex,* gave the traditional attack cry of "tallyho" and fired a stream of bullets that promptly blew up a Judy dive bomber. Perhaps ten minutes later, the count of downed enemy planes was nearing seventy, with the survivors gamely pushing on toward the center of the fleet. Attacks on carriers *Wasp* and *Bunker Hill* left nearly a hundred sailors wounded and four dead but at an additional cost of nearly thirty more raiders.

Meanwhile, nearly three hundred fifty miles east, Admiral Ozawa was following the battle from a conference room of the flagship *Taiho*, not hugely different from his adversary. As Ozawa processed the usual grossly overestimated reports of damage from his flight leaders, the battle suddenly came shockingly close to home. *Taiho* was Japan's new "supercarrier" that featured speed, enhanced watertight compartments, and space for an especially large air group. However, this morning, the *Taiho* was now in the periscope sights of the submarine *Albacore*.

Commander J. W. Blanchard was now submerged nine thousand yards from the thirty-three-thousand-ton prize that conspicuously flew the eight rays of a rising sun, the flag of the commander of the Japanese Fleet. When the primitive computer on *Albacore* signaled a "correct solution" for a possible attack, its captain questioned the information and simply fired six torpedoes on his visual sighting. A half minute later, one torpedo found its way into the side of the ship, but the Nipponese captain and crew sighed in collective relief when the torpedo burst oil and gasoline tanks but initially caused no fire.

Although *Taiho* seemed to shake off what at first seemed to be a minor hit, another American submarine closed in for a shot on a second enemy carrier, the *Shokaku*. Lieutenant Commander H. J. Kossler steered his submarine *Cavalla* into attack range. After confirming that the target was an enemy vessel "with a Rising Sun, big as hell," Kossler fired a spread of six torpedoes at a range of one thousand yards and managed three direct hits. Although Kossler counted near misses from a total of one hundred six enemy depth charges, he heard even stronger rumblings not far away and quickly realized that his torpedo spread was the death knell for *Shokaku*. When fires reached an ammunition bunker packed with bombs, the huge ship virtually disintegrated in a rain of steel.

The *Taiho*, on the other hand, might have been saved if not for the mistakes of a fledgling damage-control officer. The damage to the new flagship seemed minimal after the earlier torpedo hit, but the ship soon reeked of gasoline fumes from the fractured fuel tanks, which had been the only damage inflicted on the ship. The young officer quickly hit upon a solution of ordering every ventilation duct on the ship opened on the assumption that the air currents would suck out the smell. Now the entire ship was covered with an invisible but deadly danger as a single spark from a lit cigarette or repairman's welding arc could be fatal, and the threat became reality at 3:30 p.m., when the engine room virtually disintegrated from a spark, and the ship began a rapid journey into oblivion. One of the few lifeboats that was actually lowered carried Ozawa, his staff, and the emperor's portrait to cruiser *Haguro,* but almost seventeen hundred of the twenty-two hundred members of the ship's crew joined their vessel in death.

The bungled attempt to deal with the mortal danger facing the *Taiho* was being replicated in the air battle at about the same time that afternoon. A raiding party of twenty Zekes and twenty-nine bombers from Japanese Carrier Division Two had been vectored to attack part of the American Fleet at an erroneous location. When the strike leader found nothing but empty sea, he ordered the force to fly to Guam for refueling and new information. As the planes began circling the airbase, a flight of twelve Hellcats from carrier *Cowpens* picked them up on radar and sped toward Orote Field. As fifteen more interceptors joined the mission, several pilots simply joined the enemy landing formation and opened fire. In one of the most one-sided air battles of a one-sided day of combat, the Hellcats shot down thirty Imperial planes and so badly damaged the survivors that not one would ever fly again, for virtually no loss to the American attack force.

Now, as the sun gradually dipped toward the horizon on June 19, 1944, both Japanese and American bombers began to sort out the results of the opening day of the "Battle of the Philippine Sea." Admiral Ozawa had lost the most powerful aircraft carrier in the Imperial Navy and one of the six flattops that had participated in the raid on Pearl Harbor, but he still commanded an impressive fleet of seven carriers and a largely undamaged covey of battleships and cruisers. However, the carriers were now missing much of their primary reason for existence, as three hundred forty planes had been shot down in the roiling aerial duels that defined that day.

On the other hand, Raymond Spruance and Marc Mitscher were confirming results that were beginning to put the battle of the Philippine Sea on a short list of one-sided victories on par with George Washington at Trenton, Andrew Jackson at New Orleans, and George Dewey at Manila Bay. The swirling aerial dogfights of June 19 had resulted in the destruction of only twenty-two American planes shot down, and even with the inclusion of six additional aircraft that had landed but were beyond repair, the men of Fifth Fleet had inflicted an aircraft loss ratio of nearly twelve to one on the Imperial Navy. A total of fifty-eight named personnel, divided about equally between aircrew and deck crew, had lost their lives, while thirty times that number of Japanese seamen had died on *Taiho* alone. Now the major choice that awaited Raymond Spruance was whether to simply maintain his position and fulfill his primary task to protect the Saipan invasion beaches or take a calculated risk and sail eastward to engage Ozawa in a climactic showdown in the middle of the Philippine Sea.

Spruance spent much of the long tropical night of June 19–20 pacing around the flag plot and deck of the *Indianapolis,* torn between his Nimitz directive to protect the invasion beaches and the tantalizing opportunity to engage the now wounded Japanese Fleet in a battle of annihilation. While aircrews exchanged tales of their role in an engagement that was rapidly being called "The Great Turkey Shoot," Spruance gradually arrived at what he believed was a good compromise position. He advised Marc Mitscher that he would support an attack on Ozawa's fleet if "we know his position with sufficient accuracy;" if not, "we must ensure protection of Saipan." The first dawn searches on June 20 returned with no positive sighting of Ozawa, who had actually steamed seventy-five miles further east than the Americans calculated.

Then, as Ozawa carefully maintained radio silence, Marc Mitscher was authorized to keep steaming eastward and send out his longest-range search planes to be equipped with extra drop tanks. Then, at the very late hour of almost 4:00 p.m., an Avenger pilot flew over the tail end of the enemy fleet at the absolute maximum range of American aircraft. Within forty minutes, American carriers had turned into the wind, and, ten minutes later, the first plane in a strike force of more than three hundred aircraft was making the hop from deck to air.

As the massive air armada flew eastward, Admiral Ozawa and his staff were finalizing their after-battle report based on the claims of their surviving aircrew. Unfortunately for the admiral, he was reading one of the most grossly exaggerated battle summaries in the history of naval warfare. The admiral placed his validating signature on a report to the Emperor. The report placed American losses on June 19 at four carriers sunk, six flat-tops badly damaged, five hundred American planes definitely shot down, and four hundred more aircraft badly damaged and probably unable to fly. The consensus in Ozawa's war room was that the enemy would be fortunate to be able to launch one hundred planes and that, after their land-based planes further winnowed that total, the Imperial Fleet would change course, head east, and annihilate the remnants of the Fifth Fleet.

If the Japanese pilots had massively overstated the damage inflicted on June 19, American search planes had moderately underestimated the location of the enemy fleet on the 20th, and, as the afternoon sun began its slow descent, Mitscher's strike force was flying over an empty sea where the Imperial Fleet was supposedly steaming. Finally, sixty miles further west than expected, the first pagoda masts were sighted just as fuel gauges began moving below the critical "half" full mark. Now, with only thirty minutes of daylight remaining for their operation, the Helldivers and Avengers began pulling off in formation as sixty-eight Zeros climbed into the sky to challenge the airspace above Ozawa's task force.

Much of the American strike force quickly located *Zuikaku,* the senior carrier in the fleet, and now the last surviving member of the Pearl Harbor operation became the focal point of attention. The American planes relentlessly pounded the carrier, inflicting a pummeling that initially produced an "abandon ship" order from the vessel's captain. However, heroic work by damage-control parties began to take effect after the raiders began to search for new prey, and the elderly vessel would not meet its fate that evening.

As the *Zuikaku* was added to the American tally for the battle, the pilots searched for new prey among the six still-undamaged Japanese carriers. For twenty minutes in a fast-emerging tropic twilight, Imperial ships turned in tight circles, maneuvered into letter "S's" and threw up a multicolored barrage of antiaircraft fire that ranged from pink to purple.

Ozawa managed to scrape together a still formidable combat air patrol of seventy-five Zeros. That, combined with the intense antiaircraft fire, tended to turn what American pilots thought were fatal attacks into either minor damage or near misses. American torpedo planes did sink carrier *Hiyo,* and the Hellcats shot down fifty of the Zekes in return for a loss of twenty of the American raiders. Now, twilight had shifted into darkness and American aircrews were about to face a new deadly danger: the task of flying home in total darkness across a vast ocean with fuel gauges making their inexorable move toward the dreaded "E" indication.

As the sun sank below the horizon, the aircrews of hundreds of American planes faced a perilous journey of two hundred fifty to three hundred miles eastward to their home ships. Although a few planes dropped into the sea on the return journey, most were still flying as they neared the dark void that should, in theory, be the location of the Fifth Fleet. Then, in one of the most dramatic moments of World War II, the utter blackness of the Pacific Ocean night turned almost dazzling as dozens of lights pierced the dark.

Admiral Marc Mitscher had just made a decision that contradicted every military instinct of a twentieth-century naval commander and ordered every light in his fleet to be turned on. In a mix that was part Christmas pageant, Independence Day fireworks display, and a Hollywood movie premier, deck lights, spotlights, and searchlights beamed skyward. Multicolored flares arched above; star shells sped upward, and glowing lights outlined each carrier flight deck. If there was a miracle for American pilots in the battle of the Philippine Sea, this light show was it, as men who faced a watery grave in the pitch blackness of the ocean soon found themselves guests on ships on which they had never been.

Mitscher's command, "Turn on your lights," would soon rank with "Damn the torpedoes, full speed ahead" in navy lore, as a solitary patch of the Pacific Ocean became Times Square for an evening. Half of the planes that managed to land found the wrong carrier, and some decks featured an "all star team," with as many as nine different carrier crews aboard. Eighty planes either ditched in the sea or crashed on a carrier deck, and forty-nine aircrews either died on landing or ditched too far from the fleet to be rescued. On the other hand, Mitscher's bold gamble had resulted in survival for one hundred sixty other members of the strike force who would fly in future battles.

As the two fleets steamed apart and the prospect of a truly decisive battle receded, Raymond Spruance found himself in a position not totally unlike General George Meade had in the immediate aftermath of the Battle of Gettysburg. Meade had brilliantly orchestrated a defensive triumph that had checkmated Robert E. Lee's invasion of Pennsylvania and left the Confederate Army bleeding from wounds from which it would never totally recover. Yet, after the battle, the telegraph lines sizzled with orders from Washington to annihilate the Rebels before they slipped back across the Potomac River. Now, in 1944, Raymond Spruance had fought and won a defensive battle that badly wounded but did not annihilate the Japanese Fleet. Rear Admiral Alfred Montgomery, commander of Carrier Task Group Two, insisted, "Results of the action were extremely disappointing to all hands, in that important elements of the enemy fleet, which came out in the open for the first time in over a year, were able to escape without our coming to grips with them." Rear Admiral J. J. Clark, commander of Carrier Task Group One insisted, "It was the chance of a century missed." Marc Mitscher summarized the battle with a succinct statement: "The enemy escaped. His fleet was not sunk."

Yet, in many respects, a huge victory *had* been won. Admiral Ozawa steamed into action with four hundred thirty combat planes on his flight decks, and only thirty-five were still operational forty-eight hours later. Three Imperial carriers, including the brand-new flagship, were on the bottom of the ocean. American air losses were negligible, and vessel losses nonexistent. Raymond Spruance was under strict orders from Ernest King and Chester Nimitz to protect the invasion beaches above all else. Now, while effectively protecting those beaches, Spruance had destroyed the offensive power of the same Nipponese air arm that had devastated Pearl Harbor and allowed Imperial forces to run wild in the Pacific. The naval war still had another massive round to go on the far side of the Philippine Sea. Meanwhile, the American landing force on Saipan that Spruance had been charged to protect was fighting its own grim war to the death as American soldiers and Marines found themselves fighting in the houses and fields of an island that was the first battle for what the enemy very much considered part of the Imperial homeland.

CHAPTER X

Showdown on Saipan

The news media attention that swirled around the "Great Marianas Turkey Shoot" gave Americans a new set of naval heroes to fit in comfortably with the newly emerging ground-war stars of the now clearly successful invasion of Normandy. Yet somewhere between D-Day and the Battle of the Philippine Sea, one of the most dramatic ground battles of the Pacific War had begun a relatively short distance from Admiral Marc Mitscher's *Lexington* flag office.

At just past 8:00 a.m. on June 15, 1944, a flotilla of control boats raised the first of a series of colored flags, and twenty-four LCI craft sprinted across a line of departure as crewmen unleashed a fusillade of rockets, machine guns, and automatic cannons at the Imperial defenders of Saipan's coastline. Then a vast fleet of seven hundred nineteen amphibious tractors approached shore, reminding one defender of "the advance of a swarm of grasshoppers." The American invaders riding to shore on the clanking "alligators" may not have fully realized it, but they had left behind the phase of the war that was focused on the reclamation of territories seized by the enemy in the victorious frenzy following Pearl Harbor and were entering an even more heavily contested theater of what

Japanese people thought of as their actual extended homeland inhabited by Imperial subjects.

Saipan was an eighty-five-square-mile island roughly thirteen miles long and six miles wide that was a mix of cornfields and sugarcane plantations linked by several towns and small cities that formed much of the backbone of the Japanese distillery industry. Unlike the almost primeval jungle that faced the American invaders at Guadalcanal and New Guinea, Saipan had towns with movie theaters, baseball stadiums, and radio stations; an island railroad line; and countryside studded with farmhouses.

The mixture of native Chamorro and civilian Japanese residents now shared their island with an Imperial garrison centered on thirteen combat battalions that formed an infantry division, an independent brigade, and, unique to the Pacific War up to that point, a Nipponese tank regiment. Lieutenant General Yoshitsugu Saito commanded this mixed force in his role as commander of the Northern Marianas Army Group and could effectively depend on a combat force of about thirty thousand army and navy ground-force personnel. Saito and his men did not believe they were on a suicide mission, as Admiral Ozawa's A-Go plan for the naval offensive was expected to annihilate the American landing force while they were still fighting on the beaches. Thus, when the first American amphibious tractors rumbled ashore on the morning of June 15, there was every expectation among the Japanese defenders that the Americans were walking into a trap about to be sprung from the sea.

The men allegedly walking into this trap were the members of the Joint Expeditionary Force of Operation Forager, and they centered on the 2nd Marine Division, the 4th Marine Division, and the 27th Army Infantry Division under the command of the already nationally famous magazine cover personality, Lieutenant General Holland Smith. The three assault divisions fielded a little more than sixty-four thousand men and nearly one hundred fifty tanks, many of which were newly designed flamethrower vehicles. The men were very aware of the Allied landing in Normandy only a little more than a week earlier, and many of the GIs and Marines most likely wondered which assault force had the more dangerous task.

Thoughts of any place other than the beach directly in front of them quickly disappeared as the amphibious tractors, supported by a phalanx of one hundred amphibious tanks, hit dry ground along eleven landing beaches on the southeastern portion of the island centered on the town of Charan Kanoa and its twin landmarks of a huge sugar refinery and the soaring towers of the Saipan radio station. Unlike the Omaha and Utah beach experiences nine days earlier, the initial Marine landing on Saipan produced running gun battles between American and Japanese tanks, a duel that swirled right into the streets of Charan Kanoa. This battle was neither the bloodbath of Omaha nor the near walkover at Utah. Eight thousand assault troops landed within the first twenty minutes but were forced to contend with an ingenious network of Japanese spider holes, camouflaged trenches, and long stretches of roadside ditches, all filled with enemy defenders.

By nightfall of Jig Day, the Marines straddled a ten-thousand-yard-wide beachfront and had generally penetrated just under one mile inland from the sea. Nearly two thousand casualties were being tended by beachfront medics or medical teams in three hospital vessels. Soon after dark, the defenders began initiating their now almost traditional night counterattacks, which gained only minor penetrations at the cost of seven hundred Japanese killed and many more wounded dragged inland before dawn.

Soon after sunrise, the Japanese "banzai" attacks ended, and the Marine assault forces began the battle to control the southern half of Saipan Island. Unlike the northern sector, dominated by dense stretches of hills, the southern half of the island was a relatively flat checkerboard of towns, villages, sugarcane fields, and cornfields that painted a backdrop similar to those of many Civil War battlefields eight decades earlier. Fighting for Saipan was neither the experience of the North African desert war nor the Pacific jungle war of 1942 and 1943, and, for the first time in this theater, large numbers of civilians would form part of the cast of characters.

On this sunny, warm Friday morning, the 8th Marine Regiment was pushing along a road flanked on both sides by cornfields and cane fields when large numbers of defenders began popping up and out from the sprawling fields. Some of the Imperial troopers charged forward waving pistols and swords in close infighting that was countered by Marine units specially equipped with pump-action shotguns that poured a deadly spray of buckshot on their Nipponese assailants. In a scene that, at the time, invoked the deadly cornfields at Antietam in 1862, a fast-moving melee turned farmland into a battlefield where the action surged back and forth in a slow-but-deliberate American advance.

As darkness settled over the Saipan farmland, General Saito decided that the time was appropriate for the introduction of his most powerful offensive weapon—the 9th Tank Regiment, which represented the most powerful armored strike force so far in the Pacific islands campaigns. Saito inspected his armored phalanx of nearly fifty tanks and perhaps wondered at the offensive possibilities that might been available to him if nearly sixty additional tanks had joined his command instead of sitting on the bottom of the ocean after an enemy submarine attack on their transport convoy. However, Saito felt that a possibly unexpected night attack with the still substantial contingent that had landed safely on Saipan might be a turning point in the battle, as the A-Go naval operation was nearing its initiation.

Just before midnight on June 16, the phalanx of armor began to assemble with its infantry support forces, and at 3:00 a.m. Saturday, Colonel Tahashi Goto gave the order to advance from his command tank. Goto's objective was the Saipan radio station now in American hands, the capture of which would connect the garrison with the naval portion of the A-Go plan.

Much of Goto's force was centered on the Type 37 Chi Ha tank, which featured a 57mm main gun and two supporting machine guns. The Chi Ha would have been viewed as an obsolescent relic on most battlefields in Northwest Europe that summer, but in the utter darkness of a Pacific island, these armored vehicles might just make a major difference in the attempt to throw the American invaders back into the sea.

Several hundred yards away, Lieutenant Colonel William Jones, commander of the 1st Battalion, 6th Marines, heard a clanking noise that reminded him of shipboard briefings that suggested the presence of nearly two hundred Imperial tanks on Saipan. Now, even a quarter of that number could be decisive against a Marine line of mortar and rifle pits with no immediate tank supports of its own.

Saito expected this armored assault to penetrate to within five hundred yards of the water's edge as a huge wedge between the 6th and 8th Marine regiments, which then could be filled in by Japanese infantry after the armored victory. However, as the tanks clanked through fields and groves of trees, the American defenders quickly sharpened their tank-hunting skills and staged their own nocturnal hunting expeditions with their MIAI bazookas. While these rocket launchers were barely adequate against the Panthers and Tigers of the Wehrmacht, these weapons tore through the thin-skinned Nipponese tanks in a frenzy of destruction that left half of the armored force a flaming wreck. The Marines' task was made even easier when, to the Americans' surprise, the approaching tanks would frequently halt, the crew would jump out and sing patriotic songs and wave their swords, a trumpet would blow, and then the column would move forward through an expanding shooting gallery of startled Marines. Even the Japanese tanks that avoided a fatal bazooka strike returned without the infantrymen who had been sprawled all over the advancing vehicles as the assault force closed with the Marines. These tanks may have survived, but their decks were cleared by the sweeping tracers of the Marine defenders. A parting salute from massed American bazooka teams brought the Japanese loss of their invaluable armored support to thirty-one tanks, while seven hundred Nipponese infantry were found in the field the next morning. Seventy-three Marines had joined their adversaries in death, but Saito's outnumbered garrison could not afford this uneven exchange and still hope to hold Saipan for long.

The night armored attack achieved surprise but little else, and Saito reluctantly ordered a gradual fallback to the much hillier, densely forested northern half of the island. The fortunes of 31st Army were now largely dependent on Ozawa's A-Go naval operation, and, if the plan succeeded as expected, the American invasion force would be placed in a position similar to that of the defenders of the Bataan peninsula two years earlier, trapped between a Nipponese army in front of them and a Japanese fleet behind them, with no hope for reinforcements or supplies. Japanese planning in 1944 was still heavily organized around the "victory disease" caused by Pearl Harbor, with an expectation that any significant naval engagement would surely be a decisive Imperial victory with Midway still viewed as an isolated aberration. However, by the morning of June 22, there was still no sign of Ozawa's "victorious" fleet, and, even through the usual Japanese veil of grossly exaggerated damage claims against the enemy, Saito and his men may have had the first uncomfortable flicker that they just might be on their own against the Yankee invaders.

Meanwhile, on the American side of the battle line, General Holland Smith was facing a critical decision of his own as the Marines left the cornfields and farms behind and advanced northward. Smith's original operational plan envisioned an offensive toward the central highlands, with the 2nd Marine Division picking up the western edge of the high ground, while the 4th Marine Division took responsibility for the eastern sector fronting the Magicienne Bay. However, those two divisions had lost six thousand men in the first week of "Forager," and a large number of these casualties were front-line infantrymen. Smith's Forager complement also included the Army 27th Division, which the Marine General hoped to keep in semipermanent reserve, especially when he became convinced that this unit was not even a very good Army division, let alone a Marine contingent. Holland Smith's strong suit was not tact, and he had evaluated the "Apple Knockers," heavily recruited from upstate New York, as "a silk stocking outfit with an impeccable reputation for annual balls, banquets and shipshape summer camps which contains the entangled roots of home town loyalties, ambition and intrigue and should be broken up and replaced with anyone on earth but former members of the New York National Guard." Now, with this less-than-enthusiastic welcome to a crucial body of reinforcements, another general named Smith entered the battle for Saipan.

Major General Ralph Smith was not actually from New York, but a Nebraskan who had graduated from Officer Candidate School just before American entry into World War I. He had attended the French École de Guerre and was assigned to command the 27th Division in November 1942. He presently commanded a large force of soldiers in what was still viewed as a primarily Navy-Marine operation, and his Apple Knockers were attempting to advance against a hilly center position dominated by Japanese positions that were on even higher ground. Two of Ralph Smith's regiments, supported by the 762nd Tank Battalion, almost immediately collided with Imperial troopers ensconced on the high ground of Mt. Tapotchau, and the assault largely broke apart as the armored forces lost fifty-four of their seventy-two vehicles, which were burning wrecks surrounded by dead and wounded GIs.

As the army units pulled back to their start lines, Holland Smith fumed at Ralph Smith's lack of aggressiveness, even though the two Marine divisions had made only modest gains under somewhat more favorable conditions.

As senior ground-forces officer on Saipan, Holland Smith had every right to sack his army namesake, and in the European theater, several division commanders were fired for roughly the same failure to advance in their assigned missions. However, in this case, it was a Marine commander firing an Army general, and that Marine was also pouring out his feelings to popular news correspondent, Robert Sherwood, who made sure the "Smith vs. Smith" feud quickly made national headlines.

Ralph Smith's relief from command would soon emerge as one of the iconic new stories surrounding Operation Forager, due to its unique "Marine vs. Army" subplot. Ralph Smith would gain a measure of revenge over his Marine superior by receiving choice assignments following his Saipan experience and by living longer than virtually any other World War II general, as he lived until the eve of the new century and passed away at age 102. On the other hand, Holland Smith, in June 1944, may have fired a division commander, but he still faced a ferocious enemy now ensconced on ground that was beginning to be called by both soldiers and Marines "Death Valley" and "Purple Heart Ridge."

Yet, while leathernecks and GIs died by the score attempting to force their way to the high ground that marked the center of Saipan Island, General Saito was sending reports to Tokyo that his army was bleeding to death in this battle, and he would soon be forced to abandon the city of Garapan and make a final stand toward the northern tip of the island.

As Operation Forager extended into July, Saito was frantically cobbling together a new defense line that extended from the western town of Tanapay through the central town of Tarahoho and on to the east coast community of Hashigoru, which allowed the general to deploy his forces on a narrower front.

Ironically, Saito's fallback also proved to be advantageous to the American attackers, as Holland Smith was able to extricate the 2nd Marine Division for the upcoming invasion of neighboring island Tinian and make a final push northward with the 4th Marine Division and 27th Infantry Division moving side by side.

As the Imperial defenders evacuated Death Valley and Purple Heart Ridge to scramble northward for a final stand, the American soldiers and Marines entered a new stage of combat that entailed both rooting out Saito's rear-guard units and processing and disposition of hundreds of Japanese, Korean, and native Chamorro residents who chose to ignore Imperial warnings that the American invaders were Western barbarians who would practice orgies of rape and cannibalism that made suicide a far better option. Yet, as the Imperial defense perimeter gradually contracted, and thousands of noncombatant residents came under American control, these Saipan residents were pleasantly shocked to discover that the "Western barbarians" treated them with civility and compassion. As surrender gradually emerged as an option for the noncombatants on Saipan, a trickle began to turn into a flood, and on the single day of July 6, more than seven hundred civilians crossed over to the American lines while General Saito was establishing his final command post in a cave near the coastal town of Maksunsha on a parcel of high ground that overlooked the scene of the battle.

As Saito's aides set up quarters worthy of a senior officer, the general was joined by Admiral Chuichi Nagumo, the hero of 1941 Japan as the operational commander of the task force that attacked Pearl Harbor. However, after the disaster at Midway, the admiral had been shuttled between a series of low-profile desk jobs and was ultimately exiled to a paper command of naval ground troops who were essentially sailors who could not be utilized on its shrinking Imperial battle fleet.

Despite being senior officers in two services that were far more bitter rivals than their American Army and Navy adversaries, the two men
exchanged pleasantries, surveyed their Spartan headquarters, and waited
for Saito's aide, Major Takashi Hirakushi, to return from an inspection
trip of the shrinking Japanese perimeter. Hirakushi returned with shocking news that key sectors of the line were on the verge of collapse, as
American artillery turned strong points into kindling, and appallingly
large numbers of Nipponese soldiers seemed to have devolved into strag-
glers with little cohesion or unit identity. As Saito gradually shifted from
shock to reluctant acceptance of reality, he uttered to his aide a simple
directive, "It is time to end this battle."

Half a world away, in a battle for Europe fought between Western
cultures, even the fanaticism of Adolf Hitler and his most ardent Nazi
commanders had some limit to their expectations of how far a soldier was
expected to fight before surrender became tacitly recognized as an option.
While German troops were exhorted to "fight to the death," this did not
necessarily mean actual suicide in battle—Wehrmacht troops were honor-
bound to fight "to the last bullet," but, if overrun by superior numbers and
out of ammunition, they were permitted to surrender if all other options
had been attempted. Hitler fumed in his Wolf's Lair at any messages of
mass surrender but reluctantly accepted the reality of the situation if the
defenders had no other option remaining, short of mass suicide.

On the Pacific theater stage, the war was much more a clash between
two still-alien cultures where Americans and their British and Australian
allies initially accepted the reality of an honorable surrender as a last resort
and had moved away from this option only when it became apparent
that the Japanese enemy had little interest in following the spirit of the
Geneva Convention in its treatment of prisoners. Ironically, despite the
horror stories that began to filter out of Japanese-occupied territories such
as the Philippines, on the rare occasion when Nipponese troops were actually captured, the captives were relatively well treated by their victorious
enemies. Yet, by 1944, even though Japan was a modern industrial power,
much of the nation's military psyche was still locked in a medieval world
of samurai warfare, and otherwise educated, urbane men, such as Saito

and Nagumo, could calmly sit in their headquarters cave, drink American whisky, smoke cigarettes, trade stories, and then set in motion a mass suicide that would begin with them and end with what was expected to be the entire military garrison and Japanese civilian population of Saipan.

When Japanese warriors could no longer dream of victory, they next dreamed of an opportunity for a dramatic, glorious death. The ultimate act in this form of theater was *Gyokusai*, which meant "breaking the jewel," and was essentially an ultimate doomsday weapon, a "superbanzai" attack that, if all went well, would ensure that each Imperial warrior killed seven American adversaries before he met his own glorious end. When Major Takashi brought up the issues of the thousands of civilians who had sought shelter in the caves and foliage of the shrinking Japanese perimeter, the general replied brusquely, "There is no longer any distinction between civilians and troops. It would be better for them to join the attack with bamboo sticks than be captured."

The *Gyokusai* operation began in an atmosphere of low-key bantering and goodwill between army and navy as General Saito, Brigadier General Keiji Igeta, Thirty-first Army Chief of Staff, and Admiral Nagumo gathered in the private-quarters section of the headquarters cave and spent much of the night smoking, drinking, and sharing stories of their fondest military memories. Then Saito politely apologized to Major Hirakushi for failing to lead the coming suicide charge and sat on the ground in a rough circle completed by the two other senior officers. Each commander sat cross-legged in full dress uniform with an aide standing behind each man as a special assistant in the Seppuku ritual. The three men drew swords, bared their chests, and began the process of slicing across their stomachs as the junior officers simultaneously shot the men in the head and then burned the bodies to avoid possible desecration by the Americans.

In a very twentieth-century offshoot of this suicide pact, Saito had dictated a mimeographed final order to his garrison to engage in a banzai attack to pledge "seven lives to repay our country as we deliver still another blow to the American devils." Then, as the order was being distributed among the units and individuals who were forming along the coastal road for the human-wave assault southward, the most forward elements of the

American assault face stood in shock and fascination as they saw what was essentially an organized mob about to descend upon them.

In that moment, when darkness and dawn are caught in equal struggle, American troops first heard the sound of thousands of jogging feet just north of them and then gasped in astonishment when the size of the threat first became apparent. One American platoon commander insisted, "At 4:30 hours all hell broke loose. Out from the draw below us came thousands of Japs! It was like a mob after a big football game." A battalion commander preferred a film analogy to the lieutenant's sports allusion: "It was like a movie stampede staged in the old Wild West movies. We were the cameramen. The Japs kept coming and coming and didn't stop. It didn't make any difference that you shot one; five more would take his place."

Lieutenant Colonel William O'Brien, commander of the 1st Battalion of the Apple Knocker's 105th Regiment, assumed a role closer to George Armstrong Custer or William Barrett Travis of the Alamo as he initially faced the approaching wave with two pistols firing at the enemy and yelling encouragement to the men deployed around him. After being hit in the spine, he continued to shout, "Don't give them a damn inch," which soon became his epitaph in a Medal of Honor-winning final stand as the Japanese wave engulfed the colonel.

As the Imperial assault crested like a wave over the American-held coastal beaches, survivors fell back to the streets of newly captured Tanapag town and set up defensive positions block by block and house by house. Naval vessels poured gunfire into the human wave, and almost every American on the beach reverted to rifleman and often parried Japanese bayonets thrusts with the cold steel on the tips of the M-1s. One of the main targets of this swirling melee was a position held by two battalions of the 105th Regiment that were unfortunate enough to be in the direct path of the densest concentration of Imperial attackers. Before the human tide receded, this group of army personnel had lost four hundred men, and five hundred more were wounded, in a hand-to-hand combat that ranged from swords to tommy guns.

Then, just outside of Tanapag, between the coast road and the Saipan rail line, the Nipponese wave began to come within range of a powerful artillery formation of the 10th Marines that carefully determined that the approaching force was not a group of retreating Americans; they then let loose with a broadside of catastrophic impact on the attackers. Some of the gunmen grabbed swords dropped by the attackers and added another swashbuckling touch to a battle that seemed to reach across several centuries of technology.

Finally, like an ocean tide, the human-wave assault began to recede, and in positions that would soon achieve notoriety as "Bloody Run" and "Hara Kiri Gulch," the victorious defenders began to retrieve more than five hundred of their fatally injured comrades, gave medical care to hundreds of more fortunate participants, and began to tally an eventual total of four thousand three hundred eleven Japanese attackers who had indeed participated in a suicide attack. The *Gyokusai* had been as spectacular an operation as General Saito had desired, but rather than killing seven Americans for every Nipponese defender lost, the ratio was closer to nine to one in the other direction. By nightfall of July 7, all of the senior Japanese commanders on Saipan were dead, along with more than 97 percent of their men. Perhaps one thousand Japanese defenders and four thousand more of their civilian contingent were holed up in the northern tip of Saipan, bordering the cliffs of Marpi Point, and many of them were convinced that jumping from the cliffs into the ocean was a more acceptable end than being eaten by the widely acknowledged cannibals of the American assault force.

In a final carnival of death, horrified Americans closing in on Marpi Point in sailing vessels below the cliff watched entire families link arms and jump into the waiting sea. Japanese-speaking translation teams used loudspeakers to beg the survivors to surrender to a victor who would treat them well, and the pleas did receive some response. However, the newsreels of this final mass-suicide pact would bring cheer and joy in Japanese cinemas and stunned disbelief in their American counterparts as civilians in the United States began to seriously wonder whether the Nipponese enemy harbored even small elements of normal human emotions. This attitude would continue to grow as the ensuing battles against the Nipponese took on even more surreal elements, but in the short term, the capture of Saipan would allow another American invasion force to land on nearby Guam and restore the Stars and Stripes to the first American possession to fall captive to the post-Pearl Harbor Japanese tidal wave of victory. The battle for Saipan had ended, and the liberation of Guam was about to begin.

CHAPTER XI

Raising the Fallen Colors

On July 10, 1944, only hours after Saipan had been declared "secured" by the military, an American destroyer scouting possible landing sites on the island of Guam picked up an SOS signal flashed from a mirror and sent a small scouting party to investigate. They soon discovered that the signaler was a modern Robinson Crusoe, Chief Radioman George Tweed, the only living and uncaptured survivor of the Guam garrison taken by the Japanese on December 7, 1941. Tweed was a member of the token one 153-man Marine and Navy garrison that, assisted by eighty native Insular Force personnel, staged an Alamo-like defense of the island against a five-thousand-man Imperial brigade that was sent to take possession of Guam three days after Pearl Harbor.

On December 10, 1941, the tiny garrison deployed along the windows, walls, and roof of the Spanish-mission-style administration building in the town of Agana, and for somewhat longer than an hour an hour dueled with a Japanese invasion force that could ultimately deploy twenty-five times their number. After a furious hour-long firefight, the senior American officer, Navy Captain George McMillan, ordered a ceasefire, largely to prevent a massacre of his command, and then presided over a surrender ceremony in which an American flag that had flown over Guam for more than forty years was replaced by the Rising Sun emblem. In the confusion of the surrender, six sailors dodged enemy patrols and began a deadly game of hide-and-seek with the new masters of the island.

The escape of even a tiny handful of American personnel caused such a loss of face among the Nipponese officers that, for the next thirty-one months, fifty-man Japanese patrols crawled into caves, searched cliffs and trees in the rugged mountains, and tortured or killed any natives remotely suspected of aiding the fugitives. By November of 1942, the single radio in possession of the fugitives had ceased functioning, and one by one, five of the men were caught and executed. Tweed then settled into a solitary existence in which he lost forty pounds, consumed anything remotely edible, and wondered whether his wife had remarried and his sons forgotten him. Using a small 1941 calendar, Tweed kept revising the dates and years and put an "x" on each day, while also wondering whether he had passed the exam he had taken for chief radioman just before Pearl Harbor.

Now, two-and-a-half years later, Tweed found out that his wife had never lost hope for his survival; he had passed his promotion exam; and he was about to collect six thousand twenty-seven dollars in back pay. However, as this plucky sailor was leaving Guam, thousands of his fellow American servicemen were preparing to repay the sacrifice of the Americans and Guamanians who had fought the first battle for the island and to raise the Stars and Stripes once again over the most distant outpost of the American republic.

The plan for the recapture of Guam was still part of the overall Forager operation, but this particular aspect of the campaign was designated "Stevedore," and the personnel involved would compose the Southern Troops and Landing Forces, as Guam was roughly one hundred miles south of Saipan. This island was nearly three times the landmass of the former island but inhabited by a much smaller population of twenty-three thousand residents who were considered American nationals. They intermixed native dialects with English. and half lived in the part Spanish-, part American-style capital of Agana.

The defense of the island was primarily in the hands of Lieutenant General Hideyoshi Obata, who commanded the Japanese 31st Army and had experienced an interesting career, serving as both a cavalry and an air force officer before being assigned to infantry command and studying extensively in Britain, where he attained proficiency in English. The much larger size of Guam would give Obata somewhat of an advantage over his colleague General Saito on Saipan, as Obata would enjoy much more room to maneuver, but this situation was largely negated by the fact that his combined Army-Navy garrison of nineteen thousand was only a bit more than half the size of the Saipan garrison.

General Obata's primary adversary in the battle for Guam would be Major General Roy Geiger, who, like his Nipponese counterpart, had emerged as a ground-force commander by way of earlier air commands. Geiger had achieved household-name status two years earlier in the battle for Guadalcanal as commander of the harried, outnumbered "Cactus Air Force," which had provided crucial air cover to the besieged Marines in the seesaw island battle. Geiger's naval counterpart, Rear Admiral Richard Connolly, held an equally multiexperienced war record, as he had commanded Admiral William Halsey's destroyer screen after Pearl Harbor, transferred to the Atlantic theater in time for the Allied invasion of Sicily, and made it back to the Pacific for the invasions of the Marshalls and the Marianas. He developed a reputation for close fire support that earned him the nickname "Close-in Connolly."

Geiger's invasion force centered on III Amphibious Corps, a force of about fifty-five thousand ground troops attached to the 3rd Marine Division, the 1st Provisional Marine Brigade, and the U.S. Army's 77th Infantry Division, nicknamed the "Statue of Liberty Division." This assault force would be supported by a powerful armored contingent of about two hundred fifty tanks and tank destroyers, which would heavily outgun Obata's armored contingent of thirty-eight tanks.

Guam, like Saipan, represented a multitiered battle environment that formed around the northern plateau dominated by tropical foliage, narrow roads, and even narrower jungle trails. The center region was more densely populated, and the west coast was dominated by the city of Agana; Apra harbor with its American-built navy yard; the Orote Peninsula that contained the Marine barracks; and the town of Agat that fronted Agat

Bay and was the center of an important road network. Last, the southern region was only minimally inhabited and would play only a minimal role in the impending battle.

At dawn on Friday, July 21, the culminating battle for the Marianas began with a well-practiced choreography of an armada of American assault and landing craft moving toward the center part of Guam's west coast. The two initial landing areas, Green and Blue Beaches, centered on the town of Asan, roughly two miles down the road from the capital city of Agana, and Yellow and White Beaches which were on the southern outskirts of Agat about seven miles farther south. The Japanese defenders had nowhere as much firepower as the German contingent astride Omaha Beach six weeks earlier, but the topography still heavily favored the defenders, with the two American assault regiments, the 3rd Marines and 21st Marines, finding themselves separated by a deep gorge in the fork of the Asan River and heavy plunging fire from Japanese guns on Bundschu Ridge that towered over the landing beaches. As Captain John L'Estrange, commander of a contingent of thirty amphibious landing craft insisted, "It was the high ground that turned the beach into an inferno." The Marines found themselves fighting a battle in a natural amphitheater, with a river gorge limiting their ability to maneuver.

Meanwhile, about seven miles down the coast, the Southern Assault Force formed around General Lemuel Shepherd's 1st Provisional Marine Brigade quickly found itself in a different sort of difficulty. While the Imperial defenders along the Asan beaches contented themselves with pouring fire down on the adversary from their higher ground, their comrades to the south engaged the invaders right at the ocean's edge while supporting fire belched from a line of pillboxes and artillery batteries deployed on the Orote Peninsula that jutted out to sea, a few hundred yards north of the invasion beaches. Soon, twenty-six assault vessels were in flames from this enemy crossfire, while most of the supporting American artillery was still aboard ships, waiting for an opportunity to discharge their vital cargo.

Almost as soon as the sun slipped into the sea, the defenders of Guam began assembling for the almost obligatory night counterattack. General

Takahina Takeshi, commander of the 29th Division that formed the bulk of the Imperial garrison, used the high ground of the Fonte Plateau just inland from the invasion beaches as a staging area for an infantry-armor assault on the still-shallow American front. Imperial tanks began clanking down Harmon Road to support the infantrymen. The night of July 21–22 turned into a massive nocturnal shootout in which Marine defensive positions were overrun, recaptured, and overrun again. Shermans and Japanese Chi-Ha's dueled in darkness interspersed with star-shell bursts from the guns of the American fleet. Marine bazooka teams slipped behind the enemy tanks and destroyed six of the Japanese tanks and damaged several others.

By dawn on Saturday, six hundred dead Japanese troops lay intertwined with fifty American GIs and Marines, while four hundred Imperial troops limped or were carried to primitive medical facilities in exchange for one hundred Americans receiving more sophisticated treatment. Despite wildly inflated Japanese claims of "annihilating" much of the invasion force, their own 38th Regiment, which was the keystone of the southern defense force, was effectively decimated.

By dawn of July 22, the second day of Operation Stevedore, the American invaders had secured a foothold on Guam at a loss of roughly twelve hundred men that constituted only a small portion of the available manpower for the operation but included a fairly substantial percentage of the front-line assault companies. The Americans had total control of the air, a massive superiority in armor, and an unchallenged fleet providing fire support. However, the Japanese still held several ridge lines and the symbolically important locations of the pre-1941 American presence on Guam. Given these two realities, the first significant American post-invasion operation focused on the recapture of the prewar administrative infrastructure from the Piti Navy Yard down to the Marine Barracks on the Orote Peninsula, followed by a northward drive from the capital of Agana City to the tip of the island.

The first tangible signs of American progress emerged on the second day of the operation, Saturday, July 22, when Captain L'Estrange's company and the 9th Marine Regiment pushed down the main west coast highway and fought their way into the Piti Navy Yard halfway between their invasion beaches and the jutting mass of Orote Peninsula to the south. L'Estrange felt a tug backward in history as he walked into a now disused naval office building and spotted a calendar on a desk that was still opened to December 7, 1941.

While the 9th Marines secured Piti Yards, the 22nd Marines were pushing northward from their invasion beaches to the heavily defended outskirts of the town of Agat. The presence of much of the garrison's remaining armored force extended the battle into Sunday morning, but, as reinforcements and American armor began to arrive, the invaders were finally at the point of securing the Orote Peninsula and linking northern and southern attack forces together for the drive into that key portion of Guam's defenses.

General Takeshi was not about to allow Orote to fall without a ferocious battle, and, while his forces deployed near the gateway to the peninsula were expected to hold the Americans at bay for much of Monday and Tuesday, the general was busy organizing a major infantry-tank offensive for the predawn hours of Wednesday, July 24. Takeshi had hoarded an impressive armored reserve of twenty-five tanks to act as the tip of a multi-battalion strike just as the Americans were in the middle of a wide pivot to swing into the Orote Peninsula. The armored strike force would receive substantial support from Captain Yutaka Sugimoto's still largely intact 54th Naval Landing force, which promised to be a worthy opponent to the American sea-soldiers.

General Takeshi was so committed to the counterattack that he finally decided to support the armored and naval infantry units with almost anyone else who could possibly fight even if they had already been badly wounded. Takeshi walked through the primitive medical facilities and exhorted his men to battle even if they were reduced to a single arm or leg. Those men who could not actually fire a weapon were issued swords, knives, or baseball bats to produce a contingent that bore an eerie resemblance to the battle preparations for an American 1950s teen gang war.

Just after midnight on July 26, 1944, the Imperial counterattack lurched into motion as assault troops, liberally plied with generous amounts of spirits, moved downward from their positions on the Fonte Plateau toward newly captured American positions centered on Agat's harbor facilities. Unlike the "super banzai" attack on Saipan, where the senior Imperial commanders were more intent on their own suicides than on the outcome of the assault, Takeshi had carefully organized this gambit and felt that both sheer weight of numbers and the presence of considerable armored support could split the American assault force in two. The Japanese attackers had the initial advantage of attacking downhill, and one of the first American units to feel their impact was the Reconnaissance Company of the 9th Marines, which was deployed between the left flank of their regiment and the right flank of the 21st Marines. As the enemy troops poured downhill toward the Americans, the defenders picked off some of the initial contingent, lost several of their own men in the process, and then gradually backpedaled toward friendly units that were already forming behind them. Baseball bats and swords clashed with bayonets and M-1 rifles along a staggered battle line that was swathed in the flames of the heavier guns from both sides.

The sheer weight of the attackers punctured the line between the two Marine regiments, and the Imperial troopers rushed through the gap toward the beach, intending to destroy the American supply dumps and headquarters. One group pushed into the 3rd Marine Division field hospital and began rampaging through the grounds as walking-wounded carried more seriously wounded comrades toward a last stand on the beach. Soon Navy corpsmen were forming skirmish lines with their M-1 carbines, while two companies of pioneers were rushing up from the beach to assist the medical personnel. At least forty wounded Marines who were not carrying their more seriously wounded comrades to the beach joined the cobbled-together defense line, and at least one of the men had managed to hang on to his Browning automatic rifle during his hospital stay. Only three patients and medical personnel had been killed when the Pioneers arrived to push the banzai force back into the woods, while the doctors and corpsmen began treating the thirty men wounded in this one episode in the night assault.

Like the "breaking of the jewel" on Saipan, the banzai assault on Guam was an utter disaster for the attackers. Japanese casualties edged toward almost four thousand killed in action, including almost every officer who took part in the operation, ultimately including General Takeshi, who was killed by an American tank while directing the Japanese withdrawal from their Fonte Plateau starting point. Imperial headquarters in Tokyo commended the sacrifices of the assault force and accepted the wildly exaggerated claims of American casualties from the few officers who survived the assault. In reality, more than two hundred American troops had been killed and probably twice that number wounded, but the Japanese could not for long trade fatalities at a rate of fifteen or twenty to one. Even Imperial headquarters hinted at this in their commendation as they encouraged General Obata, 31st Army commander, to revert to entirely defensive measures as he assumed responsibility for the command of Guam in the wake of the banzai assault.

On the other hand, the American command staff was overjoyed that their Nipponese counterparts had managed to essentially throw away the offensive capability of their garrison on a reckless gamble, and they now felt the time was opportune to smash their way onto the Orote Peninsula. The Guam garrison in 1941 had been overwhelmed by far superior forces and compelled to watch in dismay as their commander lowered the American colors from the flagstaff of the Marine barracks, the first military surrender of the Pacific War. Now, brother Marines, supported by equally determined soldiers, were about to pour into the Orote Peninsula, and one of their major objectives was to restore the colors on the flagpole in front of that same building.

On July 27, only hours after the last elements of the enemy banzai attack was snuffed out, the American forces succeeded in sealing off the Orote Peninsula from the rest of Guam, and the 1st Provisional Marine Brigade penetrated the first line of Imperial defense. The first objective, the Marine barracks, was roughly halfway out on the 2.5-mile-wide peninsula, situated on high ground that was partially fronted with a mangrove swamp and a number of coconut tree groves that concealed the first line of Japanese defenders. While part of the assault force engaged in a massive firefight with the Imperial defenders, American Marines and Army armored units and ground troops crouching from heavy fire picked their way through a maze of trenches and pillboxes that were deployed along the coastal roads of the peninsula. Ironically, the ruined Marine barracks and the high ground surrounding it emerged as the strongest defense point on the peninsula.

Friday, July 28, the one-week anniversary of the landing on Guam, emerged as the turning point in the battle of Orote Peninsula, as American forces used the main coast road on the northern tip of the peninsula to push armored forces above both the barracks and the airfield and forced much of the enemy garrison back toward the northern tip of the peninsula. By dusk, the Marines had picked their way onto the barracks grounds and secured the rifle range just a bit further south, as artillery and tank fire gradually pushed the defenders even further toward Orote Point and eventual destruction.

Finally, at just a few minutes before 4:00 p.m., American units stood on the parade ground while "To the Colors" was played on a captured Japanese bugle. General Lemuel Shepherd, commander of the 1st Provisional Marine Brigade, took a long look at the battered headquarters building and gave one of the most important speeches of his long career that had begun in the trenches of World War I and would end in the Marine Commandant Office with his being a four-star general. "On this hallowed ground, you officers and men of the 1st Marine Brigade have avenged the loss of our comrades who were overcome by the numerically superior enemy three days after Pearl Harbor. Under our flag, this island again stands to fulfill the destiny as an American force in the Pacific." At a cost of one hundred fifteen killed and seven hundred wounded, the battle for Orote Peninsula had avenged the sacrifice of the one hundred fifty-three men who had faced an overwhelming invasion two and a half years earlier, and only one additional gesture needed to be fulfilled.

As Colonel Shepherd was speaking in front of the Marine barracks, Captain Charles Moore, Jr., U.S.N, Admiral Spruance's executive officer, was flying back from the United States on a special mission. Moore's father, Lieutenant Charles Moore, U.S.N., had been present at the raising of the first American flag over Guam when the island was seized from Spain in the War of 1898. Moore, Jr., had been personally delegated by Spruance to return to Washington to fetch the original flag hoisted over the island and return the ensign to be raised anew over the now largely wrecked building. The return of this flag symbolized to the twenty-five thousand Guamanian residents their at best difficult and at worst hellish experiences as part of the Greater East Asia Co. Prosperity Sphere, now in its final days.

Yet, for the moment, Imperial forces still held large swaths of the embattled island, and General Hideyoshi Obata, commander of 31st Army, was determined to ensure that the approximately half of the garrison that still survived would make the Americans pay to fully occupy their former possession. The action was now shifting northward, as the capture of the Orote Peninsula and the gradual push across the Fonte Plateau forced Obata to deploy his surviving forces along a new defense line extending from the town of Dededo just east of Tumon Bay across the ridge of Barrigoda just inland from the island's east coast. Those two towns were about ten miles below the northern tip of Guam but only half that distance from the spot Obata had chosen for his final stand: the high ground of Mt. Santa Rosa, a few hundred yards inland from the east coast.

General Obata's only orders from Tokyo were to extend the defense of Guam as long as possible and inflict the heaviest possible casualties on the invaders before organizing some sort of final banzai attack at his discretion. Obata intended to replicate the Saipan operation by withdrawing across successive lines of defense until he reached Mt. Santa Rosa, but he faced the difficulty of defending a wider island with far fewer first-line combat troops than his colleagues on Saipan.

Meanwhile, General Roy Geiger prepared his northern offensive with precise detail and careful planning. First, units from the 77th Infantry Division were dispatched to the southern tip of Guam to ensure that Obata had not hidden significant units that would smash into the American rear as Geiger's men pushed northward. Once it was apparent that the south was clear, the army regiments were swung northward to link up with the 3rd Marine Division for a powerful thrust northward from the now American-controlled center of the island.

On July 31, 1944, the American northern offensive began as troops swung out from Agana and moved north as they gradually spread eastward. The northern half of Guam featured substantially more challenging topography than the only moderately wooded south, as the combination of dense vegetation, hilly terrain, and fewer roads than the more densely populated south created a battlefield with few landmarks, limited visibility, and fewer opportunities to utilize the attackers' devastating artillery support. Yet, northern Guam was not trackless jungle, and Army and Marine tanks and other vehicles could support the drive if and when the engineers and foot soldiers could clear the narrow roads of the thousands of mines the enemy had planted to delay the advance.

The small-scale battles along the few available roads turned into a major firefight when the Americans arrived on the outskirts of the eastern flank town of Barrigada, which contained a huge reservoir and major water pumping facility that both sides needed. A combined tank/infantry force of soldiers and Marines smashed into a determined contingent of Imperial troops who were expected to hold this position long enough to form a reserve line to the north. As Stuart light tanks approached a nearby Buddhist temple, Chi-Ha's swung into action from behind a heavily walled greenhouse that adjoined the reservoir. The battle swung back and forth in the twilight hours of August 2 and ended in at least a temporary stalemate as the Americans held the water works, and the Japanese still deployed in the adjacent town.

The battle around Barrigada and its valuable waterworks was a test of wills between American and Japanese soldiers, but it also demonstrated that the "Smith versus Smith" Army-Marine controversy on Saipan was not about to be repeated on Guam. The commander of the 77th Army Division, General Andrew Bruce, was a hard-fighting graduate of Texas A&M, who, like many of his Marine compatriots, had spent part of the prewar era in Panamanian jungles fighting in close quarters with little sense of a front line. Now Bruce readily secured General Geiger's permission to virtually ignore his own flanks and simply ordered the combined forces of GIs and leathernecks to ignore small pockets of enemy resistance and lunge for the main body blocking the road northward. Army and Marine Shermans lumbered toward the reservoir while 155mm "Long Tom" guns dropped shells on Imperial formations. The remnants of the troops and tanks around the reservoir were forced back toward their last stronghold at Mt. Santa Rosa.

By August 8, an attack force of eight Army and Marine regiments was spread across the width of Guam, while air strikes and the guns of battleships, cruisers, and destroyers pummeled the retreating Nipponese forces. Yet, the dense foliage of northern Guam nullified much of the American advantage and reduced much of the battle to small-unit actions, as American transportation personnel attempted to link the assault regiments in some form of coherent formation. Even as the often intermixed Army and Marine units plunged ahead, the defenders were still able to cobble together occasional infantry-armor counterattacks that temporarily forced the Americans into a defensive posture. Yet, as the invaders ground inexorably northward, General Obata began to dither on whether he really wanted to make Mt. Santa Rosa his final stand or attempt to pull back another six miles to Ritidian Point, the absolute tip of Guam. Yet, Obata's decision began to matter less and less, as the general was losing the ability to communicate with increasingly fragmented units, and the general himself remained ensconced on Mount Mataguac, about three miles west of Santa Rosa.

On the morning of August 8, all three regiments of the 77th Infantry Division converged on Santa Rosa and stormed into a headquarters area covered with five hundred corpses but no live defenders. Apparently most of the Japanese troops had decided to meet their fates on some other point on Guam. The next morning, a Japanese armored contingent of five tanks lurched into a predawn assault on nearby Marine positions, and the leathernecks consolidated a little further to the rear to deflect the attack. The battle for Santa Rosa had, in effect, fizzled out as the surviving Imperial troops simply melted into the jungle.

Three days later, a battalion of the 306th Infantry overran Obata's personal headquarters on Mt. Mataguac just after the general committed suicide after a final message to headquarters in Japan. The *Gyokusai* that the Americans both expected and somewhat dreaded had never occurred, and intelligence estimates suggested that more than seven thousand Japanese soldiers had simply melted into the jungle, eventually to fight to the death in a lonely duel or occasionally surrender to the new conquerors. Now the American flag once again flew over an American territory that would ultimately emerge as an important base in the Cold War to come. Roughly twelve hundred Marines and two hundred soldiers had died in Operation Stevedore, while more than eighteen thousand Japanese defenders had paid the ultimate sacrifice for their emperor. The American capture of Saipan's neighboring island, Tinian, sandwiched between Forager and Stevedore, had exposed the Japanese home islands to a ferocious new danger, the B-29 Superfortress, which could now fly from its new Marianas bases and rain destruction on the Nipponese homeland with final incendiary and then nuclear weapons. With Chester Nimitz's navy now poised in the Marianas, and Douglas MacArthur's army peering northward from the tip of New Guinea, it was obvious to both sides that the next Pacific war headline would emanate from the region of the Philippines, as MacArthur's pledge to return would dominate the next campaign. One more great sea battle remained in 1944, but before that moment, the eyes of the free world would be riveted on France and the battle to restore the tri-color flag to the highest points of the City of Light.

CHAPTER XII

Days of the Liberators

On Wednesday morning, June 7, 1944, D-Day was officially over, and what would soon be called the Normandy Campaign was about to begin. The Allies had landed successfully over a fifty-mile swath of beachfront which was not yet a complete battlefront subject to possible ferocious enemy counterattacks. The Anglo-Canadian and American landing armies were now on French soil, but each force faced particular challenges different from the other. The British and Canadian forces had been assigned the better battleground in terms of terrain, as the country around the key city of Caen was generally flat farmland or gently rolling landscape that was relatively easy to traverse. However, the ease of movement had attracted most of the ten German armored divisions that were eager to duel the often inferior Allied tanks over this countryside. Their Panzer IV, Panther, and Tiger tanks could outgun most of the Cromwells, Churchills, and Shermans that British and Canadian forces would employ, and German Panzer commanders were eager for the battle to begin.

At first glance, the land around Utah and Omaha beaches appeared to be fairly similar to that of their British-Canadian. The first ten miles inland from the beach was relatively open if more sprinkled with bogs, marshes, and rivers than the British-Canadian battlefield. However, like a

Grimm Brothers fairytale, the cheerful summer tableaux near the beaches changed abruptly into a sinister maze of "hedgerow" country, a natural series of fortresses with a German enemy seemingly behind every corner. Here, that mainstay of so many Civil War battles, the sinister "sunken road" that always challenged the attack force, linked up with a bevy of hedges that had been designed by French farmers to keep their livestock in and were now utilized by German soldiers to keep the Americans out of the interior of France.

During the first days of the Battle of Normandy, the greatest victory the Allies achieved was the simple act of landing an assault force that largely defied comparison to any previous amphibious operation. The Allies soon landed eight hundred seventy-five thousand men and one hundred fifty thousand vehicles centered on British Second Army's fifteen divisions and American First Army's thirteen divisions that faced four hundred thousand defenders who had to rely on the terrain and their superior tanks for any hope of slowing down the enemy drive inland. The two senior American commanders, Dwight Eisenhower, supreme commander of all Overlord forces, and Omar Bradley, commander of American First Army, were initially filled with optimism when the enemy failed to throw the invaders from the beaches on June 6 and when "Lightning Joe" Collins's forces swept northward up toward Cherbourg from the Utah beach landing zone. However, Collins's divisions were merely in search of a good port and harbor to sustain the army; in reality, the drive for Cherbourg took much of Collins's army away from the interior of France. The drive inland on the "mainland" front of Overlord had to go on through the hedgerows, and the German defenders felt that they could hold this terrain indefinitely. While Dwight Eisenhower's position as Supreme Commander forced Ike into a more global view of all Allied operations, Bradley's world was the GI's world, and from general down to private, this world had, at least temporarily, been reduced to the perspective of the nearest enemy-held hedgerow. Lieutenant General Omar Nelson Bradley's initial environment was the small-town world of the son of a Missouri schoolteacher with a meager salary that turned to no salary when he died. Bradley escaped a future of rural poverty when he secured an appointment to West Point in a plebe class that also included Dwight Eisenhower. Like Ike, Bradley largely missed out on combat in World War I but had secured a number of career-advancing staff appointments that by 1942 had made him deputy commander to Eisenhower in the North African campaign. The bespectacled Missourian spent most of 1943 commanding II Corps from Tunisia to Sicily and then was ordered to England for a senior command in Overlord.

Bradley's bookish appearance and, on the surface, mild demeanor caught the attention of correspondents, who carried generally favorable stories about the "GI's general"; their reports overlooked the reality that Bradley was potentially as ruthless and ambitious as any other commander. Now Bradley's temper was fraying, as the initially successful drive inland was threatening to devolve into a World War I-era stalemate against the backdrop of an American high command and general public who expected the most motorized army in the history of warfare to use all of those vehicles to speed in the general direction of Adolf Hitler's Wolf's Lair.

For a time, in high summer of 1944, Overlord developed into the Battle of the Bocage, a hedgerow war in which young American junior officers nicknamed "ninety day wonders," after the course length of the Officer Candidate School, were commanding small units of Americans against equally young German junior officers who used clever cover and concealment to turn each hedgerow into a minifortress. Contrary to the most pessimistic accounts in the American press, the GIs were not exactly stopped cold, but every time they managed to capture an enemy hedgerow, another, almost identical, one appeared in front of them. Meanwhile, in Bradley's First Army headquarters, the Missourian could easily detect in Army Air Force reconnaissance aerial photos that the hedgerows *did* have a finite limit, but the major problem was to break out of this bleak country sometime before the relatively dry campaign season ended.

Bradley's big prize beyond the hedges was Brittany and its desperately needed ports and harbors, and, as the boscage-country shootouts reverberated through the summer air, the Missourian was busy piecing together a plan designed to break out from the current position around St. Lo to the city of Avranches, the gateway to Brittany and the sea. The code name for this operation was Cobra, and, if all went well, the American forces would see not only the ocean but perhaps the Eiffel Tower before the end of the summer.

Six weeks after D-Day, the American First Army revolved around four multidivision corps, of which VII and VIII Corps would be the lead units for Cobra. Much of the responsibility for the American breakout from the hedge war rested on J. Lawton Collins, the veteran of the Pacific War who had gained significant victories from Guadalcanal to Cherbourg. Collins was energetic, popular, and extremely open to suggestions from any member of his VII Corps.

Collins's divisions, covered on the flank by the men of General Troy Middleton's VIII Corps, would be the nucleus of a fourteen-division breakout of almost one hundred fifty thousand men along a relatively small sector of the German defense line in Normandy. The assault troops were encouraged to supplement their "official" weapons with fast-firing Browning automatic rifles and Thompson submachine guns and would be aided in breaking out of the hedges by clever additions to standard Sherman tanks. One of the most important new devices was the brainchild of a sergeant in the 102 Cavalry regiment, Curtis Culin. Culin insisted that the steel beams the enemy had placed on the invasion beaches to rip the bottoms out of landing craft could be recycled into "tusks" that could be attached to the front of Sherman tanks that would then rip through enemy-held hedges. Over five hundred of these converted "Rhino" tanks would be ready to literally rip open the front when Cobra commenced.

Omar Bradley's breakout plan was based on the expectation that the attacking force could smash through the enemy front lines before the Germans could fully react, and much of that activity was based on the Army Air Force promise to bomb St. Lo with more than sixteen hundred planes at the opening of the battle. At 1:00 p.m. on July 24, the aerial armada appeared over a battle site that was almost entirely clouded over, and, while some planes were recalled and others actually hit enemy targets, enough bombs fell "short" and killed or wounded more than two hundred American troops. The next day, a theoretically better planned bombing operation in slightly better conditions systematically tore apart the elite Panzer Lehr division, killing or wounding nearly 70 percent of the German personnel. Unfortunately, confusion in orders between air and ground units resulted in six hundred American casualties with one hundred or more deaths, including that of Lieutenant General Lesley McNair, Commander of Army Ground Forces who had been visiting several units and asked to view the operation as close to the front as possible. Despite these losses to "friendly fire," the American assault force was able to advance more than a mile into enemy territory and set the stage for a massive breakout the next day.

Wednesday, July 26, 1944, turned out to be a key moment in the liberation of France and its capital city. Collins paired together an impressive strike force of the 1st Infantry Division and the 2nd and 3rd Armored Divisions that poured down a key road network under the cover of American Thunderbolt fighter-bombers. Sherman tanks were drafted as pickup armored personnel carriers as GIs clutched any handhold they could locate, and eight or nine men somehow found room as their powerful "bus" pushed through German lines far faster than marching speed.

One by one, key French towns slipped into American control—St. Gilles, Coutances, Morigny, all changed hands as German forces sought an escape exit. Sometimes a German Panther would appear briefly, fire a devastating round that turned an American tank into a flaming wreck, and then desperately seek cover from the ubiquitous Thunderbolts diving from the sky. On July 29, one group of P-47s hit the jackpot when they flew over a German traffic jam of five hundred German tanks, trucks, and half-tracks that tied up one of the roads that led to the battle area. As one formation ran out of ammunition and flew off, a new one quickly arrived to replace it in an aerial massacre that left one hundred twenty tanks and two hundred sixty-six other vehicles smoldering or flaming wrecks.

Meanwhile, the men and vehicles of Das Reich, the 2nd Panzer Division, slammed up against an American armor and infantry roadblock on the road to Coutances. These SS tankers had spent much of the war leaving a trail of atrocities over much of Europe, with their most publicized handiwork the massacre of the entire population of the town of Oradour-sur-Glane, who had the misfortune of merely being in the path of the tankers on their way to Normandy beaches. Now the black-clad tankers found themselves pitted against people who could actually fight back, and in a series of firefights from one crossroads to another, the Panzers dueled with American 105mm cannons, M10 tank destroyers, and Shermans, while fighter-bombers nipped at the German flanks. When the melee ended, Das Reich had lost their division commander and most of their tanks in a one-sided engagement in which German losses outnumbered Americans fifteen to one.

Operation Cobra had not only decimated perhaps the most hated military unit in the Western theater but damaged or destroyed more than two-thirds of the entire mobile power of the German Seventh Army and opened the way for a race to both the Atlantic Coast and Paris in the near future. German troops were still relentless in defense, but, when the action spilled over from the hedgerows to more open country, Allied airpower usually gave the edge in the ground battle to the Americans. The Germans seemed to be on the run, but more than once in the European war, the Wehrmacht turned on its pursuers and inflicted a bloody nose on their adversaries.

As Adolf Hitler processed the collapse of his Normandy front, his intelligence reports indicated the return of one of the Americans' most feared commanders, George S. Patton. That scion of a wealthy Confederate family had almost seized defeat from victory in both North Africa and Sicily by a pair of slapping incidents in military hospitals where the general was unable to control his volatile temper and nearly found himself packed off to an obscure post in America with a job as a supply officer. However, Patton did manage to regularly beat German armies, and, while Dwight Eisenhower warned him that his lack of self-discipline was still a major issue between them, the volatile general now found himself back in command of the superb Third Army. Patton, now a general whose high-pitched, squeaky voice and permanently brown, tobacco-stained teeth stumps belied a genuine ability to both motivate troops and scare enemies, was on the move to capture the port city of Avranches and the Breton peninsula, which would prove an excellent launchpad for a drive into the heart of France.

Meanwhile, several hundred miles to the east at Wolf's Lair in Rastenburg, Germany, Adolf Hitler carefully followed Patton's progress and evaluated his military potential in the context of the American Western films that the Fuehrer still idolized. Hitler saw the Third Army commander as a saloon poker player or riverboat gambler who was reckless, self-absorbed, and overconfident and who "doesn't care about risks and acts as if he owned the world." The German dictator insisted that Patton was overplaying his hand, and the German Army was about to teach him a lesson in humility. The lesson would be Operation Luttich, which would turn the long weeks of German retreat into a major renewal of fortune for the hard-pressed Wehrmacht.

Adolf Hitler used his extensive knowledge of American Western movies to attempt an analysis of Patton's probable objectives. The Fuehrer insisted that the Third Army commander was a "Cowboy general," who was tempting fate by leaving part of his force isolated or overextended, a detachment that would now be the first victim in a planned German counteroffensive. Through an impressive sleight of hand, four German armored divisions that had been contesting the British advance in the eastern part of the battlefield were pulled off the line and sent west to smash into American units advancing into the town of Mortain.

This picturesque town of two thousand people featured cobblestone streets that led out to nearby high ground that, at its peak, offered a breathtaking view of the provinces of Normandy, Brittany, and Maine, and on a clear day a glimpse of the Atlantic Ocean. The defensive linchpin of Mortain had the dull military title of Hill 314, which was soon occupied by a battalion of the American 30th Division. These GIs were members of the "Old Hickory" division that boasted a lineage back to service with Andrew Jackson at the Battle of New Orleans in its 117th Regiment and a link to Pickett's Charge at Gettysburg with a 120th Regiment that could be traced back to the 1st North Carolina Confederate regiment. Now, those troops found themselves thousands of miles from American battlefields, occupying a region referred to locally as "Norman Switzerland," due to its majestic peaks. Roughly six hundred of these men now occupied Hill 314—three companies of GIs that would soon face the armored might of Hitler's new offense.

At a few minutes past midnight on August 7, 1944, the most alert of "Old Hickory" heard an insistent rumbling noise just below their position. What they heard was the sound of two dozen German tanks leading an infantry force into an attack on the town of Mortain. By morning, the American soldiers in town were either dead, POWs, or scrambling for higher ground as the German victors celebrated the first victory in Operation Luttich. The GIs above on Hill 314 were becoming an American island in a sea of German field gray. Yet, unlike sieges in earlier wars, the Americans still had a direct connection to friendly forces through radio transmissions between the GIs and fighter-bomber pilots circling above them.

One by one, the outer positions of the defenders were overrun, and the defenders of Hill 314 found themselves in a slowly contracting circle. While each German attack whittled down the garrison by a few more men, American air strikes were inflicting far more German casualties with no substantial breakthrough. As Hitler analyzed reports in Wolf's Lair, he became increasingly obsessed with the battle, which now bore some resemblance to settlers circling their wagons against hostile Indian attacks in his favorite film genre. Units that were beginning to achieve success in other areas of the Luttich battle were reassigned to the battle for Hill 314. Hitler, in his frequently self-contradictory manner, gave orders that other units should push right to the sea at the same moment those forces were cannibalized to feed the Mortain attack. In turn, as those units pushed eastward, Allied Thunderbolts, Mustangs, Typhoons, and Hurricanes began circling over them, blowing men and vehicles to pieces. When the fighter-bombers ran low on fuel, their place in the air was taken by hundreds of Flying Fortresses that destroyed German ground units from a higher altitude.

While the small garrison on Hill 314 had no hope of defeating the German offensive entirely on their own, their position was rapidly being improved by events far from Mortain. First, on August 8, First Canadian Army launched Operation Totalize, an offensive aimed at capturing Falaise, over twenty miles inland from the current battlefield. Then, elements of Patton's army captured the city of Le Mans, which prevented the 9th Panzer Division from adding its heft to the Mortain operation. Suddenly, Hill 314 seemed more of a trip for the attacker than the defenders, and by Saturday morning, August 12, American scouts spotted two shocking realities: the ground below Hill 314 was empty of live Germans, and a relief force of GIs was just arriving on the scene. At a cost of just under twenty-five hundred casualties, including one hundred sixty-five killed, the 30th Division had blunted a massive German counteroffensive that had cost several Panzer divisions most of their tanks and supporting vehicles. Even more important, while Hitler was focusing on Mortain, George Patton's XV Corps had burst through weakened German units and was initiating an offensive that would not stop until American troops were marching through the Arc de Triomphe in Paris.

The commander of XV Corps, General Wade Hampton Haislip, was a namesake of two important Southern generals who each made their mark on military history. General Wade Hampton, Sr., was a South Carolinian who was one of the commanding generals of the largest invasion of Canada during the War of 1812. His son, Wade Hampton, Jr., began his role in the Civil War by organizing a unique combined "legion" of South Carolina infantry, artillery, and cavalry units, and ended the war as one of Robert E. Lee's senior cavalry commanders. Now, the namesake of these two generals commanded a force far larger than either of them had and was emerging as George Patton's "hammer" on a Normandy front that was now cracking wide open. Haislip commanded a mixed force of three infantry divisions: the U.S. 4th Armored Division and the French 2nd Armored Division, the highest-profile unit in Charles de Gaulle's Free French Forces.

As Operation Luttich petered out and multiple British Canadian offensives in the east finally began to shred the enemy line in that area, Omar Bradley and George Patton, while frequently disagreeing over exactly what they wanted to accomplish, decided to unleash Haislip's forces in an attempt to trap much of the German Army in a giant pincer that was just beginning to emerge in the area around Falaise Gap. Omar Bradley and George Patton were about to initiate a debate that would soon spread through the Allied command structure as to whether the major prize in a germinating Allied offensive was the capture of the

German Army north of the Seine River, the liberation of Paris, or some combination of the two goals.

As Frenchmen in both occupied and liberated France celebrated the Feast of the Assumption on August 15, 1944, the debate over future Allied goals was further complicated by the welcome news of Operation Dragoon, the Allied invasion of southern France. On a day that Hitler admitted was "the worst day of my life," an invasion force that included American divisions, the American Canadian Special Services Brigade, regular French divisions, and French underground forces achieved total surprise and overran German coastal defenses from Cannes to Cape Benat on the Mediterranean coast. While German units on this new Southern front reeled from the Allied attacks, Hitler received word that his senior commander in the North, Gunther von Kluge, had disappeared from the battlefield and was feared to have defected to the Allies.

While the field marshal was actually walking across the French countryside on foot after his staff car was destroyed by Allied fire, the Fuehrer had nightmares that his senior commander was secretly negotiating to surrender the entire German Army in the north, and, when Kluge reappeared at his headquarters, he was arrested by military police and ordered to report to Wolf's Lair for "consultations." The field marshal avoided the journey by taking poison, but Hitler responded by appointing a safely ardent Nazi, Field Marshal Walther Model, as the new commander of an army of ninety thousand men that was now being squeezed into a pocket thirty miles by fifteen miles centered on the town of Falaise.

Now, while the capture of Paris loomed ever larger on the horizon, a single road from St. Lambert to Chambois emerged as the center of the Battle of Normandy, as surviving German units traveled down the road to their goal of two still-functioning bridges over the Dives River, while Allied forces attempted to seize the high ground and turn the passage into an avenue of death. As the Allies gradually seized the high ground, a battle mixed with brutality and occasional chivalry raced across the sunlit French countryside. When a long line of German ambulances drove along the road, Allied soldiers on the heights held their fire all the way to the Dives River. Yet, when General Paul Hausser, commander of German

Seventh Army, walked along the road with some of his surviving men, artillery fire fragments ripped into him, and he completed the journey semiconscious on the back deck of a Panther tank. Even Colonel Kurt "Panzer" Meyer, an SS commander who was fortunate to escape postwar execution for his killing of British prisoners, shed his habitual arrogance, ditched his trademark motorcycle, and dodged between rocks and trees until he finally swam the Dives with the last twelve men of his command still fit to fight.

As the Falaise pocket finally swung fully shut, Allied commanders received mixed messages of success. Of the ninety thousand German soldiers caught between the front lines and the Dives River, when the Western front began to crack on August 7, a little more than thirty thousand were being processed as Allied prisoners, and ten thousand more were being buried by Allied graves registration units. However, fifty thousand survivors, including four corps commanders, were now, at least temporarily, safe on the far side of the Dives, and they would form a veteran corps of leaders for Hitler's new "Volksgrenadier" regiments that were sweeping up older men, younger teens, and wounded veterans into a new army to defend the German homeland. On the other hand, the nine invaluable Panzer divisions that had formed the strongest link of the German defense of Normandy had been reduced to a combined twenty-five tanks from their original D-Day force of fifteen hundred. However, while senior Anglo-American commanders congratulated themselves on an impressive victory in Normandy and yet pointed politely accusing fingers at each other for the escape of a relatively large number of enemy soldiers, a relatively junior French commander was about to determine the next objective of the Allied juggernaut budding in France.

Captain Phillipe de Hautercloque had begun World War II as an obscure company commander and been evacuated from Dunkirk to England after the collapse of the Western Front in May of 1940. However, unlike the vast majority of his French comrades who decided to return to France after that nation's surrender, Hautercloque chose to remain in England with the small group of men who joined Brigadier General Charles De Gaulle's army in exile. After changing his name to Jacques Le Clerc to lessen the possibility of German retaliation against his family in occupied France, the captain became a favorite of De Gaulle and was rewarded with command of the French Army's most powerful combat unit, the 2nd French Armored Division.

Le Clerc's assignment to Wade Hampton Haislip's XV Corps paired an officer who viewed himself as a daring incarnation of the Three Musketeers with an American leader who was reared with the legends of the Confederate cavalry in the Civil War. News of the German disaster at Falaise now spurred Charles De Gaulle to utilize his status as a head of state, as well as an army commander, to prod senior American and British officials into reluctant acceptance of the need to liberate Paris before the Germans had the time or inclination to destroy the city. On the other hand, Dwight Eisenhower viewed the liberation of the City of Light as something between a useless diversion and a logistic nightmare, as he wanted to smash German divisions in the field, not feed hoards of hungry Parisians.

However, while Ike carefully planned the next Allied offensive, the Gendarmes of Paris hugely improved De Gaulle's hand when they occupied the police headquarters, raised the French tri-color over it, and dared the German occupiers to come and take down the flag. General Dietrich von Choltitz, the German commander of the city, was a nervous, overweight epicurean who had been enjoying his safe post until this incident but now received direct orders from Hitler to destroy the city using his twenty-five-thousand-man garrison as the agents of destruction. De Gaulle, who now had his eyes fixed solely on the endangered capital, promptly ordered Le Clerc to ignore any Allied order and push his tanks into Paris without delay.

As Hitler fumed and demanded information on when exactly Paris had been put to the torch, French tanks, enjoying massive American armored and infantry support, pushed through gaps in a teetering German defense line and began to make their move toward the City of Light. While Choltitz dithered about the consequences of surrender, German units and Parisians who now realized that they had picked the wrong side in this war began to remove as much booty as possible and streamed out of the city ahead of the Allied tanks. Outside the city, the French tanks, paired with units of the American 4th Infantry Division, rumbled into the outer perimeter of Paris on the evening of August 24 and the next morning entered a city enjoying its first taste of freedom in four years.

On this day that would enter the French calendar as Liberation Day, Charles De Gaulle entered the city as its greatest modern hero, even as pro-German collaborators took pot shots at the adoring crowd. While Dwight Eisenhower and other Allied leaders exhaled in exasperation, the first major objective of Operation Overlord had been accomplished. Paris was once again an Allied capital city. French, British, and American flags were hanging in the summer heat from almost every balcony, and Parisians mended frayed outfits to turn out as proud partners in an Allied victory. For just a little while, visions of a quick end to the war shimmered in the haze, and people remembered the sudden, unexpected surrender of the Kaiser in the previous war. However, as the summer days almost imperceptibly shortened toward autumn, "victory fever" was about to meet the cold reality of a German Army that was not yet a spent force.

CHAPTER XIII

Redemption at Leyte

At twilight of March 11, 1942, a balding, late-middle-aged man wearing a leather bomber jacket clambered onto a creaking, ramshackle dock and took a final look at the stunningly beautiful tropical peninsula that loomed just two miles across the bay. The general then shook hands with his new host, Lieutenant John Bulkely, U.S.N., and ushered his wife, toddler son, and the boy's nanny aboard one of the smallest combat vessels in the American Navy, PT-41. After the hearty command, "You may cast off, Buck, when you are ready," General Douglas MacArthur, commander of all forces in the Philippine Commonwealth, began a dramatic journey through Japanese-infested waters to rendezvous with an Army Air Force bomber that would carry him another fifteen hundred miles to Batchelor Field near Darwin, Australia. Soon after his arrival at the airfield, MacArthur met with American and Australian press representatives and explained that he had been ordered by President Roosevelt to leave the Philippines in order to oversee the establishment of a powerful relief force that would be assigned to throw the enemy back out of the commonwealth. As a final exclamation point to his speech, MacArthur insisted that now that he had successfully journeyed through enemy lines, "I shall return," to orchestrate final victory in the currently besieged islands.

While MacArthur, his family, and many of his senior military officers were now relatively safely ensconced in Australia, the general had left behind a besieged garrison on the Bataan Peninsula and nearly adjacent Corregidor Island, while most of the rest of Luzon and other Philippine Islands were now being integrated into the Japanese puppet empire—the Greater East-Asia Co. Prosperity Sphere. The general had left behind an American contingent of about twenty thousand men centered on a single all-American Army regiment, a badly understrength Marine regiment, provisional brigades of beached sailors and grounded airmen, and an air force of four battered P-40 fighters.

This force was supported by a numerically impressive contingent of almost sixty thousand Filipino soldiers, who, although eager to fight and personally brave, had received almost no actual military training and now, like their American allies, were slowly succumbing to starvation and disease on a Bataan battlefield that had almost no food supply beyond the meager stock brought in from Manila before the enemy began the siege.

The commander of this beleaguered garrison, Douglas MacArthur, was one of the most humorless, egotistical, self-promoting commanders of American forces in World War II, but he was personally supremely brave and fully expected to die fighting in his Corregidor headquarters. Only a presidential order forced his escape, and now he began to bombard Roosevelt with demands for massive reinforcements so that he could go right back to Bataan and annihilate the Nipponese. MacArthur would haggle, threaten, and flatter his commander-in-chief both from a distance and in person, but it would take thirty months for a return to become feasible, and in that time the men he left behind suffered starvation, humiliation, torture, and death that made a mockery of the Nipponese promise that, although they had not signed the Geneva Convention on treatment of prisoners, they would abide by its spirit. Their interpretation of that spirit would produce the Bataan Death March, the most systematic mistreatment of American captives in the nation's military history. Even when the march terminated in assignment to prison camps, Yanks were dying at a rate about two hundred times the rate of their countrymen who had been captured by the Germans.

However, now, in the late summer of 1944, MacArthur was ready to return to the Philippines as he had promised, and he would enter the island of Leyte with more than two hundred thousand ground troops backed by the most powerful naval fleet in history. MacArthur's sense of theater and the dramatic initially implied a landing at Bataan or Manila, but Luzon Island was teeming with Japanese troops who nearly outnumbered his own vast array, and the less-defended beaches of Leyte offered a better initial landing point for a march northward to reconquer the battlefields of 1941–42.

Douglas MacArthur's return to the Philippines would be supported by an invasion force that was larger than any single operation in the Pacific theater up to this point in the war. The general planned to walk ashore very early in the battle, and behind him would come a powerful array of American power typical of the latter stages of World War II. The invasion force would include the 1st Cavalry Division, a militarily robust force that had shed their horses but still maintained a brawny roster of four regiments; the 7th Infantry Division, a regular army unit that had already fought the Japanese in the snow and ice of the Aleutians campaign; the 24th Infantry Division, which had originally been tasked to defend Pearl Harbor, Hawaii, from an expected Japanese invasion and had then crossed the green hell of New Guinea to arrive at the gateway to the Philippines; and the 96th Infantry Division, the only "rookie" outfit among the four initial assault divisions that had drawn excellent reviews in training and now waited for an opportunity to create its own distinctive reputation. Once these units had established a beachhead, they would be joined by the 32nd Infantry Division, which had only recently been involved in the liberation of Guam.

MacArthur's status as Southwest Pacific Theater commander essentially placed all relevant air, naval, and ground forces of that region under his command, so the GIs of this operation were in turn placed under the command of 6th Army commander General Walter Krueger. Ironically, Krueger began his career training to become an officer in the German Army, as his father had held command positions under the kaiser, but, when the younger Krieger's mother was widowed, she had brought her teenage son to America, where Walter was introduced to life in a new army during the Spanish American War and the Philippine Insurrection. Now, like MacArthur, Krueger was returning to the Philippines but at an enormously higher rank than when he left.

All throughout the Philippines in September and much of October, rumors spread among a population still loyal to the United States that MacArthur would soon keep his promise to return, and the word "Leyte" began to achieve even greater prominence. At 6:00 a.m. on Friday morning, October 20, the American bombardment fleet moved into position and plastered the invasion beaches while combat planes flew over five hundred sorties against Imperial defenders who had nowhere near the fortification array that defended Omaha beach four and a half months earlier. Douglas MacArthur, peering through his binoculars on the bridge of the cruiser *Nashville,* noted with satisfaction that "thousands of shells with a roar that was incessant and deafening created ugly pillars of smoke that began to rise on the beaches while overhead swarms of airplanes darted in and out of the maelstrom."

Meanwhile, soldiers less prone to such imagery and viewing the battle from a less Olympian perspective wolfed down their traditional preinvasion breakfast of steak and eggs and clambered down into invasion craft that formed assault lines that looked remarkably like Omaha or Utah beach activities. As the landing craft arrived near the beach, an occasional Japanese shell decimated or even annihilated an unlucky group of invaders but, unlike Omaha, never seriously threatened the success of the operations as officers still clambered ashore, shouted, "Follow me," and slogged through the sand toward enemy gun emplacements. While the men of D-Day shivered in the cold and damp of the Normandy beaches, these Americans literally gasped for breath in an environment where both temperature and humidity flirted with one hundred, and already heavy packs now seemed like blacksmiths' anvils on their backs.

While the choreography of the Leyte invasion resembled that of Omaha and Utah beaches, the Nipponese defenders had no Erwin Rommel or the Todt Organization's carefully constructed rows of lethal impediments and dozens of blockhouses. While the landings were not walkovers, far more men cleared the beach unwounded than the warriors of Overlord. While the senior leader of Overlord waited until after D-Day to personally come ashore, Douglas MacArthur would likely have come ashore in the first landing craft if senior lieutenants had not extracted a small bit of caution from the general. Less than four hours after the landing beaches were secured, MacArthur's party hopped from a landing craft fifty yards from the beach, and the general half-walked, half-waded at the front of a small entourage until he actually touched Filipino soil for the first time in two and a half years. The general prodded an occasional Japanese corpse, sucked on his corncob pipe, and then sauntered up to a newly arrived communications truck and announced his return to all concerned with the simple acknowledgment, "People of the Philippines, I have returned, the hour of your redemption is near . . . rally to me." The mighty American Army was now in the Philippines to avenge the deaths of their comrades at Bataan and Corregidor and the Death March that followed. However, the ability to expand a small beachhead into a totally liberated nation would be heavily dependent on what transpired back out in the sea from which MacArthur had just arrived. The landing on Leyte essentially engaged a huge, invisible tripwire that would set almost every seaworthy craft in the Imperial Japanese Navy in motion in an attempt to destroy the invasion force and the American fleet that supported it.

In twenty-first-century American leisure culture, one of the surest ways to initiate an argument or even a brawl is to steer a conversation in a tavern, house party, or sports stadium to the topic of an NFL or major collegiate football team that is dividing quarterback duties between two equally qualified players. Almost as soon as a professional or major college coach announces his intention, two separate camps seem to form, each highlighting the strengths of "their" quarterback and the negative qualities of the other member of this platoon. Statistics such as pass completion rate, interception frequency, and overall yardage create an "apples and oranges" debate that energizes newspaper correspondents, sports talk radio hosts, and denizens of sports bars all the way into the stands, as each game progresses. If this level of contention can be raised by the platooning of two men competing in a college game, it is fascinating to speculate about the emotional volatility in "platooning" two senior commanders at the peak of a World War. Amazingly, this is exactly the reality of the command structure in the United States Navy in the period leading up to the colossal naval battle of Leyte Gulf.

As the naval war shifted toward the heart of the Japanese Empire during 1944, admirals Ernest King and Chester Nimitz faced a growing quandary. The Pacific Fleet that would eventually carry the war to Japan had grown so rapidly that the armada's commander was now charged with oversight of a flotilla many times the size of that of any admiral in history. At the moment, the officer with the task was Admiral Raymond Spruance, an enormously competent but rather defensive-minded commander. On the other hand, General Douglas MacArthur, as senior commander of the adjacent Southwest Pacific theater, experienced overall command of a second major fleet under Admiral William Halsey. King and Nimitz were becoming concerned that naval operations in that theater were about to enter a nautical cul-de-sac in what was increasingly becoming a land campaign in that region.

Ernest King and Chester Nimitz may have had very different personalities, but neither man lacked imagination, and the jointly agreed solution was to essentially create a platoon leadership system for the far more important fleet that would be pushing the Japanese from the Marianas and Philippines all the way back to the Inland Sea and Nippon itself. When Raymond Spruance commanded this vast assemblage of ships, he would be the senior officer of Fifth Fleet; then, after a major campaign, Spruance would return to Pearl Harbor to plan future operations, and William Halsey would establish a command over the same vessels that would now be designated Third Fleet. In essence, one admiral would fight as the other planned, and this rotation would continue all the way to Tokyo Bay if necessary. This plan looked especially appealing when Raymond Spruance had fought a brilliant but essentially defensive battle in the Philippine Sea, which had protected the landing force and decimated Japanese naval air assets but left the Imperial Fleet mostly intact. Now that the Americans were about to initiate an invasion of a much more psychologically important part of the Japanese Empire, King and Nimitz expected Halsey to act far more aggressively and essentially annihilate the enemy fleet as the army liberated the Philippines. William "Bull" Halsey was now in command of Third Fleet, which was really Spruance's Fifth Fleet with a new senior admiral. Yet, the American senior admirals were not the only officers pleased with this change.

The senior commanders of the Imperial Japanese Navy were now determined to risk the entire Nipponese fleet in a massive throw of the dice designated the SHO-1 (Victory-1) operation. This exquisitely overcomplicated plan of multiple feints, strikes, and parries suited the Japanese affection for misdirection and complex subtleties that seemed a part of the very Nipponese existence. William Halsey was a salty, aggressive, impetuous leader who seemed likely to accept the bait the Imperial commanders would dangle in front of him. Since the Battle of Midway, the aircraft carrier had become the key piece on the maritime chessboard, and now the entire remaining carrier force of the Japanese Navy would be dangled in front of him. The core of the SHO-1 plan was to use Admiral Jisaburo Ozawa's carrier fleet as a lure to draw the American fleet northward toward Japan, while the still-formidable surface units of the Imperial Navy staged a multiple-pronged attack on the vulnerable Leyte landing areas that would now be shorn of their most powerful protectors. Admiral Soemu Toyoda, Chief of the Naval General Staff, and Admiral Ozawa fully expected to lose most of their carriers, but, since those vessels could launch only minimal air units after the carnage of the Marianas "Turkey Shoot," the loss of these vessels seemed a small price to pay for the annihilation of the American beachhead at Leyte.

While Ozawa's carriers sailed south from the Inland Sea to attract Admiral Halsey's attention, Admiral Takeo Kurita sailed northward from Brunei with a powerful surface fleet that included five battleships, ten heavy cruisers, two light cruisers, and fifteen destroyers jointly tasked with the obliteration of the American beachhead to the north. On the evening of October 22, 1944, Admiral Kurita's fleet sailed through the treacherous narrows of Palawan Passage between northern Borneo and the southern tip of the Philippines, and his appearance was almost immediately discovered by a pair of American submarines. Commander Daniel McClintock, skipper of the *Darter,* moved silently toward the port flank of the stately flotilla of more than thirty vessels steaming confidently in a double row less than one thousand yards away. Only moments later, the cruiser *Takeo* was wreathed in flames and limping back to Brunei, while Kurita's flagship *Atago* was in its death throes, which forced the admiral to jump into the water before the vessel sank eighteen minutes later. While *Darter* had to be abandoned when it beached on a nearby reef, the loss of a single submarine (with the rescue of its entire crew) was a tiny price to pay for eliminating two major enemy vessels before the formal battle had even begun.

When word of the shootout at Palawan Passage arrived on Admiral Halsey's bridge on the battleship *New Jersey,* the colorful mariner ordered the Seventh Fleet of his Vice Admiral, Thomas Kinkaid, to screen the Leyte operation from the south, while Halsey's own Third Fleet searched for developing threats from the Nipponese homeland. In essence, the naval plan for the Leyte operation would be one in which Kinkaid's fleet, jokingly identified as "Douglas MacArthur's personal Navy," would stay relatively close to the invasion beaches, while Halsey's more powerful array of aircraft carriers and new battleships would be free to challenge any foray from the north. Admiral Kinkaid, who had tangled with the Japanese Navy from the shores of Alaska to New Guinea, commanded a fleet centered on older battleships that had either been raised from the mud of Pearl Harbor or fortunate enough to be somewhere else on December 7, 1941, and a covey of "escort" carriers that were miniature versions of fleet carriers built on the hulls of freighters and tankers. If this fleet was the initial force to encounter the main Japanese force, Kinkaid's mission was to delay the enemy until Halsey's far more powerful fleet arrived while knocking down the numbers of the Nipponese flotilla. What was not expected among the American high command as the Leyte operation progressed was that the bait of the Nipponese carriers would entrance Halsey to the point of near disaster for the American campaign.

The object of William Halsey's soon-to-be-undivided attention was Admiral Jisaburo Ozawa's nominally powerful array of six carriers; *Zuikaku,* the last surviving vessel from the six carriers that launched the attack on Pearl Harbor; the light carriers, *Zuiho, Chitose,* and *Chiyouda;* and two new dual-purpose vessels, *Hyuga* and *Ise,* two powerful battleships that had been retrofitted with flight decks to replace part of their big-gun array. Until overextended Japanese shipyards could build more aircraft carriers, this sextet represented the entire remaining carrier air component of the Imperial Navy. Even more daunting was that the Battle of the Philippine Sea in June had reduced Ozawa's air fleet to a mere eighty fighters and thirty-six bombers and torpedo planes, only a tiny fraction of what these vessels were designed to carry. Ironically, the Japanese high command now welcomed the destruction of these ships, as this event would mean that their gambit had worked, and, while William Halsey was busy attacking Ozawa, Admiral Kurita's powerful surface fleet would be rampaging off the coast of Leyte.

While Ozawa's search planes desperately attempted to attract the attention of Halsey's scout units, more than one hundred fifty Japanese planes took off from airstrips in the Philippines and flew out to sea in search of prey. They soon found Rear Admiral Frederick Sherman's Task Group Three, and within minutes dogfights filled the sky as Sherman's carriers launched reinforcements for the already airborne air cover. Commander David McCampbell, who had already achieved distinction in the Marianas battle, promptly splashed seven of the intruders, while other American pilots knocked down thirty-five more raiders only a few minutes into the battle.

However, unlike the recent Turkey Shoot off Saipan, these swirling dogfights allowed a single Imperial attack plane to penetrate the American air screen, and the pilot dropped a well-placed bomb on the carrier *Princeton.* The flames quickly roared through the hangar deck, and soon turned the vessel into a raging inferno that no number of damage-control parties could contain. When the fire spread to the ship's torpedo-storage compartments, the *Princeton* was doomed, and on this October 24 afternoon, the carrier plunged into the deep Pacific waters as the vast majority of the crew was being rescued by destroyers.

Revenge for the loss of the *Princeton* was not long in coming, as American search planes had discovered Admiral Kurita's main attack force, which had entered the Sibuyan Sea on its way to Leyte Gulf and the American invasion beaches, led by the two super-battleships,

Yamato and *Musashi*. Soon, planes from six American carriers were buzzing over Kurita's main assault force like angry wasps as the enormous fleet sent up waves of antiaircraft fire. *Yamato* took two bomb hits that struck no vital areas, but its twin *Musashi* shuddered under nineteen torpedo and seventeen bomb strikes, which sent her to the bottom in the early evening with nearly half of her crew. The only compensation for this enormous loss was that Admiral Halsey quickly accepted the greatly exaggerated pilot "confirmation" of many other Japanese vessels sunk and concluded that Kurita's Center Group fleet no longer represented a threat to the Leyte invasion area. As Third Fleet pilots finally located Ozawa's carrier fleet, the most powerful segments of the American cover force now headed northward, leaving only Admiral Kinkaid's far less formidable Seventh Fleet as the sentinels against a Japanese surface attack.

Just after midnight on October 25, a double echelon of Japanese ships began to enter the narrow waters of Surigao Straits that separated Leyte from neighboring Dinagat Island. The lead flotilla, commanded by Vice Admiral Kiyohide Shima, was formed around two heavy cruisers—a light cruiser and four destroyers—while a more powerful force under Vice Admiral Shoji Nishimura followed a dozen miles behind with two battleships, a heavy cruiser, and an additional four destroyers. These two task forces were under orders from Admiral Toyoda to pass through the Surigao Straits and arrive off Taccoban in Leyte Gulf around dawn to form the southern flank of a pincer in concert with Admiral Kurita's strike force sailing down from the north. This huge combined force would then annihilate the American amphibious craft, transport, and supply ships and much of the beachhead itself while Admiral Halsey ran on a wild goose chase after Ozawa's cruiser.

Japanese battle plans did not fully take into account the aggressive nature of Seventh Fleet commander Admiral Thomas Kinkaid, a feisty but popular sea dog who, according to one fellow admiral, was "a noisy Irishman who loves a good fight." Kinkaid had set up a multiple-echelon welcome for the Nipponese intruders, and the tip of this nautical spear was a flotilla of thirty-nine PT boats that sat in Surigao Strait on this humid tropical night with their engines idling and their crewmen straining to hear the sound of an enemy closing from the south.

Shima's force expected opposition in the straits, but these Nipponese officers expected a straight-up slugging match with American equivalents of their own vessels. Yet the battle opened with tiny "mosquito boats" attacking in groups of three and challenging the enemy at what was considered the Japanese forte—night fighting. As Japanese crews switched on dozens of powerful searchlights and opened fire, the PT boats zigzagged through the fleet, firing their torpedoes at the vessels lunging toward them. A dozen of the small craft quickly took hits, but PT-137 hit light cruiser *Abukuma* with a torpedo that knocked the vessel out of the battle and made the warship a sitting duck for American fliers to sink the next day. As other Imperial ships attempted to swat away the nocturnal menace, they were unwittingly slipping into a cleverly designed trap orchestrated by Rear Admiral Jesse Oldendorf, who was waiting behind the PT boats with six battleships and several destroyer squadrons.

As Shima's ships began to encounter Oldendorf's screening vessels, Admiral Nishimuro's heavier squadron arrived to supplement the attack force, and the new combined fleet pushed confidently forward. American destroyers closed in and fired torpedoes and guns and scampered northward to suck the Imperial ships into a killing zone as the battleships that had been pulled from the mud of Pearl Harbor sought to obtain their revenge on this October night. In twenty minutes, battleships *Yomushiro* and *Fuso,* heavy cruiser *Mugami I,* light carrier *Abukuma,* and six destroyers disappeared from the Japanese order of battle with huge numbers of their crewmen lost. At dawn, with American PT boats nipping at their flanks, the mighty fleet pulled back from Surigao Straits with only six of the seventeen vessels that had entered a few hours before, and only one of their survivors was a capital ship. Seventh Feet had, at a cost of thirty-nine men killed and one destroyer badly damaged, effectively annihilated Toyoda's southern pincer and left the fate of the entire SHO-1 operation on the shoulders of Admiral Kurita, who was now approaching Leyte Gulf from the north. The southern threat had been largely neutralized by second-tier battleships that were not fast enough to hunt with the new battlewagons constructed since Pearl Harbor. Now, the guardians of the northern approach to Leyte were equally second-line vessels, aircraft carriers that were too small to be designated "fleet" or even "light" carriers, but in the current situation, with their equally small escorts, they held the future of MacArthur's liberation of the Philippines in their hands.

The American Navy may have enjoyed enormous assets in the Leyte campaign, but, when Admiral Takeo Kurita's northern strike force appeared off the island of Samar at the entrance to Leyte Gulf at dawn on October 25, all of the sacrifices of the Imperial Navy up to this point in the battle seemed worthwhile; the long passage to the invasion beaches was guarded only by three small groups of "jeep" carriers and their equally small destroyers and destroyer escort consorts. While the "big boys" of the American fleet were busy annihilating Japanese surface forces at other gateways to Leyte, Admiral Kurita was nearing a target area guarded by the three "taffies" that constituted the final line of American defense. At first, neither Kurita nor Rear Admiral Thomas Sprague, commander of Escort Carrier Group 77-4, could fully comprehend what events could have placed these two mismatched fleets in direct confrontation with one another. The David-versus-Goliath battle began when Kurita, still half-convinced that the sprinkling of tiny carriers and escorts were part of an enormous plot by Admiral Halsey to trap the Japanese fleet in the gulf, reluctantly ordered his vastly superior fleet to close distance and open fire on the nearest enemy formation, Admiral Clifton Sprague's Taffy 3 flotilla.

At almost exactly 7:00 a.m. on this tropical morning, Kurita ordered the warships to attack "Halsey's Fleet," and brightly colored dye marker shells began dropping around Sprague's six escort carriers and seven escorts. One of the strangest battles in modern naval warfare had now begun. Almost any hit from Kurita's battleships could virtually vaporize "Ziggy" Sprague's "jeep" carriers, but, as the vast splotches of purple, green, red, blue, and yellow dye tinted the sea around them, American planes roared off the stubby flight decks, and puny three-inch and five-inch guns answered the Imperial behemoths. As Sprague noted the "horrible beauty" of the potentially fatal multicolored barrage, he ordered his outgunned ships to sail into a series of torrential cloudbursts that provided temporary shelter.

A running battle that was steadily drawing ever nearer to the invasion beaches entered its critical phase as destroyers *Hoel, Hermann,* and *Johnston* laid smoke screens and fired from their main batteries as the Taffy planes made runs on the enemy ships' decks. Most of the shells and a later spread of torpedoes initially either missed the ships or caused minimal damage, but then Japanese luck began to change as the heavy cruisers were forced out of the fight from Taffy 3 bombardments and air strikes. In turn, carrier *Gambier Bay* slipped under the waves, riddled with Japanese shells, and was soon joined by destroyers *Hoel* and *Samuel Roberts*. Then, in an almost suicidal dash, *Johnston* confronted five Imperial cruisers that promptly switched their massive firepower to this isolated intruder, which was then surrounded by an entire Imperial destroyer squadron that made a running circle around her like a lone covered wagon attacked by circling Indians. Sixty percent of Johnston's crew would die with the ship, but the survivors viewed a rare glimpse of Japanese chivalry in this war as the senior captain of the attack force saluted his adversaries while his crewmen threw barrels of food and water overboard to sustain their now shipwrecked adversaries.

After dispatching this small covey of light vessels, Admiral Kurita became convinced that the Taffies were merely bait set by Halsey, who was waiting with the main part of the fleet just over the horizon. The admiral in essence declared victory and then set sail for home waters, leaving Ozawa's "bait" force to fend for itself. As Kurita retired, Admiral William Halsey was ensconced on the bridge of the gleaming new battleship *New Jersey,* choreographing what was essentially the ritual execution of the Imperial aircraft carrier fleet. At Cape Engano, only one hundred fifty miles north of Halsey's flagship, a cloud of Helldivers and Avengers, protected by scores of Hellcat fighters, swept through a weak screen of Imperial interceptors and dismembered the core of Japanese naval air power. Carrier *Chitose* was on the bottom of the sea in little more than an hour; *Chiyoda* blazed on her upper decks, while flooding below, and soon foundered. *Zuiko* slipped under the waves as a flaming wreck, and *Zaikaku,* last survivor of the Pearl Harbor raid and Ozawa's flagship, capsized soon after the admiral shifted his flag to a light cruiser.

By nightfall of October 25, 1944, Douglas MacArthur's ground forces could concentrate on liberating the Philippines with no interference from the Imperial Navy. The American Navy would begin to draw an ever-tighter nautical cordon around the islands, while hundred of airplanes would sweep aloft from newly constructed bases and control the air space over American ground forces. Now the 1942 siege of Bataan and Corregidor was being reversed, and the desperate Imperial Army units would fight with diminishing supplies and little prospect of reinforcements. The last great naval battle of World War II had ended in a more one-sided American victory than that of Horatio Nelson at Trafalgar, and Japanese offensive power was now largely centered on the young, barely trained pilots who would become the instruments of the Divine Wind, the suicide pact of the Kamikaze warriors.

Yet, while American newspaper headlines touted victories on all fronts, life on the home front was still a series of adventures, conflicts, and challenges for everyone, from young children pining for the return of their favorite candy bar to the local grocery store, to parents and adolescents engaging in a growing "generation gap" conflict. And, finally, Governor Thomas Dewey of New York and President Franklin Roosevelt were conducting an emotional, if peaceful, campaign to determine who would be the commander-in-chief of American forces when the now-looming victory finally became reality.

CHAPTER XIV

The Home
Front War

American service personnel stationed overseas, from the battlefront in France to the carrier decks of the Pacific fleet, received a vivid portrait of the nation they were fighting for when the September 25, 1944, issue of *Life* magazine finally reached them. The most widely read print media source in the war now devoted a "letter from home" written to the men and women serving outside the nation's borders. The extensive number of articles and accompanying photographs attempted to provide a snapshot of what these Americans were missing at the moment but would hopefully experience in the not-too-distant future. Addressing the male majority of personnel, the introductory article insisted, "Most of you remember the good food, the pretty girls, the clean bathrooms. . . . They will be waiting for you. America is mostly the same, but there *are* boom towns, new factories, and the country is more tough minded, more determined but overall, never has America seemed such a mighty and explosive force, but we will need your help when you get back."

If the American experience has always been a series of paradoxes and contrasts, the American home front in 1944 was at the high end of this curve. The economy had nearly doubled in size even from the 1929 prewar peak and was many times the level of the 1933 nadir of the Depression.

Unemployment was nearly nonexistent; generally, only adults between jobs, medically disabled people, or those needed at home tended to be outside the huge army of workers, which, in turn, had created the greatest spending boom up to that point in history. Adjusting prices for an inflationary economy of a seven-decade-length, newspaper and magazine articles and radio news commentaries alternately bragged and cautioned about people buying $4,000 cigarette lighters, $1,000 children's nightwear, $70,000 mink coats, and $600 black-market tickets to the new Broadway show *Oklahoma!*

The most optimistic or hopeful pundits suggested that perhaps this huge spending spree would be translated after the war into an upsurge in purchases of refrigerators, automobiles, and houses that might prevent the still-hovering specter of economic depression from returning. Critics also admitted that the same people who were overpaying for often frivolous purchases were also largely responsible for already producing two hundred thousand airplanes, fifty-one thousand landing craft, eight thousand ships, sixty thousand tanks, three hundred eighty thousand artillery pieces, two million machine guns, and ten million rifles within thirty-three months of Pearl Harbor—enough not only to lavishly equip American armed forces but also to supply much of the Allied war needs as well.

Yet, even in an American domestic society that had avoided most of the physical destruction that was ravaging Europe and Asia, three major "wars" or conflicts occupied the attention of huge numbers of Americans who were not actively involved in open battle with the Axis enemy: the need to function in a wartime economy riddled with both legitimate and not-so-legitimate shortages and inequities; an increasingly publicized conflict between adults attempting to maintain their authority and value system and a massive cohort of children, teens, and very young adults who seemed determined to create a new authority structure; and, finally, a looming presidential election that would determine whether the incumbent president's already unprecedented three terms would be extended even further or whether another governor of New York would put the Republican party back into the White House for the first time since the depths of the Depression. Like the actual shooting war, each of these three conflicts had geographic and social peculiarities but still created a clearly discernible hostility and belligerence that often brooked little compromise or negotiation from the contending adversaries.

The most substantially intrusive home-front conflict for most Americans not in uniform in 1944 was the labyrinth they traversed almost every day due to the whims and peculiarities of the innocuously titled "War Production Board." This nonelected body regulated everything from the availability of butter at the family dinner table to the campaign to abolish vests from the traditional men's business suit. The simple reality of home-front life in 1944 was that the armed forces had first call on just about any manufactured product or service, and civilians were expected to make do with whatever goods or services remained after the military demands were satisfied. The irony of this situation was that during the Depression years of the 1930s, there were usually plenty of goods on offer but few people with the money to pay for them, while by 1944 many Americans enjoyed the highest wages of their lives but found their relative wealth often useless when they attempted to purchase even necessary items such as food, clothing, and transportation.

Food rationing was one of the most discussed and argued topics among civilians in 1944, even if most Americans realized that their diets were significantly superior to their counterparts' in almost every other major war society. Every American civilian over the age of thirty days had his or her own personal ration book of color-coded, point-valued stamps that was issued regularly at a local school or similar public distribution point. Since women did most of the food shopping in 1944, one of their major tasks was to balance a number of ration points in the collective ration books for the needs and desires of each family member for multiple meals each week. Unlike the recent Depression era, when shoppers literally counted out pennies to pay for sufficient nutrition for family members, customers in 1944 tended to focus on the number of ration points required for each item, with the actual monetary cost usually a secondary factor.

One of the primary elements of the battle of the ration books was that America in 1944 was essentially a society of adult consumers interested primarily in consuming red meat, coffee, and cigarettes, all of which were now in short supply. This was an era when chicken and turkey were not even fully considered meat products by rationing authorities, as poultry was no more than a "real" meat substitute, coffee was a virtually universal adult beverage in a society where bottled water was seen as a European fetish, soft drinks and fruit drinks were usually relegated to children or teens, and something approaching two-thirds of adults were moderate to heavy smokers. The very popularity of these items made them the central point of the food rationing system. Many civilian adults were forced to desperate measures, such as eating out in restaurants much more frequently than ever before, as ration coupons were not required (although subject to "meatless" Tuesday and Friday regulations); switching from favorite cigarette brands to less popular brands that were more likely to be available in stores; and reusing coffee grounds to squeeze every available cup from a finite household supply. Finally, as will be discussed in more detail later, more than a few consumers delved into the black market of under-the-counter deals and purchases of counterfeit ration coupons, which seemed less exorbitant in price in view of the booming economy in which they lived.

The amounts set aside for each civilian for products that were in limited supply were both highly specific and yet subject to change if unforeseen circumstances developed. For example, at the beginning of 1944, it was expected that each American would receive ration coupons for one hundred thirty-two pounds of meat during the next twelve months, compared to one hundred thirty-one pounds in 1943, because a record level of pork production would slightly outweigh rising shortages in the availability of beef. On the other hand, the enormous use of cheese products in military ration packs slashed civilian availability to a paltry one ounce a week for the foreseeable future and sent housewives scrambling to find cheese substitutes for their favorite recipes. The drop in cheese availability was, however, partially compensated by the War Production Board's announcement that each civilian would be entitled to four additional eggs for the year 1944, as the annual allotment was raised to three hundred forty-nine.

While the vagaries of food availability evoked attention in everything from magazines to dialogue in popular films, the impact of clothing rationing created its own minor crisis in many families. Male white-collar workers often complained about the government-mandated elimination of vests from all suits, which created a major fashion change away from a well-dressed business appearance that had been standard since Colonial times. The enormous need for military footwear had reduced civilian men to continuous dealings with shoe repair shops that, in turn, were constantly short of replacement soles. The need for military headgear threatened to freeze in place the changes in men's hat styles, as more and more males had to fall back on their prewar chapeaux that had sat forgotten in a hatbox at the back of a clothes closet.

While the clothing restrictions for men seemed to be resented primarily as an intrusion into normal fashion progress, American women in 1944 were often beginning to view the new, more casual "war work" styles as a welcome break from the traditional fashion demand of appearance over comfort. The most noticeable impact of the war on women's fashions was an explosion in the substitutions of trousers for skirts, first in war plants and eventually in leisure use. At the very end of the 1930s, pants were just beginning to enter girls' and women's wardrobes, but now the practicality of war work fashion pushed this trend more rapidly to the point that the Rosie the Riveter iconic look now included pants, bandanas, work gloves, and even welding masks as the new fashion statements in a war society where substantial opposition to more comfortable female clothes was branded by its enthusiasts as "unpatriotic."

While food and clothing rationing usually allowed consumers to substitute some less popular but still acceptable products for the items in shortest supply, the ongoing gasoline shortage was the most publicized and debated aspect of the entire War Production Board program. By the eve of Pearl Harbor, the American love affair with its automobiles had been developing for nearly two generations, while the same fondness for cars had been responsible for major cutbacks in trolley, bus, and train services that could not provide the unique freedom of private automobile use. Then, the concept of a heavily mechanized military campaign against the Axis powers had all but halted all private automobile production and reduced the average family gasoline ration to a paltry three gallons a week.

By 1944, odometer reading had become a national pastime, as each excursion in the family car was parsed according to distance, importance, and the availability of shorter alternate routes.

Family dinner conversations, backyard chats with neighbors, and discussions around the office water cooler shifted increasingly to the best way to get from one point to another in a war society where the traditional freedom to roam was now significantly curtailed. Newspapers and magazines ran increasing numbers of features on the "new bootleggers," as stolen or counterfeited gasoline ration coupons were emerging as the coin of the realm in the wartime underworld. Reports suggested that as much as 40 percent of all gasoline was being purchased with stolen or faked coupons that only an expert could detect as bogus. As gangsters destroyed, stole, or counterfeited the lifeblood of the transportation system, they set up a huge pyramid where gasoline coupons were sold to "filling station" attendants at anywhere from one cent to ten cents above the normal cost of a gallon of gas, while some war workers who qualified for generous allocations because of the nature of their jobs would sell their personal coupon supply to acquaintances for fifty cents above the normal purchase price.

One of the major rivals to the rationing war in public communications and the national news media in 1944 was adult shock and even revulsion at the behavior of a significant proportion of the nation's adolescent population. During 1944, some psychology and sociology textbooks and some print media sources began substituting the term *teen-ager* for the traditional word *youth* to describe Americans who were no longer young children and yet had not reached adult status. These Americans were usually just below military age but beyond traditional childhood and were identified increasingly with an institution that had been expanding rapidly over the past quarter century—the high school.

On the one hand, many adults in 1944 viewed this burgeoning high school population with anything from bemusement to actual respect for their war contributions. Teenage fashions, from outlandish zoot suits for boys and rolled-down white athletic socks paired with saddle shoes for bobby-soxer girls, were featured in magazine articles and depicted in a wide range of films, from the intense drama of *Since You Went Away* to the youthful hijinks of *Janie*. Adult-oriented productions highlighted the efforts of teen Boy Scouts who by late 1944 had collected almost three million books, nearly forty million pounds of rubber, twenty million pounds of tin, and more than three hundred million pounds of scrap metal for the war effort in their war drive. More generally, these publications praised high school students as a group that purchased significant numbers of war bonds and replaced adults in the workplace so that those adults could enter the military.

However, these positive views of adolescent Americans in 1944 were at least partially contradicted by more disturbing reports in national news magazines and the documentary film series *The March of Time,* which had just released a disturbing expose titled "Youth in Crisis." A congressional subcommittee, chaired by Florida congressman Claude Pepper, was charged with investigating soaring wartime juvenile delinquency and related health and education issues while holding public hearings that included witnesses such as Andrew Jackson Higgins, the developer of the iconic invasion landing craft, and Father Flanagan, the founder of Boys Town in Nebraska, as well as the mayors of Cleveland and New York City.

The editors of *Life* magazine dispatched reporters to twenty-seven cities across the nation to study the growing delinquency crisis, and they discovered that for many teens, their antisocial behavior had developed as a strange cocktail of an attempt to emulate their older peers in uniform by "playing war" combined with the frustration of not being taken seriously by adult Americans. For example, in Connecticut, a group of ten boys stole a tractor from a farm and ran it back and forth through a cemetery in a simulated "tank battle," smashing gravestones as "enemy forts." Other teens formed "commando groups" that fought mock battles only slightly less dangerous than a real battle, as they used guns and knives to "play war" by invading restaurants and nightclubs which sometimes resulted in fatalities to either the teens or the adults. By 1944, FBI agents admitted that they were actually spending as much time tracking down preteens and teen saboteurs as chasing genuine Axis agents. One gang of three preteens had managed to derail a troop train in New York by building a fire on the tracks, while another brand of junior marauders accomplished a similar result by planting dynamite on the rails.

Adolescent and even preadolescent girls developed a slightly different set of wartime fantasies in their role as "Victory Girls," which frequently included offering sexual favors to servicemen, sometimes by operating in large packs. Local groups of girls adopted clever code names, such as "khaki wackies," "cuddle bunnies," "patriotutes," "chippies," and "good time Janes," which most of the girls in the group saw as an honor, not an activity that should be ridiculed or disparaged. Victory Girls could be found anywhere men in uniform congregated, which was, in essence, just about anywhere in the United States. In Indianapolis, adults complained that fifteen- and sixteen-year-old girls attempted to pick up servicemen as soon as they arrived in the bus terminal. The train station of Portland, Oregon, was replete with "girls twelve and up" whenever a troop train arrived or departed, often shocking military police with their ability to discover the timing of a secret operation. At Chicago's Navy Pier, sailors admitted, "It is almost impossible to either enter or exit without being virtually kidnapped by giggling Victory Girls." A major complaint by servicemen was that thirteen- and fourteen-year-old girls were so heavily made up that the young men were seldom aware of the girls' very young age.

While America in 1944 dealt with growing generational conflict, the year was also the date of the great quadrennial battle known as a presidential election, and most citizens believed that this year's version was going to be a barn burner. Both President Franklin Roosevelt and Governor Thomas Dewey were intelligent, compassionate, patriotic men, but between them lay a vast political chasm.

Roosevelt had already assured his place as the dominant American politician of the first half of the twentieth century by steering the nation at least partially out of the greatest economic disaster in the history of the Republic. More recently he had emerged as an effective, and in some cases brilliant, commander-in-chief, who was heavily responsible for the appointment of those military leaders who by autumn of 1944 were sending the enemy reeling back toward their own soil. On the other hand, the ravages of polio, a four-pack-a-day smoking habit, and the stress of orchestrating the nation's largest war were visibly taking an enormous toll on the health of a man who was still only in his early sixties but now often resembled someone ten or even twenty years older.

On the other hand, Thomas Dewey was a full generation younger than his opponent: the father of young children and a popular, successful governor of the most populous state in the union. Dewey was an excellent speaker who had energized a party that had not mounted a serious challenge to recover the White House since Roosevelt's first election twelve years earlier. In rapid succession, Herbert Hoover, Alf Landon, and Wendell Willkie had been dispatched from contention by one-sided electoral votes that had an air of inevitability as soon as the party conventions had ended. Now Dewey presented a really serious challenge to the incumbent with his youth, his glamorous background as a crime buster, and his ability to avoid significant political gaffes.

Perhaps the most notable aspect of the 1944 presidential campaign was that, unlike many of its earlier counterparts since 1920, the national debate was much more over the future than the past. The ongoing war had clearly proven that the United States could never again return to total national isolationism as Warren Harding had promised in 1920, yet the economic issues of the Depression-era 1930s had, at least temporarily, largely disappeared, and the political debate would be over the ability to continue prosperity, not restore it.

The man who carried the reborn hopes of Republicans that the oval office was not a semipermanent fiefdom of the Democratic party, Thomas Edmund Dewey, was a forty-two-year-old governor of New York who had been largely raised and educated in Michigan in a small-town, middle-class environment of a largely prosperous America of the first two decades of the twentieth century. Like John Kennedy a decade and a half later, much of the Dewey brand revolved around the fact that, if elected, he would become the first president born in the twentieth century, which, in turn, was crystallized by the presence of a young, attractive wife and photogenic young children. Thomas Dewey also had the great good luck of not being Herbert Hoover, Alf Landon, or Wendell Willkie, all of whom had gone down in crushing defeat in a series of Roosevelt landslides. Now, in 1944, most pundits of both parties admitted that this election would be the closest race since 1916, when Woodrow Wilson eked out a victory in a tight contest with Republican Charles Evans Hughes.

The highly influential circle of American news magazines was naturally energized by a presidential election that might actually be something other than a landslide and by an extensive "Day in the Life: Feature on Governor Dewey" in *Life* magazine that described the governor as a man with a keen, productive mind, a genius for putting other people to work, and an ability to profit from his mistakes with a governing style "more purposeful than theoretical." Yet even highly complimentary features on the governor could not help noting a certain fussiness and a need for privacy of a man who kept the door closed while working alone, pushed a button under his desk to signal a person to enter, disliked talking on the telephone, and smoked the same number of Marlboro cigarettes each day.

On the other hand, like his predecessor in the governor's mansion, Franklin Roosevelt, he swam multiple laps in the gubernatorial swimming pool, seldom wore a hat in an era in which that absence was still culturally daring, and was enormously warm and affectionate to his wife and two young sons. Paired with his only slightly older running mate, Governor John Bricker of Ohio, the candidates made a highly photogenic ticket, which challenged the Roosevelt ticket even by attracting celebrities to their camp. For example, while teen heartthrob Frank Sinatra emerged as a major campaigner for the president, the Dewey campaign met that challenge with the equally popular Shirley Temple, who had successfully made the transition from child to teen film roles.

During the run-up to the election, Franklin Roosevelt rallied his now dissipating strength for a final supreme effort to retain his presidency. For example, in a driving, icy rain, the President rode in an open car through four of the boroughs of New York City, climaxed by a long speech before a huge crowd in Ebbets Field. The president also reluctantly bowed to the demands of the socially conservative, often segregationist Southern wing of his party by removing liberal Vice President Henry Wallace from his ticket and substituting Missouri senator Harry Truman, who proved much more acceptable south of the Mason-Dixon line.

While the 1944 election occurred in approximately the same stage of World War II as the 1864 election had occurred in the Civil War, Dewey and Roosevelt were far more in accord with the prosecution of the conflict than Lincoln and his opponent, former General George McClellan. McClellan largely accepted a party platform that hinted at an immediate end to the war after the election based on concessions to the Confederacy, ranging from reunion that included the maintenance of slavery in the nation to recognition of the Confederacy as a legitimate nation. Both candidates in 1944 favored all-out prosecution of the war until total victory, and it is likely that a Dewey presidency would have been no more lenient toward the defeated Germany and Japan than the incumbent.

Yet despite relative accord on the prosecution of the war, it was obvious in 1944 that there was a strong divergence on how the nation was going to win the peace and function in a postwar world. By election eve, voter registration had reached an all-time high, and most people agreed that the result of the election would deeply affect the fate of the nation that their children would inherit. Dewey slammed the administration and its current treatment of former enemy and now new ally Italy; alleged corruption in running New Deal programs; and America's role in a proposed world body that would follow the war. In a time just before the emergence of television, people flocked from miles around to see the presidential candidates speak at rallies that seemed like giant county fairs. People wanted to see what the candidates looked like in the flesh, even if they were at a distance, and even loyal Roosevelt supporters were privately shocked at the president's haggard, deeply lined face and gaunt appearance, especially when compared to Dewey's youthful vigor.

Yet when Election Day arrived, the man who had shepherded the nation through its greatest economic crisis and to near victory in its greatest war coasted to a victory far more comfortable than most political analysts had predicted. Compared to the three previous elections, Republicans had made substantial gains, as the president barely won in several states that he had carried easily in previous elections. While Roosevelt actually carried thirty-six of forty-eight states and limited the challenger to a swath of America running from northern New England through much of the

Midwest, the popular vote of twenty-four million to twenty-one million was the closest election since Charles Evans Hughes had lost to Woodrow Wilson in 1916. The GOP had also increased its control of governors' mansions to an almost even twenty-three statehouses and had lost three other governorships by paper-thin margins.

Given the obvious rapid decline of Franklin Roosevelt's health, leaders of both parties tacitly acknowledged that the real political showdown would come in 1948, when Dewey would still be a relatively young governor of the most populous state, and his opponent would most likely not be someone named Roosevelt. Most of the news media stressed the ability of the Republic to even hold an election in the middle of a massive war in which 19,183 American service personnel had died in the month preceding the election, and many of the greatest military challenges still lay ahead.

By November of 1944, the presidential election had been settled, but the home front still roiled with the challenges of soaring draft calls, arbitrary and confusing ration policies, and a fear that many adolescent Americans had lost their sound moorings. However, as these domestic issues were analyzed and debated, the increasing hope and expectation that the war in Europe would be over by Christmas was about to be rudely shattered on the autumn battlefields three thousand miles across the sea.

CHAPTER XV

Autumn of Shattered Dreams

As the still balmy air of early September wafted over the rapidly expanding dominion of "liberated Europe," the generals and soldiers of the burgeoning Allied Expeditionary Force began to sense that the Home by Christmas predictions that were left unfulfilled in so many previous wars might actually occur in the transformative year of 1944. The anticipated street-by-street battle against the Germans to liberate Paris had never occurred, and now lines of prisoners were being marched out of the city as the French tricolor flag fluttered over virtually every public building in the City of Light. A German army that seemed invincible when it marched into France four years earlier was now beating a hasty retreat toward the outer defenses of the fatherland itself. General Dwight Eisenhower, master of the Allied forces that now stretched from the Normandy beaches to the gates of Germany, grew so certain of impending victory that he cheerfully bet five pounds with 21st Army commander Bernard Montgomery that the war in Europe would be over by Christmas, while more junior generals were mapping out possible stop lines in the heart of the Reich that would reduce the possibility of friendly fire incidents between the eastward-moving Anglo-Americans and the Soviet forces about to sweep westward toward Berlin.

From documents of Allied headquarters to reports of newspaper correspondents, a sense of impending victory seemed to permeate the autumn campaign season. One of the major impediments to early victory now seemed to be the difficulty that Senior Commander Omar Bradley and General Bernard Montgomery were experiencing in deploying their sixty available combat divisions in an increasingly crowded battlefront. Ironically, one of the plans to ease this situation marked the first hint that the impending doom of the Third Reich was not quite as imminent as originally expected.

General Bernard Montgomery had just surrendered command of all Allied ground forces as directed by the timetables of Operation Overlord, although the sting of his losing authority over American ground forces was eased by his simultaneous promotion to the coveted rank of Field Marshal. Now, Montgomery was interested in finding a way to best utilize his still formidable Anglo-Canadian army to achieve some major victory that would shorten the war while also easing the crowding of the Allied battlefield. Monty's plan, code-named Market Garden, was designed to use an airborne army of British, Polish, and American contingents to get behind the current front lines near the Belgian-Dutch border, with a special interest in securing a lodgment on the Rhine River at the Dutch city of Arnhem. While the bulk of the ground forces and about half of the airborne forces would be deployed from Montgomery's command, the 82nd and 101st American Airborne divisions would be assigned to snatch six major bridges located midway between the British airborne forces at Arnhem and the main British ground force sixty miles to the west at the Belgian-Dutch border. If all went according to plan, the American paratroopers would hold open the main road separating the two British forces and allow General Brian Horrocks's XXX Corps to link up with British 1st Airborne Division and secure the Arnhem Bridge as the jumping-off point for a thrust into the Third Reich.

Operation Market Garden actually started out with substantial success, as on the almost perfect late summer morning of September 17, 1944, British 1st Airborne division parachuted into an area about seven miles from the Rhine, with Colonel John Frost's battalion dropped into the suburbs of Arnhem itself. For a brief moment, it appeared that Market Garden was a rousing success, as the British and American airdrops caught the German defenders totally off guard. However, within hours, the operation began to unravel at slow-motion speed.

First, Frost's parent unit, General Roy Urquhart's First British Airborne Division, was supposed to rush into Arnheim to reinforce the small advance contingent, but it found itself hopelessly scattered throughout the Dutch countryside while also landing almost on top of a crack German SS Panzer Corps that hugely outgunned them. The Germans essentially split Frost's battalion from the rest of his division and then began annihilating both forces in a one-sided battle of tanks against small-caliber weapons.

The nearest relief force was a contingent of American paratroopers that had landed on the west side of the Waal River at Nijmegen, only a few miles from the British drop point. However, each time the paratroopers neared a span across the river, a German demolition unit blew the bridge and kept the British forces safely contained from aid. In one act of sheer desperation, Major Julian Cook's battalion of the 505th parachute regiment received the unenviable order to cross the river in daylight and capture a damaged-but-still-standing bridge from the opposite side while British tanks stood ready to move from the west bank once the GIs had removed the explosive charged from the span.

On the afternoon of September 20, after repeated delays and problems in supplying craft that could carry Cook's men across the river, six small flotillas of canvas and plywood contraptions arrived, most of which were missing their vital oars. Cook and three hundred fifty men, largely using rifle butts as oars, started across the river under the dubious cover of British smoke-screen shells that were less than fully functional. They quickly became the backdrop of a live-action shooting gallery for the German defenders on the far bank of the river.

Only half of the American troops arrived safely on the far shore, but these survivors quickly engaged in a deadly duel with the German defenders, who ranged in age down to preteens and who proved to be among the most zealous combatants. In a particularly fierce shootout, where little quarter was given, the paratroopers pushed the defenders back across a railroad embankment, while the most audacious Germans spurned cover to get a clear shot at GIs who were hanging from the underside of the bridge attempting to dismantle explosive arrays. Cook's relatively small contingent of unwounded survivors cheered as British tanks crossed the now-captured bridge and then relapsed into near shock as the tankers encamped near the bridge and brewed tea as they admitted that they could not go further toward Arnhem without British infantry support that was somewhere near the tail end of a ten-mile backup on the road behind them.

While the two American airborne divisions fought their way from one bridge to the next, John Frost's battalion in Arnheim was gradually squeezed into a perimeter only a half-block wide with German forces now in control of the rest of the city while the rest of British 1st Airborne division was trapped in a slightly larger pocket a few miles away. Frost, who was suffering from multiple wounds, had the single consolation that as his command was whittled toward extinction and then surrender, the normally ferocious SS troops demonstrated a chivalry rare in their conduct of war, including excellent care for the wounded paratroopers and effusive compliments to the surrendering combatants. This rare show of humanity, in turn, convinced General Urquhart to entrust his thousands of wounded men to German medical care while he slipped over a river back to the Allied lines with the two thousand ambulatory survivors of the ten-thousand-man landing force he had commanded at the start of Market Garden.

While Bernard Montgomery cheerfully indicated that Market Garden was a 90 percent success on the premise that the Allies had liberated a modest portion of Holland and *almost* reached the Rhine, analysts on both sides saw the battle as a clear German victory, with the main consolation for American leaders being the excellent account of themselves given by the American airborne units and the fact that the rest of the battle was a British show. However, the failure to secure a bridge across the Rhine at Arnhem meant that the river would have to be crossed somewhere else, and as autumn turned toward winter, that alternative route increasingly seemed to be on the far side of a virtually impenetrable forest that rivaled the woods of the scariest fairy tales for its air of malevolence.

Once Montgomery's British Army was at least temporarily stalemated in its attempt to cross the Rhine through Holland, American forces began to focus on a new gateway to that last major natural barrier to the Nazi heartland. This gateway was the gloomy, spectral woodland of the Hurtgen Forest, which was fronted by the ancient city of Aachen. After the failure of Market Garden, General "Lightning Joe" Collins's VII Corps was tasked with penetrating Hitler's vaunted West Wall, often also called the Siegfried Line, which extended in two directions from the first city inside the Reich's border, Charlemagne's ancient capital city of more than one hundred fifty thousand people.

As the Northwest European autumn gradually morphed from warm sunshine to the cloudiness and chill of approaching winter, General Collins set up corps headquarters in the town of Stolberg, while Hitler poured more than twenty thousand reinforcements into Aachen to defend the cradle of the Holy Roman Empire to the death. All that now remained was a Wagnerian musical score to accompany one of the most ferocious street battles on the Western Front. By the midpoint of October, German soldiers, backed by a shrinking pool of ardent Nazi civilians, fought an urban guerilla war against American tanks, bazooka guns, and riflemen. GIs and Landsers fought from opposite ends in a movie theater, on alternate floors of apartment buildings, and from blackened, stalled-out streetcars in a street fight that gradually pushed toward the city center. By the time the defenders reluctantly began to abandon the city, nearly 90 percent of Aachen's buildings were destroyed or severely damaged, but the Germans retreating out of the city could be consoled with the grim satisfaction that their retrograde monument was actually driving the Americans into an even more hellish battleground than the bloody streets of Aachen. If the Americans were to gain the Rhineland from this direction, they had to enter the haunted woodlands of the Hurtgenwald.

One of the minor ironies of the American experience in World War II was that the primary official narrative of the naval aspects of the war was entrusted to a Harvard historian who, at the beginning of the war, secured a personal audience with President Roosevelt, secured a commission as a commander in the navy, and ultimately returned to Harvard as an admiral. Samuel Eliot Morrison viewed and recorded both the Atlantic and Pacific theater battles from the war rooms and bridges of senior fleet officers, often discussing tactics with them over dinner and cigars. On the other hand, the most noted historian of the army experience, Dr. Forrest Pogue, recorded the ground war from the much more lowly perspective of a sergeant who would never be permitted the same level of personal access or perspective as his naval counterpart. Yet Sergeant Pogue was, like Admiral Morrison, an excellent historian, and when he was informed that the road into the German heartland led through the Hurtgen Forest, he immediately compared the coming campaign to the spring of 1864 when General Ulysses Grant's Army of the Potomac attempted to march on Richmond through the Wilderness of eastern Virginia.

This World War II version of the Wilderness campaign was centered on a two-hundred-square-mile swath of dark, desolate vegetation interspersed with a few small towns and primitive roads, startlingly similar to the environment faced by the Union Army as it lurched south toward Richmond.

The Hurtgen Forest was the physical link between the German frontier centered on Aachen and the Roer River, which represented the last natural barrier to the Rhine a bit further east. Just as General Grant had believed that he had to push through the Wilderness in order to eventually confront the Confederate Army in more open ground, First Army Commander Lieutenant General Courtney Hodges insisted that control of the Hurtgen Forest and its massive system of dams that could conceivably flood the approaches to the Roer was a vital component of the impending drive to the Rhine. However, what the commander of First Army, who was at best tolerably qualified, did not seem to fully appreciate was that those dark and haunted woodlands essentially negated the very assets that made the American Army such a formidable force in 1944; the tanks, air support, massive artillery support, and ability to move faster and further than the enemy would be only minimally employable in the upcoming battle.

The agony of Hurtgen began on October 6, 1944, when elements of the 9th Army Division pushed into the wet, dripping foliage with the objective of closing in on a German position around a terrain that featured the less-than-reassuring title of Deadman's Moor. Like people suddenly transported to the environment of Sherlock Holmes's adventures in *The Hound of the Baskervilles,* young men in olive drab slowly pushed forward until German artillery turned the trees into lethal projectiles, as airbursts created a fusillade of splinters tearing through the unprotected men. Even soldiers who had grown up in the most heavily wooded areas of the United States marveled at the sheer terror of navigating though a dark labyrinth where the enemy always seemed to remain invisible.

As the 9th Division casualties soared, General Hodges threw in the 28th Infantry Division, a unit formed from Pennsylvania National Guard units and now commanded by one of the heroes of Omaha Beach, General Norman Cota. "Dutch" Cota had been rewarded for his gallantry on D-Day with command of this Keystone State unit, but now, instead of contending with German defenders deployed behind massive man-made defenses in a relatively finite area, he was facing an enemy scattered throughout a huge battle zone and able to utilize their natural environment to seemingly baffle every American thrust. Now combat engineers often proved more valuable than artillery or tanks, and it was the sappers who gradually improved what were essentially cart tracks—narrow but usable roads capable of at least equipping and feeding an expedition into the Hurtgen's dark interior.

As the GIs pushed their way through a maze of natural barriers and German ambushes, new units were constantly fed into the operation. As casualties mounted, tempers frayed at Corps, Army, and Theater Headquarters. Senior commanders could see the Roer River and even the Rhine shimmering not that far ahead of the battlefield in a sort of optical illusion where the goal point always seemed nearer than it really was. Since Hitler, in essence, maintained a mirror image view of his adversaries, the Fuehrer howled at any German retreat from what he considered a "perfect" defensive battlefield. However, in this case, the stalemate essentially favored Hitler because it forced American attention away from a far larger operation that was about to emerge: Operation Watch on the Rhine.

The American focus on the Hurtgen battle in the late fall of 1944 allowed Hitler to cobble together his riskiest offensive of the entire war.

The fact that German armies had twice since 1914 used the Ardennes Forest as a route into the heart of their enemies' defense lines did little to discourage American senior commanders from reducing the defensive screen along that vital front to a pair of battered veteran divisions in desperate need of rest and refitting and two rookie divisions that could experience combat on a limited basis on a "ghost front," which neither side seemed to covet. Hitler's plan was to strike this weakly held segment of the Allied line with a major portion of an attack force of twenty-five divisions nine days before Christmas, when the short winter days and normally heavy cloud cover largely negated the massive Allied air power that the Germans could no longer match. The operational goal was to brush past the American defenders, cross the Meuse River, recapture the key port of Antwerp, and neuter the Anglo-American power long enough to swing much of the Wehrmacht eastward and smash the expected Soviet winter offensive in its tracks. The outcome of this victory could be anything from buying time to fully utilize Germany's new jet airplanes and long-range rockets to negotiating a separate peace with the Western Allies that would allow the Reich to narrow its enemies to its Communist nemesis.

Using a combination of brilliant deception tactics and lackluster Allied intelligence, Hitler was able to mass three armies, six hundred thousand troops, along an eighty-five-mile start line extending from Monschau near the Hurtgen Forest to Echternoch, just north of Luxembourg City. At 5:30 a.m. on December 16, 1944, the powerful German assault force smashed into a badly outnumbered American force that believed it had been deployed in a rest area. Dwight Eisenhower, following the German offensive from his heavily guarded headquarters outside Paris, probably quickly realized that he was about to lose his bet with Montgomery, but, unlike his French counterparts in 1940, he showed little sign of panic, and the first inkling emerged that Watch on the Rhine just might become a great opportunity for the Allies. Instead of the Allied forces forced to root out the enemy in defensive positions of their own choosing, the Germans were now out in the open, facing the prospect of massive destruction from the air whenever any semblance of flying weather returned.

Eisenhower's initial concern regarding how well the either inexperienced or worn-out front-line units would fight was quickly eliminated as word spread along the Allied lines of the German interpretation of the Geneva Convention near the Belgian town of Malmedy. When a thirty-three-truck convoy of American field artillery personnel halted in Malmedy for a lunch break, they were surrounded by a vastly superior Panzer SS force that induced them to surrender. As the nearly two hundred GIs were herded toward a nearby snow-covered field to be processed and identified, German machine guns hidden in nearby trucks let loose with a fusillade that killed most of the men, from combat soldiers to medics, followed by more close-in atrocities by individual SS personnel, who began systematically murdering most of the men who still clung to life. While the Germans were able to bag an enormous haul of seven thousand American prisoners from two American divisions trapped along the Schnee Eifel Heights around the town of St. Vith, word of the massacre at Malmedy quickly ensured that this would be the last major surrender to the enemy, as GIs now were determined to fight to the death against an enemy that showed no quarter.

Watch on the Rhine was in many respects simply an updated, winter-based version of the German Ardennes offensive of May 1940, which defeated the entire French Army within six weeks. In that earlier campaign, masses of French soldiers effectively decided that it would be better to sit out the war in German POW camps than to die for what they increasingly viewed as a lost war. Now American GIs hunkered in far worse weather conditions against far greater odds and effectively decided that they could beat this massive enemy advance.

Even as ground was grudgingly abandoned in the center of the line, the flanks were beginning to hold, and firebreaks were beginning to be established in formerly unheard-of Ardennes towns. The community that would soon gain a level of fame comparable to Lexington Green, Gettysburg, or the Alamo was a nondescript crossroad community named Bastogne, which, just as the German tidal wave began to surge forward, morphed into a bastion held by an outnumbered-but-determined garrison centered on units of the 101st Airborne Division, elements of the 9th and

10th Armored Divisions, combat-engineer companies and other assorted forces that were turning this small Belgian community into the most identifiable location in the war at Christmas of 1944.

The legendary status of Bastogne probably began when a delegation of officers from the units surrounding the town approached acting 101st Division Commander General Anthony McAuliffe with a polite invitation to capitulate in the face of overwhelming odds. The nonplussed general sent a terse one-word reply of "NUTS" to the offer, and soon the single word was gaining headlines in American newspapers during the tense holiday period. That clear-yet-catchy American refusal turned Christmas Eve in Bastogne into a parody of "Peace on Earth," as German bombers hammered a church that had been turned into a hospital, long-range guns pounded the residential areas, and Wehrmacht reinforcements were rushed to the scene for a massive Christmas Day assault.

On the evening of December 24, a reconnaissance battalion of the 2nd Panzer Division reported to headquarters that they had advanced to within six miles of the Meuse River, and an unusually jovial Adolf Hitler congratulated his senior generals on the progress of Watch on the Rhine. German radio programs were interrupted as victory announcements replaced Christmas carols, and emotions soared even higher on a report that a captured American jeep containing a small scout party of three soldiers actually arrived at the approach to a bridge on the Meuse at the town of Divant and was prevented from crossing only by striking a stray mine.

On Christmas morning, an attack force of the 15th Panzergrenadier Division smashed into the American foxholes on the north side of Bastogne and initiated a donnybrook that rolled across the snow-covered fields as dozens of individual firefights broke out in the normally peaceful grounds. American tank destroyers that had been rushed into Bastogne just before the German siege now used their superior speed and the cover of the snow-covered trees to begin picking off enemy tanks before they could rumble into the town proper. As these battles raged on this nominal day of peace, few people were yet aware that the German Christmas attack on Bastogne represented the high tide of Watch on the Rhine. The last week of 1944 would be spent fighting on a battlefield where the balance of power was gradually shifting in favor of the Americans, as clearing skies brought their enormous air power back into play, and the bold long-range drive of George Patton's tanks checkmated the German Panzer Army.

The autumn of 1944 had truly been a season of shattered dreams for Americans who hoped that the European war would be over by the end of the year. Yet, as the seasons almost imperceptibly shifted in the days just before Christmas, the dreams of peace and victory began to emerge, if ever so gradually. On New Year's Eve of 1944, American GIs were still sitting in foxholes around Bastogne instead of holding victory parties in occupied Germany. Americans continued to die in large numbers, not only in Belgium but also in Italy and in the still only partially liberated Philippines. The map of Axis occupation was clearly shrinking but still controlled the lives and deaths of far too many people for whom 1944 had been a beacon of hope but also an everyday reality of an ongoing dance with death. Yet, exactly a year earlier, Paris and Rome were still under German occupation; the Japanese fleet still represented a powerful threat to the liberation of much of the Pacific; and Operation Overlord was still viewed as a risky gamble. Now, the dictators were fighting with their backs to the wall. Tokyo would soon be joined by Berlin in the murderous hell of man-made firestorms; Germany was about to be invaded from both east and west. Increasing numbers of American servicemen were bantering the phrase, "Home Alive in '45!"

Perhaps the dream of victory in 1944 had been shattered by the reality of Arnhem, the Hurtgen forest, and Malmedy, but in this same season the American stand at Bastogne, MacArthur's drive toward the liberation of Manila, and the rumblings of the most massive Soviet offensive yet in the east brought hope that this New Year's Eve of 1944 might just be the last time a calendar was replaced in a nation at war with the Axis. The Longest Year was about to end, but perhaps the next New Year's Eve celebration would celebrate the end of a 1945 that would be the year that America's heroes came home.

Epilogue 1945

On the frigid, snowy evening of Sunday, December 31, 1944, an American officer wearing the three stars of a lieutenant general hunched over a makeshift desk in a ramshackle, temporary headquarters in the now world-famous town of Bastogne, Belgium, and composed the first General Orders for the year 1945. General George Patton had driven through a small American-held corridor squeezed between German lines and delighted the American defenders with his gruff, salty humor and insistence on the certainty of victory. Now he was at work on a special New Year's greeting to the personnel of the XIX Tactical Air Command and his own Third Army as Order Number 1 for New Year's Day, 1945.

"From the bloody corridor at Avranches to Brest, thence across France to the Saar, over the Saar into Germany, and now onto Bastogne, your record has been one of continuous victory. Not only have you invariably defeated a cunning and ruthless enemy, but also you have overcome by your indomitable fortitude every aspect of terrain and weather. Neither heat nor dust nor floods nor snow have stayed your progress. The speed and brilliancy of your achievements are unsurpassed in military history." As this message was being delivered to Patton's men around midnight of this new year, all guns in the Third Army fired a massive cannonade for twenty minutes at the German lines as a New Year's greeting that inflicted the first casualty of 1945 on an increasingly besieged Third Reich.

However, in towns a bit further to the east, out of range of American guns, German pilots who were just getting into the swing of holiday festivities were stunned to receive confirmation that a long-planned aerial offensive would begin at dawn on New Year's Day. The code words "Varus—Teutonicus" set in motion the Luftwaffe's own New Year's greeting to Allied air force personnel by initiating "Operation Baseplate," a massive simultaneous attack by more than one thousand German planes on American and British airfields supporting the ground forces in the Battle of the Ardennes.

Senior pilots such as Josef "Pips" Priller, one of the only Luftwaffe officers who actually was able to strafe the invasion beaches on D-Day, developed a new sense of optimism as they joined dozens of other squadrons, including the largest concentration of jet-propelled planes that had ever been sent on a mission. This giant raid was the most massive offensive undertaking since the Battle of Britain more than four years earlier and was timed to smash into Allied territory just as the American and British pilots were preparing their own missions.

At one Spitfire base in Holland, a dozen planes were being prepared for a patrol just as sixty German fighters slashed across the field and virtually annihilated the squadron. Allied antiaircraft gunners fired in helpless fury as they attempted to focus on jets that were simply too fast to bracket. Yet, in turn, often inexperienced German pilots wasted time and ammunition firing at hangars, repair facilities, and offices instead of concentrating on fighter revetments, allowing the now fully alerted Allies to fully engage the intruders. On the frigid New Year's morning, aerial dogfighters swirled across the sky as Spitfires and Mustangs gained altitude to exact retribution for their dead or wounded comrades on the ground. Their German opponents would tally a sensational roll of more than three hundred kills during ground attacks and aerial duels, but huge gaps were now forming in the German formations as the defenders began to take their revenge. As squadrons landed on the friendly fields of Fuerstenau, Nordhorn, and Varrebusch, headcounts revealed that nearly three hundred of their comrades had not returned. While the Allies had lost far more planes than pilots, most of the missing Luftwaffe aircraft meant the loss of both, which turned an essentially drawn battle into a virtual German defeat.

Several hundred miles south of the Battle of Baseplate, other American pilots were in the air providing top cover for a taste of New Year's at home that had somehow been transferred in a unique form to northern Italy. American P-38 Lightnings were flying leisurely patterns over Beita Stadium in Florence because below them more than twenty-five thousand American and Italian guests had congregated for the 1st annual Spaghetti Bowl between the football teams of Fifth Army and 12th Air Force. The game had been so heavily publicized that German propaganda broadcasts to American personnel had promised a German presence at the event in the form of Luftwaffe raiders, which would provide a very different type of excitement than gridiron action.

Like the traditional bowl games that would be played later that day in the American Southeast and Southwest, the Spaghetti Bowl featured elaborate floats for a bowl queen and her princesses, drum majorettes, cheerleaders, a fifty-six-piece band, hot dogs, and the prospect of socializing between American fighting men and army nurses, WACs, and much of the eligible young female population of Florence. While running back John Moody, a black All-American from Morris Brown College, scored two touchdowns for the army team, and former Texas Tech fullback Edward Shanks countered with tallies for the air force, excited servicemen wrapped blankets around their dates, cheered lustily, and occasionally glanced upwards at the protective screen of fighters, perhaps wondering if the Luftwaffe would make good on their promise "to join the party."

Half a world away, in the Philippines capital city of Manila, the Imperial Japanese occupiers celebrated the third anniversary of their capture of the Luzon metropolis but were forced to downgrade their usual insistence to the populace that the Americans would never return. Now, General Douglas MacArthur was on relatively nearby Leyte Island with seven American Army divisions poised for a return to the nerve center of the commonwealth. While Japanese officials continued to insist that the Filipinos should have accepted their status as a conquered people, they conveniently ignored the stark differences between their own invasion force and the vast array available to the approaching Americans. Only weeks after Pearl Harbor, Imperial forces had conquered Luzon with a fleet of eighty warships and two hundred fifty landing boats. Three years later, MacArthur was preparing to make the leap between Leyte and Luzon with a fleet of eight hundred warships, twenty-five hundred landing craft, nine hundred amphibious vehicles, and almost total control of the skies above the landing zone. On this New Year's Day, it was clear that the battle for Leyte had largely ended; the battle for Luzon and Manila was about to begin.

Meanwhile, back in a United States that had largely escaped the direct horrors of the war, 1945 began with a mixture of satisfaction that 1944 had been a year of decisive movement toward ultimate victory and a national debate on when that victory would actually occur. Slogans ranged from the optimistic "Home Alive in '45" to the less effusive prediction of "The Golden Gate in '48," with little inclination to consistency on the part of either the general public or the news media. One popular weekly news magazine ran a sobering editorial in its first issue of 1945 with the provocative theme, "Should We Draft American Women?" The article gave dire statistics that insisted that American war factories were short seven hundred thousand workers, the Women's Army Corps was below enlistment quotas, and the service was short eighteen thousand nurses and that these gaps argued for a National Service Act such as the one in Britain. Citing the activist role of Eleanor Roosevelt, "the most active First Lady in history," and "the status of women charging at lightning speed," the editorial board of the Time-Life empire called for a "complete civilian draft of able-bodied men and women" based on polls that showed that women were more willing to be drafted than men and the presence of millions of extra women in the workforce compared to 1941.

Yet even media outlets that called for a universal national draft were carrying a rapidly expanding series of advertisements centered on the return of servicemen to their families in an impending postwar society. Uniformed men, usually healthy, handsome, and self-assured, were depicted embracing their pretty, well-groomed wives, fiancées, or girlfriends in romantic reunion scenes that hinted that postwar America was going to be far more prosperous and exciting than the gray, dismal world of the 1930s. Children returning from school or outdoor play were portrayed in utter shock and delight with the surprise realization that "Daddy's Home!" Appliance companies such as General Electric and Philco depicted reunited families gathered in the living room, sampling the most exciting addition to their postwar home: a new television set that allowed them to actually see Bob Hope, Jerry Colonna, or Frank Sinatra on their own "widescreen" seven-inch or twelve-inch television set. Household appliance ads extolled the advantages of "all electric" kitchens and a new generation of washing machines that would replace the tedious job of feeding clothes through an attached "wringing" device that was replaced by an automatic "spin dry" feature built into the machine itself. Auto ads enticed drivers to a near future where the still relatively "boxy" autos of the 1930s were giving way to streamlined new models.

Even as the war reached a seeming climax on all fronts in January of 1945, Hollywood producers were releasing films that either featured the conflict more as a side issue or did not feature it at all. The most heavily promoted movie of January 1945 was the eagerly anticipated *National Velvet,* which MGM producers insisted was their best film in more than a decade. A just emerging star, Elizabeth Taylor, played Velvet Brown, a twelve-year-old daughter of a British butcher who defied gender and class restraints to win the British Grand National Steeplechase in a lush Technicolor adventure that evoked excitement from a wide demographic audience. Another must-see film for family audiences was *Janie,* which focused on contemporary American teenagers in which bobby-soxers and their boyfriends clearly placed the ongoing war backstage as they frolicked through a seemingly indulgent adult world.

January of 1945 in America perfectly fitted the Roman dedication of the month to the god Janus, who looked both backward and forward. Americans on the home front followed the ebb and flow of the battle in the Ardennes that was now increasingly called the Battle of the Bulge, as the initial penetration of American lines now began to appear as a protrusion ripe for destruction. The concept of annihilation of the enemy intruders took on new purpose as magazines, newspapers, and theater newsreels began featuring the grim pictures of the massacre of American prisoners at Malmedy. Horror, shock, and the desire for revenge all permeated the American mindset as photos depicted clearly designated medical personnel riddled with bullets and other GIs shot repeatedly in the face or coldly executed as they writhed in pain on the snow-covered fields. A visceral hatred that had so far been limited primarily to the Japanese enemy was now creeping into the American psyche regarding the war with Germany in these early days of 1945. The Malmedy massacre soon became the tip of an emotional iceberg as Allied forces pushed deeper into the occupied regions of the Reich and discovered the first clues that concentration camps were actually extermination centers, even though not yet fully comparable to what would be discovered as the GIs moved further east.

On the other side of the planet, General MacArthur's forces were now entering the main island of the Philippines, and within a few weeks Americans would be liberating some of the gaunt survivors of the Bataan Death March and the nurses who had stayed behind to tend the besieged garrison; by the end of January, forces were breaking through the outer defenses of Manila. The campaigns of the just-ended "Longest Year" of 1944 had created the conditions in which the bloodiest war in history could finally end in 1945. This sense of climax was particularly noticeable on a frigid, late January day in the nation's capital.

On January 20, 1945, a relatively small audience of five thousand invited guests shivered, stomped their feet, and exhaled frosty breaths of air as the gaunt, increasingly feeble President of the United States prepared to take his fourth and final oath of office. Most of the spectators who had not personally seen the sixty-two-year-old president in recent weeks involuntarily gasped at the gaunt commander in chief who stood before them. A shadow of the earlier lion of the White House emerged as Chief Justice Harlan Stone administered the obligatory oath, but the brief, five-hundred-sixty-eight word, six-minute presidential address illustrated the failing stamina of the president. Roosevelt challenged his supporters, and a large radio audience, to follow the still-raging war with a new international outlook based on the Americans' new role as citizens of the world and members of a unified human community. In a stunning visual image that revealed how much the war had changed America, only two dignitaries wore the traditional top hats that symbolized a special status of wealth and power, while the remaining guests were dressed not unlike the crowd beyond the platform.

This final wartime inauguration symbolized the seeming contradictions of an America that was both engaged in its largest war and basking in its greatest economic boom at the same moment in time. The inauguration planners observed the austerity of the war by featuring a meatless menu for the inauguration dinner. Yet the guests were hardly forced into a Spartan diet, as they savored a meal centered on terrapin, capon, lobster thermidor, cream cake, and champagne. In turn, the reality of war status was emphasized by the prominent presence of General George Marshall and Admiral King; yet the mood of the evening was enormously softened by the humor of comedians Bob Hope and Jerry Colonna.

For a final time, Franklin Roosevelt entered a new term as president of a nation approaching the end of a war and the beginning of a still uncertain but exciting peace in a month that stood suspended between two realities. The Longest Year of 1944 was now over, and Americans were eager to discover what new adventures waited for them in a 1945 that might very well end in peace.

A Note on Sources

From the time I first envisioned this project devoted to the American wartime experience in 1944, I was convinced that the best way to understand Americans' world on the home front and on the war front was to devote much of my research activity perusing the sources that people of that time consulted to understand the domestic and military aspects of the conflict. Therefore, for much of the past twenty months, I immersed myself in 1944 America at the libraries of the University of Pennsylvania and Rosemont College, both of which feature original magazines and newspapers of the era. I supplemented my research by numerous virtual excursions on eBay to fill in any gaps in these collections.

I investigated articles, editorials, letters to the editor, and advertisements from most 1944 issues of *Time, Newsweek, United States News, Life, Fortune,* and *Foreign Affairs* and extensive selections from *Ladies' Home Journal, Good Housekeeping, Saturday Evening Post, Seventeen,* and *Look.* I also consulted a wide variety of newspapers from a mix of large cities, medium-sized cities, small towns, and some of the emerging suburbs.

Another fascinating source of documentation for this book came courtesy of my father, who served in the United States Army Air Force between 1942 and 1946 in ranks ranging from 2nd lieutenant to major. His appointments to the Command and General Staff School in Fort Leavenworth, Kansas, and as information and education officer at a large airbase produced a variety of fascinating documents ranging from evaluations of American performance in key battles to educational pamphlets and books on topics ranging from correct behavior in liberated nations to hints on differentiating between Chinese allies and Japanese enemies.

The American war experience in 1944 has produced a formidable array of books that extends well into triple figures. Since this is my third book on World War II, I have consulted a rather high percentage of these sources but will list here mainly those works most valuable in developing this project. An excellent place to begin my examination of the American plan for victory in Europe in 1944 is General Dwight Eisenhower's *Crusade in Europe,* written four years after the war and an excellent personal and operational chronicle of the big picture in Northwest Europe. At the opposite end of the command structure of the battle for Northwest Europe is the much more recent (2007) *Brothers in Battle, Best of Friends* by two members of the Band of Brothers: William Guarnere and Edward Heffron, who chronicled the war from the individual foxhole perspective. The simmering rivalry between British and American commanders during the drive through France is effectively related in David Irving's *The War Between the Generals* (1981), which is relatively evenhanded in its criticisms of egocentric commanders on both sides of the Anglo-American divide in 1944.

The command decisions that led to the battles of Cassino and Anzio are discussed in length in Mark Clark's somewhat self-serving but generally informative *Calculated Risk* (1950), while a much more human and interesting view of that general emerges in Maurine Clark's *Captain's Bride, General's Lady* (1956), which presents a very different side of the general and an excellent portrait of home-front Americans who waited impatiently for even the briefest news of their loved ones engaged in combat. Other excellent accounts of the purgatory that was the Italian campaign in winter 1944 are British author Peter Caddick-Adams's

Monte Cassino: Ten Armies in Hell (2013) and Duane Schultz's *Crossing the Rapido* (2011).

The attempt to drive the Luftwaffe from the skies before Overlord can be viewed from a variety of viewpoints. John McManus's *Deadly Sky: The American Combat Airman in World War II* (2000) and Donald Miller's *Masters of the Air* (2006) placed Operation Point Blank — Big Week in the broad perspective of aerial battles of 1944. Bill Yenne's *Big Week* (2013) and *The Point Blank Directive* (2012) by Douglas Keeney provide detailed analyses of the specific battles. Adolf Galland's *The First and the Last: The Rise and Fall of the German Fighter Forces* (1954) is the definitive account from a Luftwaffe pilot perspective.

An excellent starting point for any exploration of the Pacific War is E. B. Potter's biography of Chester Nimitz, titled simply *Nimitz* (1976) and then proceed to two volumes of Samuel Morrison's magisterial chronicle of the navy in World War II: *History of Naval Operations in World War II, New Guinea and the Marianas* (1951) and *Leyte* (1963). Robert Sherrod presents a correspondent's eye view of the battle for Saipan in *On to Westward* (1944). Francis O'Brien's *Battling for Saipan* (2003) focuses on the role of army ground troops in the battle, and Guy Gabaldon's *Saipan: Suicide Island* (1990) views the battle from the viewpoint of a Marine enlisted man. The naval battle of the Philippine Sea receives an excellent treatment in William Y'Blood's *Red Sun Setting* (1980). The ground battle for Leyte Island receives most extensive coverage in Nathan Prefer's *Leyte, 1944: The Soldiers' Battle* (2012) and Gerald Astor's *Crisis in the Pacific* (1996). The sea battle command decisions receive significant attention in E. B. Potter's *Bull Halsey* (1985) and Theodore Taylor's *The Magnificent Mitscher* (1954).

Two recent magisterial accounts of Operation Overlord and its aftermath are Anthony Beevor's *D-Day* (2009) and Rick Atkinson's *The Guns at Last Light* (2013), while Stephen Ambrose provides the most readable oral histories of the battles in *D-Day* (1994) and *Citizen Soldiers* (1997). An excellent analysis of the positive and negative aspects of American ground combat in Europe in 1944 is Michael Doubler's *Closing with the Enemy* (1994). The breakout from Normandy to the liberation of Paris is chronicled in Alwyn Featherston's *Battle for Mortain* (1993) and Martin Blumenson's *The Duel for France* (1963), while Hitler's massive counterattack in the Ardennes is chronicled in John Toland's classic, *Battle: The Story of the Bulge* (1959), and the more recent works, John McManus's *Alamo in the Ardennes* (2007) and Leo Barron and Don Cygan, *No Silent Night* (2012).

Index